D0242914

Boat to Boardroom

— Alex Alley and Paula Reid —

High performance lessons for leaders and teams using the
Global Challenge Round-the-World Yacht Race

FASTPRINT PUBLISHING
PETERBOROUGH, ENGLAND

BOAT TO BOARDROOM
Copyright © Alex Alley & Paula Reid 2009

All rights reserved.

No part of this book may be reproduced in any form by
photocopying or any electronic or mechanical means,
including information storage or retrieval systems,
without permission in writing from both the copyright
owner and the publisher of the book.

ISBN 978-184426-612-8

First Published 2009 by
FASTPRINT PUBLISHING
Peterborough, England.

Printed on FSC approved paper by
www.printondemand-worldwide.com

Foreword by David Chapman, Sponsor

A FEW WEEKS AGO I DECIDED AS A New Year's Resolution to read *A Brief History of Time*, after telling myself repeatedly, 'Yes I must read that', for what I thought was a couple of years. I was stunned to have a 20th anniversary edition duly land on the doormat. For anyone whose ambitions are more adventurous, postponing goals can have greater consequences. The 2004-5 Global Challenge was the last race of its kind. Those who put it off will now never go.

The 12 skippers and 180 core crew who sailed the whole race committed themselves to something truly life-changing. They discovered more about themselves in a few months than some of us do in a lifetime, and had a serious race to compete in too. It's hardly surprising then that the event also provided an opportunity to study lessons in teamwork and leadership.

The structure of relationships in the project was rather complex. The Company employed the skippers, the technical staff, race managers and marketers for their side of the enterprise, and provided training. The core crew and leggers (who sailed one or more of the seven legs) were fee-paying customers of the Company and also under the orders of the Skipper. Then there were Boat Sponsors, and many Corporate Sponsors with lesser rights and obligations. Each had their demands and objectives, inevitably adding to the Skippers' already difficult role. Topping it off were the 'Families and Friends' who had contributed in varying measures in time, effort and money to help finance a crew member's dream, and who felt a serious sense of ownership as they followed progress and often visited 'their' boat around the globe.

The result was a real mixture of motivations, and everyone involved in the race has his or her own set of experiences. For one participant it might be changing into kit, still wet from the last watch, at midnight on a 30 degree angle in the freezing Southern Ocean. For another it might be the sheer quantity of Cloudy Bay consumed when a boat finally reached Wellington. (You know who you are!) One of my favourites was watching our legger housewife novice transform into winning transatlantic race crew member celebrating on the podium in La Rochelle.

It's not hard to see the parallels in the people you meet in the course of your job. The fact they're sitting next to you does not mean their motivations, abilities and experiences are the same as yours. Yet you're part of the same team with the same objective and your leader has to get you all sailing in the right direction.

The race gave me the opportunity to watch such leadership and teamwork develop within that hothouse atmosphere, from a safe distance. Paula and Alex, on the other hand, were in the thick of it. All 'normal' life was there, but outside its comfort zone: people leaving and joining the team, relationships good and bad, problems arising and being resolved, mistakes and successes, goal setting and budgeting. Not to mention a great deal of fun.

Above all though, in my view, the real 'challenge' for all the stakeholders was in managing and harnessing the inevitability of *change* while staying focussed on the original objectives.

There were many moments that will stay long in the memory, but the stand-out was certainly Leg Two. The race took on extra meaning for us during December and January as the boat struggled with all sorts of issues, and we ourselves were coming to the end of a messy boardroom battle that culminated in the takeover of Stelmar by OSG. Boardroom swings seemed matched on a daily basis by events on board the boat, as each success was checked by another setback, to such a degree that it seemed only fitting that *Team Stelmar* should finally reach Wellington on the very day that OSG finalised the takeover. Decent shipowners don't ever leave crew stranded, and it's a testimony to OSG that they unhesitatingly honoured Stelmar's commitments to the Team in full for the remaining five legs. Only this time with lobsters. But that's a story for another day.

David Chapman

January 2009

Alex Alley & Paula Reid

Introduction

BOAT TO BOARDROOM USES THE EXTREME case study of the 2004/5 Global Challenge round the world yacht race to demonstrate leadership and teamwork in action.

Sailing is quite simply the most effective sport at facilitating team development and learning. It encompasses all the key ingredients of high performance, leadership, strategy and tactics, crisis planning, teamwork, motivation, communication and personal development.

The Global Challenge is dubbed 'the world's toughest yacht race' because it is for amateur crews and sails 'the wrong way' around the world; against the prevailing conditions, past Cape Horn and twice into the Southern Ocean, covering 35,000 miles. In 2004/5 *Team Stelmar* experienced the biggest challenge of all the boats, suffering from two separate medical evacuations in the Southern Ocean and having to sail an extra two thousand miles. However, they also celebrated two podium places, won the most trophies overall and set a new speed record for this class of boat.

Alex and Paula were both core crew on *Team Stelmar* and have been delivering the story and the lessons to companies and organisations ever since they returned. They have been speaking, training and facilitating in workshops and on boats and felt it was about time that all these experiences were captured in a book.

Boat to Boardroom was written with the intention to be two books in one. Team Stelmar's amazing story from the race – acting as an extreme case study – and nine business Chapters covering leadership and teamwork.

The book is designed to be accessible and practical, enlightening and inspiring with stories, tips and anecdotes.

Each business Chapter includes definitions and descriptions of the subject, linking the Global Challenge actions and learnings to the business world, and then summarises with a handy list of lessons. There are also leadership and teamwork scenarios and exercises that can be carried out in the workplace to drive the learning home in an engaging way.

Please feel free to read either the story or the business Chapters first – or just look up the lists of lessons if you are in a hurry. The business Chapters reference the story of the Global Challenge yacht race, using it as an extreme case study. They can stand alone, or be read in conjunction with one another. There are inevitably overlapping messages, but each Chapter has been written with unique content. So, for instance, if you are leading a team, you will gain fresh insights and tips from reading all nine Chapters.

Sit back and enjoy the story as an armchair sailor, and then put the business lessons into practice.

List of Skippers and Boats in order of finishing:

1. Andy Forbes   BG Spirit

2. Stuart Jackson   Barclays Adventurer

3. David Melville   BP Explorer

4. Duggie Gillespie   Sark

5. Eero Lehtinen   SAIC

6. Clive Cosby   Team Stelmar

7. James Allen   Me to You

8. Amedeo Sorrentino   VAIO (Sony)

9. Matt Riddell   Samsung

10. Dee Caffari   Imagine It. Done (Unisys)

11. Loz Marriott   Pindar

12. Paul Kelly   Team Save the Children

Challenge 72' Class Yacht

Apparent Wind Range	Mainsail	Headsails	
0 - 18 Knots	Full Mainsail	Genoa	
16 - 22 Knots	Full Mainsail	No 1 Yankee	Staysail
22 - 25 Knots	Full Mainsail	No 2 Yankee	Staysail

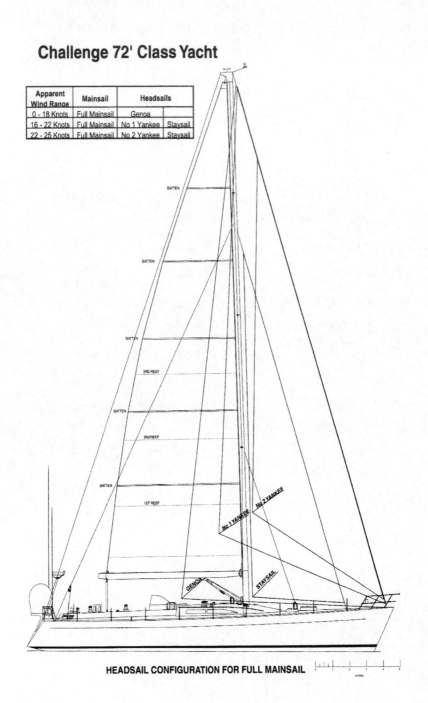

HEADSAIL CONFIGURATION FOR FULL MAINSAIL

Challenge 72' Class Yacht

General Arrangement

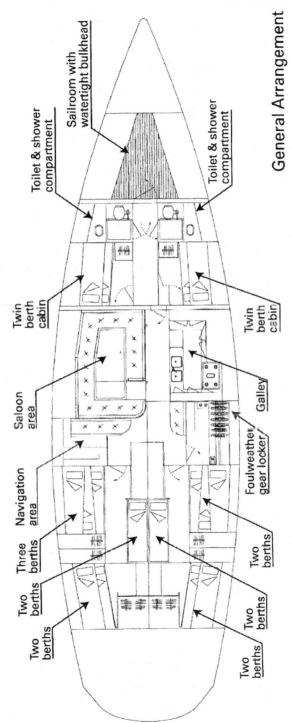

Sailroom with watertight bulkhead

Toilet & shower compartment

Toilet & shower compartment

Twin berth cabin

Twin berth cabin

Saloon area

Galley

Foulweather gear locker

Navigation area

Three berths

Two berths

Two berths

Two berths

Two berths

Two berths

Contents

Page

The Story of the Global Challenge:

Pre Start   16

Leg 1: Portsmouth to Buenos Aires   26

Leg 2: Buenos Aires to Wellington   57

Leg 3: Wellington to Sydney   88

Leg 4: Sydney to Cape Town   100

Leg 5: Cape Town to Boston   113

Leg 6: Boston to La Rochelle   129

Leg 7: La Rochelle to Portsmouth   135

The Business Chapters:

Chapter 1: Leadership   149

Chapter 2: High Performance   179

Chapter 3: Strategy and Tactics   209

Chapter 4: Crisis Prevention and Management   226

Chapter 5: Teamwork – the Basics   256

Chapter 6: Advanced Teamwork   283

Chapter 7: Motivation   306

Chapter 8: Communication   341

Chapter 9: Personal Development   362

The Global Challenge 2004/5

THE GLOBAL CHALLENGE ROUND THE World Yacht Race was conceived by Sir Chay Blyth and first ran in 1992/3 as the British Steel Challenge. There were ten boats, each 67' long and made of steel. They were designed to be very labour intensive for the 14 crew on each boat, not having any of the comforts of a cruising yacht. The next race in 1996/7 saw the introduction of four more yachts and a new title sponsor - BT.

The race ran every four years and in 2000/1 the boats were changed. The new fleet was only 12 boats strong, but each steel boat was 72' long with a crew of 18. Much more powerful and much faster than the older boats, these were to compete in two round the world races.

After a multimillion pound refit in Plymouth, the yachts were re-branded and sent out for the 2004/5 race. This was to be the last race as Challenge Business struggled to find a title sponsor and subsequently folded six months after the 2004/5 event finished. The yachts were sold off privately. This was quite sad as a large part of our lives was tied up in our boat, with many memories, both good and bad.

The crew was made up of a Skipper employed by Challenge Business – the race organisers - 15 'core crew' doing the whole race and two 'leggers' who would only be on board for one leg before being replaced by two more leggers for the next leg and so on.

In 2004/5 the boats carried 12 sails: a mainsail, a genoa, a staysail and storm staysail, three Yankees, four spinnakers and a trysail. The sails were heavy, especially when wet, but very strong. If a sail was damaged - and they were often - then they had to be repaired by hand, there was no luxury of an electric sewing machine. Everything on the boat was over-engineered to cope with the rigours of the Southern Ocean and ten months of racing round the world.

The 2004/5 race followed a different route to the previous one due to the hurricane risk around the Caribbean. From the start in Portsmouth, the boats sailed south down the Atlantic, crossing the equator, and finishing in Buenos Aires some five weeks later.

After a stopover of about 2½ weeks, the race restarted, heading south again, around the notorious Cape Horn and into the desolate expanse of the Southern Ocean, skirting Antarctica bound for Wellington. A leg of about six week's duration. In Wellington the boats would be lifted out and checked for signs of damage. From there the boats had a short sprint of about seven days across the Tasman Sea to Sydney. After a break of a couple of weeks, the teams prepared to head back into the Southern Ocean again, this time bound for Cape Town. Another six week epic in the frozen waters. From Cape Town the teams headed north-west up the Atlantic, crossing their outbound track and officially circumnavigating the planet. The destination this time was Boston. After Boston there was a relatively short leg of about 16 days back across the North Atlantic to La Rochelle in France, and from there there was another sprint leg back to Portsmouth and the finish.

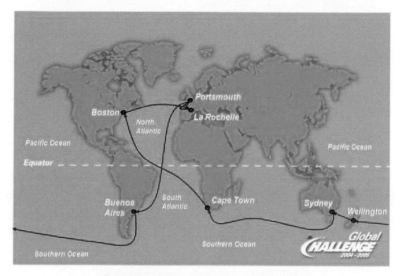

The Global Challenge 2004/5 route

Pre Start
October 3rd 2004, 13:59
Southsea Castle, Portsmouth

A GROUP OF DIGNITARIES, including HRH Princess Anne, huddle together, bracing themselves against the wind on top of the battlements of Southsea Castle overlooking the Solent. They are watching the 12 yachts jostling for position at the start of the 2004/5 Global Challenge Round the World Yacht Race. The boats charge for the start line as Princess Anne pulls the firing cord on the starting cannon at precisely 14:00.

The first boat across the line is Team Stelmar, our boat. The race has started, next stop Buenos Aires, 6400 miles away.

The race may have started, but for some people the challenge began over four years earlier, when they signed up as crew and began the training programme set by Challenge Business. A huge commitment in the crew's lives, which would involve each of them raising the £26,750 needed to pay for the berth on board. On top of that, many of them gave up their jobs and put the real world on hold. This was it.

The next three years included a series of training sails during which the skippers would make notes on each and every crew member on their different strengths and abilities. This was kept secret in a crew dossier. Each training sail built on the skills and knowledge of earlier sails. As the event was aimed at 'amateur' crews, there was a lot of basic sailing taught to the novice sailors, and every five-day training sail had a different selection of crew. Rarely did the same people sail together twice.

In the January before the race start, at the London Excel Boat Show, all the crew volunteers gathered for the team announcements. For several days before, the Challenge trainers had sat down to divide up the volunteers into the 12 teams, as equally as possible, with the same mix of experience, age and gender. They did a good job.

Each team had a paid Skipper, employed by Challenge Business and 15 core crew, who were to do the entire ten-month race. This was the day to find out who was on which boat and who the skippers were.

Late in the afternoon, everyone gathered in one of the conference rooms above the arena in Excel. There were some familiar faces from training sails, and many more unknown. The atmosphere was tense as Sir Chay Blyth gave an introductory speech before, one by one, the core members of the teams were announced. The 7th team to appear on the screen was ours. This was our new 'family' who would be sailing round the world together, and our Skipper was called Clive Cosby, one of the youngest skippers in the race at 28 years old. Once we had been given our colour-coded shirts (ours were white with CREW written on the back in large black letters) we all lined up for the first of many team photos.

We were an eclectic bunch.

The **final** line-up of the 16 core crew on *Team Stelmar* doing the whole race, was as follows:

Clive Cosby	28	Skipper
Alex Alley	33	Sales Manager
Julian Smith	34	Project Manager
Kate Stainsby	34	Physiotherapist
Mike Morgan	54	Software Engineer
Newton Scott	57	Director
Nicko Brennan	28	Software Engineer
Paul Goodman	47	Long Distance Lorry Driver
Paula Reid	37	Conference Director
Phil Beck	36	Systems Engineer
Richard Parson	38	Funeral Director

Robert Hooykaas	47	Private Asset Manager
Ruth Newton	27	Doctor
Sue Lyons	46	Secretary & Ballet Dancer
Tim Johnston	27	Accountant
Tim Wright (Wrighty)	38	VP International Marketing

Outside Excel there was a group of black cabs waiting to take us away for our first team meal to start the process of getting to know each other.

We headed for the Gaucho Grill in Canary Wharf to begin the team bonding; the idea being that as our first stopover was Buenos Aires in Argentina, then it would be good to begin sampling the delights of Argentinean cuisine.

At this point we had no boat sponsor so we became 'Team 7' and one of our first jobs as a team was to come up with a brand.

Two weeks after the Excel announcement we had our first team get-together at Hayling Island sailing club in Hampshire. We were not there to sail, but to get to know each other and do some team building and brainstorming. We came up with a logo for 'Team 7' and created our values which we would all buy into and live by for the duration of the event. They were 'Safe, Happy and Fast'.

The first priority was to be a safe boat. The sea is a dangerous, volatile environment, especially the Southern Ocean where the winds blow at storm force for days on end and the water temperature is only a few degrees above freezing. If you were to fall in, hypothermia would set in within minutes and the chances are that you would freeze to death before drowning.

Then there is the danger within the boat itself. Seventy-two feet long with a mast towering 100' above the sea, the forces involved are massive, with the ropes controlling the sails carrying literally tonnes of load.

Our next value was to be a happy boat. Each crew member had made a huge sacrifice to take part and it would be miserable for them if it wasn't a happy experience. Also, living in close proximity to 17 others for prolonged periods meant that everyone had to be tolerant of each other.

The third value went hand-in-hand with the second. If the boat was a happy one then it would be easier to make it a fast one, and if it was fast, then the team would be happy.

During the race our supporters would wave banners with 'Safe Happy Fast' printed on them. These were good values which work in life generally - not just on the boat - and it was a great boost for us to see them flying when we left each port.

It was during one of these weekend sessions at Hayling Island that the first crew nickname was born during a game of touch rugby on the beach. Tim Johnston, a 6'4" tall ex-rower from Oxford University and one of the fittest members of the crew, got the ball and ran so fast that Alex said he was like a flash of lightning. From that point on he was known to everyone as 'Flash'. After several weekend get-togethers in Hayling Island, we were given our first real team bonding experience when we were taken to *HMS Excellent* in Portsmouth Royal Navy Dockyard.

The DRIU, as it is known, is a Damage Repair Instructional Unit. Literally a full-size section of a Navy warship, several storeys tall, which can be filled with water and rocked up to 20 degrees to simulate an attack situation.

After a short training session, which included learning how to plug holes in a sinking ship, we were led into the simulator to begin our task. Waiting in the onboard storeroom, we heard the sound of explosions and rushing water, then the lights flickered and went out and the dim emergency lighting came on. We all headed down the stairs to the flooding room to begin plugging the holes with wooden wedges and mallets. What we didn't realise was that the waist-deep water was fed directly from outside and, as this was February, it was only eight degrees. After the initial shock, adrenaline took over and we all performed well as a team. Before we knew it, the 45 minute session was over and we headed back for a hot shower and debrief.

The purpose of these sessions was to see how we would work under pressure in an unfamiliar environment and who could take on which roles on the boat.

As we got to know more and more about each other's strengths and weaknesses, thoughts turned to more specialist roles for the race.

Under the race rules each boat had to have a medic. Our doctor – Ruth, who was a General Practitioner - went on courses to learn more about the injuries you may get on an ocean racing yacht and to get familiar with the very comprehensive medical kit on board the boats.

Another role was that of engineer who would take care of the engine, generator, water-maker and other systems on board. This job fell to Phil who was an ideal candidate because he dealt with systems in his job. The task of looking after the rigging went to Alex, with huge sailing experience and yacht design knowledge. The sails were looked after by the whole team but led by Wrighty, Rob and Paul, who went on a sailmaking course with Hood Sailmakers. Nicko took the role of Navigator, again a regular racing sailor with excellent skills on a computer. Julian was responsible for the safety on board and Paula was in charge of communications.

———————————

During our time together we had presentations from previous crews about what to expect during the race, with tactics and tips on getting the best out of the boats. As all 12 boats were identical, every little helped.

A lot of time was spent discussing the sort of food to take with us. With no fridge on the boats, we had no fresh food, except for the first couple of days after the start. From then on it was either boil-in-the-bag or freeze-dried expedition food. The former is individually packed and precooked and typically consisted of 'stew' type meals. They can be eaten cold straight from the packet or heated up by placing in a pan of boiling water. The advantage is that it is very easy to prepare and ideal for a quick fix in stormy conditions. The down side is that they are very heavy and weight was a big consideration when provisioning the boat. The freeze-dried option was much lighter but took a bit more preparation as the 'cook' had to soak the powder to rehydrate it before cooking. These meals were usually noodle or pasta based. In the end we decided to take mostly freeze-dried food with just a few boil-in-the-bag meals for the very roughest of days. It was all very high calorie food, over 5000 per day, per person for the Southern Ocean legs, and included three chocolate or energy bars per day, every day! Good news for the chocoholics.

Time was also spent deliberating over which meals should be eaten on each leg. We wanted lighter food for the legs through the tropics and more hot meals for the cold Southern Ocean legs. Eighteen people eating three meals a day for up to 40 days at a time equates to over 2000 individual meals for the first leg alone. The food had to be measured out, packed into vacuum bags and labelled with day and leg number and whether they were for breakfast, lunch or dinner. The first leg food was packed on the boat just before the start and all the other food was stored and then shipped to each port.

Sorting out the food was in itself a massive task. We had to decide on what to take and order enough for 18 people for the entire race, plus a 10% surplus for emergencies. The food pack was a team-build event in its own right. We hired a huge marquee for the weekend and had all the food delivered there as well as two industrial vacuum packing machines. The entire crew, along with friends and family, worked around the clock in shifts opening packets of food, weighing out the contents, vacuum-packing and labelling each pack before bagging them in the day bags. Between Friday evening and Sunday night we had most of the food packed and stood back looking at a mountain of black bags, all marked day by day, leg by leg.

It was at the end of this mammoth food-pack weekend that Clive gave us the good news that we had finally been allocated a boat sponsor. This was a Greek shipping company called Stelmar, originally owned by Stelios of EasyJet. We now had our race identity as we changed from the temporary Team 7 to Team Stelmar and it was a very proud moment for us all as we drank champagne out of plastic cups on the harbour side. Everything had started to come together.

Our sponsor was great, led by the ever happy David Chapman who was our main contact. Although the sponsors were not obliged to supply the crew with anything (having already spent a large sum of money sponsoring the boat), we were very lucky and soon we were sporting Team Stelmar branded kit. We went from a ragtag bunch to a very professional-looking team - but looking good was not enough, we had to **be** good.

———————————

Several weeks before the race start all the teams had to complete a qualifying sail. This was a chance for the organisers to test various systems and for the crews to see how they would stack up against the competition in a 'race' situation.

There was a mock start on the start line off Southsea from where the boats would sail out past the Needles, into the English Channel and then along the South Coast, heading eventually for the Fastnet Rock off Southern Ireland. Although not officially a race, there was a very competitive atmosphere across the fleet.

All the time we were gathering data as to how best to sail the boat, which sails to use in what wind strength, and how best to trim our particular boat.

During the four days, each boat would receive a message from Race Control notifying them of a disaster on board. The team then had to go through the simulation and report back to Race Control. After a couple of days we received our first message - we had been holed below the waterline by a submerged object.

In this instance we were not required to do anything, only to discuss what we could do to save the situation. We all decided that the best course of action was to pass a sail under the boat, like a sling, and use the outside water pressure against the sail to cover the hole and stem the flow. We told Race Control of our intended action and were informed that we had passed the test, but to await further instructions over the next day or two.

The following day we received another message telling us that a crew member had been hurt on the foredeck and this time we were to act out the simulation. We decided to use our biggest crew member for this which was Flash, thinking that if we could get him down below decks then we could get anyone below.

We set up the foredeck with Flash lying down immobilised with some tomato ketchup splashed around for added realism. When we were ready the call went out of 'man down' and we swung into action. The boat was turned away from the wind to stabilise it, then with Ruth the medic in charge, we opened the foredeck hatch and very carefully passed Flash down through it and along the corridor onto the saloon table. At this point we contacted Race Control via the satellite phone to tell them what we had done. Again we passed.

Towards the end of the qualifying sail, all the boats were to congregate in Poole Bay for another mock start and then to finish off Southsea. The pace was hectic and *Team Stelmar* showed herself to be one of the front runners with slick crew work and good boat speed. It was at this point that another crew nickname was born. On noticing how Alex was jumping around the boat looking for extra boat speed, Kate said it was like watching Tigger from *Winnie the Pooh*. From then on, Alex became Tigger the Rigger, or Tigs for short.

Once back in port Clive announced the watch system and who would be on which watch. We were to run a system of two 6-hour watches during the day: 06:00-12:00 and 12:00-18:00; then three 4-hour watches during the night: 18:00-22:00; 22:00-02:00 and 02:00-06:00.

We decided on names for the watches, the 'Grunters' and the 'Groaners'.

The first leg Grunters consisted of: Mike, Newton, Paula, Phil, Rich, Rob and Ruth, with Adrian Stafford-Jones as the legger. (Adrian was one of the team's sub-sponsors and ended up joining the crew for four legs.)

The Groaners were: Alex, Julian, Kate, Paul, Sue, Flash and Tim, with Tony Rogers as the legger.

Race day was fast approaching. The food was packed, kit organised and we were sail training as much as we could, as well as going to the gym to increase our strength and fitness.

On the Thursday before the race start, all the crew were down in Portsmouth completing final preparations and making sure everything was ready and in place on the boat. Sails were marked up and carefully folded in their bags and stowed in the sail locker in the bow of the boat.

Everyone was now in race mode. Work had been left behind and the whole team were now living in the crew hotel in Southsea.

There was a final corporate sail for the Stelmar executives to take their clients out for the day to schmooze them. Everything went well; it was a sunny day with a good breeze. By the end though everyone was tired and feeling the pressure. In 48 hours time we would be leaving the UK for nearly a year.

The next day was the crew briefing in the cinema at Gunwharf Quays, Portsmouth, where the fleet was based.

We covered the race rules, leg details, tips and safety, as well as the start procedure and start line details. After the briefing we had one final check that the boat was ready. All the food was packed, systems checked, all 12 sails on board. We were ready.

On Saturday we were given a day to rest and spend with family and friends. There was a carnival for the teams, although only Paula and Mike made it from *Team Stelmar*.

Leg 1

Portsmouth – Buenos Aires

6400 miles

IT WAS A GREY, BLUSTERY MORNING when the crew woke. After so much training and preparation we believed we were ready. Most of us just wanted to get on with it and get going. The waiting was over.

Outside, supporters were beginning to gather under the fluttering flags, staking their claim for a spot where they could see the yachts leave.

The last few bits of personal kit were taken to the boat and we all met for a crew breakfast at the Loch Fyne restaurant in Gunwharf Quays, where a large Team Stelmar banner hung from the wall. Many of the crew went for a full English breakfast, knowing that this was the last real meal they would be eating for well over a month. Others went for a lighter breakfast, perhaps feeling slightly nervous. We then had 30 minutes to say our goodbyes before heading back to the restaurant for a final briefing and team talk at 09:30 before walking down to the boat together at 10:00.

As with many plans, things did not go smoothly for us. Clive was determined we walked to the boat en masse, but we wasted precious 'goodbye' time, as at 10:10 we were still not all together and Julian was saying a long goodbye to his girlfriend, holding the rest of the crew up. Friends and family were not allowed onto the pontoon after 10:30.

Eventually we all got through the security gate onto the pontoon and were able to walk to the boat together, in a show of strength. However, at 10:28 Paula's sister came running onto the pontoon to tell her that their mother had been involved in an accident. During a surge in the crowd, she had fallen down some steps and broken a leg in three places. Paula ran back up, through security and back into the crowds to see her mother lying pale and supported by two paramedics. One final hug and she had to go back to the boat and get ready to leave.

Paula:

I was extremely nervous that day because I had had only two months preparation time, having joined the team very late in the day, plus force eight gales were predicted! I had been upset by the delay in getting onto the pontoon, knowing this was cutting short my time for goodbyes. All my crew were wrapped up in their own worlds, so it also felt quite lonely. Then I had to say goodbye to my Mum who had already admitted to feeling very worried and stressed about what I was about to do. I left her lying on the concrete floor, white as a sheet, not actually knowing at the time what was wrong with her. As we pulled away from the pontoon, everyone was waving goodbye, but I was just scanning the crowds for the ambulance. This was a horrible way to start the race on top of everything else.

A difficult time for everyone, but we had a job to do which we had been planning for a long time.

There was a release of balloons and confetti cannons as our boat theme tune, *Praise You* by Fatboy Slim, blasted out over the PA system in the marina. It was our turn to leave and it was very emotional as we saw the ambulance make its way through the crowd towards Paula's mother while we untied the boat and headed out to the start line. We all lined up along the port side of the boat waving to the crowds and could make out Team Stelmar flags and 'Safe Happy Fast' banners amongst them.

We had chartered a small ferry as our supporters' boat which followed us out towards the start area. The boat was packed with several hundred people and had a 20' Team Stelmar banner along the side. (To help raise crew funds for better kit and food, we had sold tickets for the supporters' boat and it was sold out.) There was a big cheer as we hoisted our mainsail. We left the headsail down until nearer the start time, making sure we made the right choice as to which one to use given the wind strength at the start.

Twenty minutes to go and the first gun fired indicating the starting sequence had begun. Ten minutes later and a second gun fired - time to make our decision as to which headsail to use. The wind was blowing around 20 knots so we decide to use the Number 2 Yankee (No.1 being the biggest and No.3 the smallest).

We circled round, trying all the time to judge our run to the start line to perfection, making timed runs from a known position. Yacht racing starts with a 'rolling' start; the skill is being on the line at full speed when the starting gun goes off. Any boat over the line before the gun would be given a penalty which in this case would mean having to wait at a designated area for one hour.

Another gun fired; five minutes to go. The engine had to be turned off at this point. We positioned ourselves in what we believed was a good place and began to 'power up' the boat, catching more wind in our sails by altering our angle to it. *Team Stelmar* heeled over and surged forward, spray coming over the deck as the bow cut through the choppy water. One minute to go and we were at full power, charging towards the line.

Bang! The gun went and we had judged the line to perfection. We were first across, much to the joy of our supporters who went wild.

Next stop Buenos Aires, over 6000 miles away.

The first few hours were very busy, with lots of tacking down the Solent towards the Needles. It was quite chaotic on board. Normally the boat is sailed by one watch, but on start day all 18 crew were on deck with everyone helping out. The problem was there were too many people and everyone kept getting in each other's way which slowed us down. By the time we got to the Needles we had dropped down the fleet to 9th place. Lessons learned for later.

The wind was building all the while and by the time we passed the Needles and headed out into the English Channel, it was getting towards 30 knots, so we put a second reef in the mainsail to make the boat more controllable.

The last of the spectator and press boats left us and turned to head back home while we carried on powering out to sea; we suddenly felt very alone.

3rd October 2004, 18:00 hrs

Poole Bay

We finally broke into the watch system, with the Grunters heading down for some food and sleep. This was easier said than done as it was only 18:00 and still light outside; also the adrenaline from the start was still flowing. Sleep for them was going to be difficult, especially with the motion of the boat, which was getting rockier all the time.

On deck things began to settle into more of a routine; a routine that would last for ten months. The helm rotated every hour to maintain concentration, the sails were constantly trimmed and every 15 minutes someone logged data in the cockpit. This was a system we had developed on Team Stelmar to help improve performance. We had a laminated sheet by the wheel in the cockpit on which we would record boat speed, wind speed, wind angle, heading and sail combination. We could then compare it to previous records to make sure we were at maximum speed for the conditions. In reality it was academic as the onboard computer recorded everything continually, but it made the on-watch crew focus on the performance by filling it in.

At 22:00 the Grunters came up on watch. The scene was very different from when they went down below four hours earlier. It was now pitch black with some very large waves around. No sign of land but occasionally there would be a white navigation light pitching through the darkness - the masthead light of the competition. The conditions were getting worse by the hour and Nicko popped his head up from the navigation area to inform everyone that it was forecast to continue doing so for the next few days. Not the nice gentle start everyone was hoping for. Instead we were heading straight into a storm. It was a good test of boat and equipment, as well as the crew.

For four hours the Grunters worked at maximising the boat speed and by the time they came off watch at 02:00 they were all very wet and tired. Sleeping would be easier this time, despite the violent motion of the boat with wind now gusting to over 40 knots.

Moving around on deck was getting difficult too. Everyone was clipped on with their safety lines as soon as they came out of the hatch onto the deck. The strength of the wind coupled with the motion of the boat - now well heeled over - meant that the only way to go forward was on hands and knees. This was getting tough.

The Groaners decided to change down to the storm staysail, a 'bullet-proof', strong, thick orange sail that was rated for huge wind strengths and, as the name suggests, is used in storm conditions. With Alex on the helm trying to keep the boat stable and make the foredeck as safe as possible, the foredeck team, led by Wrighty, dragged the heavy sail bag along the side deck into the darkness towards the bow. It was hard work. With waves coming over the boat and heavy rain and spray making it difficult to see, the team toiled on.

Trying to make yourself heard above the noise was impossible and we developed a series of hand signals to communicate between the bow, the snake-pit in the middle of the boat, and the cockpit and helm at the back.

The staysail was pulled down and the storm staysail was ready to go up. Everything went like clockwork, until there was a problem with the staysail sheet (one of the control lines) which had come loose. We were unable to control the sail, and it flogged spectacularly in the storm force winds, eventually completely ripping in half from front to back. The sail had to come back down to be repaired. Without enough power to drive the boat easily, a huge wave swept across the foredeck and once the spray had cleared there was one less man on deck.

Wrighty had been swept overboard!

Everyone immediately went into autopilot and began a well-rehearsed drill of 'man overboard'. Thanks to our value – 'Safe' - Wrighty was still clipped on and was being dragged through the water. As another big wave washed over the deck he was caught and pulled back on board by Flash and Julian. It would have been a very different story had he not been clipped on.

Wrighty was taken below decks and given a hot cup of tea and an examination by Dr Ruth. Battered, bruised and slightly shocked Wrighty was given the all clear, but it served to remind everyone of the importance of being clipped on and the dangers of the environment we were heading into.

After the chaos had died down and Challenge Business had been notified, it was decided to have a communication embargo of the incident for fear of worrying friends and family back home.

All this and the race was only a few hours old.

For the first few days, many of the crew were seasick. It was very stormy and choppy as we headed across the Channel to France and then on across the Bay of Biscay. The wind increased all the time, touching almost 60 knots as we rounded the notorious Cape Finistere at the north-west corner of Spain. However, the sailing was very exhilarating as the wind was now coming from behind and we were able to get the boat surfing down the waves.

During this time, Alex was hit by a wave while driving and physically knocked to the floor. This made us decide that someone should ride 'shotgun' to the helm in such conditions, ready to grab the wheel and stop the boat going out of control.

It became an on-going challenge as to who could get the highest speed from the boat. The top speed we recorded was 16 knots while surfing down the waves.

Sunday 10th October 2004, Day 7

485 miles off the Moroccan coast

We had been at sea racing for a week and already the storms of the first few days were a distant memory, apart from the tattered storm sail sitting below decks waiting for repair. The initial seasickness had gone, only to be replaced with a bout of sickness and diarrhoea. Everything on the boat was cleaned and disinfected twice a day. The weather was getting much warmer the further south we went. The sky was blue and we were heading towards the steady trade winds which would help us on our way.

Due to the length of time the first leg would take, and the five hour time difference between the UK and Buenos Aires, we decided to gradually 'lose' time as we sailed. So every Sunday at the 18:00 watch change we had 'Happy Hour'. This involved all the crew getting together on deck and spending an hour together until 19:00, at which point the clocks were reset to 18:00 and the watch changed over.

This was the only real time watches got to mix. Usually there would be a quick changeover when everyone would update their opposite number, share knowledge of what had happened and how everything was set up, before rushing below deck to get fed and go to sleep.

Happy hour was a chance to chat properly and let your hair down. Sometimes we would make up fancy dress with whatever we could find on board; marker pens, bin bags, tape, etc. This first Happy Hour was themed 'school disco' and the ingenuity of some of the crew was mind boggling. It's amazing what can be achieved with some black bags and tape!

Life on board was now well and truly into a routine of sailing, eating and resting. We had a rotating 'mother duty' system. Apart from the Skipper, Navigator and Watch Leaders, everyone had to do mother duty which involved cooking and cleaning for everybody while on duty. As there were seven on a watch (excluding the Watch Leaders) everyone was 'mother' for one day a week.

Around the saloon table was a mass of white Ripstop nylon from a torn spinnaker which was being carefully stitched together by a 'sewing circle' who would rotate, day and night, to get the sail ready for the next time we needed it. The storm staysail remained at the bottom of the pile. This sailcloth was so thick that needles kept breaking, so when a spinnaker came down for repair, the staysail would remain at the bottom of the pile.

Repairing a spinnaker 'blow out' was a major job. It required unpicking double row stitching from the edge tapes of the sail before restitching the sail back in. These sails were the size of a tennis court and the repair work would often take a team of three people working round the clock two or more days.

We were at a decision point, tactically, during the race. We were comfortably with the leading pack of boats heading south as we passed Madeira. The next obstacle was the Canary Islands, a tactical cross-roads which can either help or hinder. Before the race we had sought expert knowledge about each of the legs and one piece of advice we were given, by a Navigator from the previous race, was to stay well clear of the Canaries with their high mountains for fear of being trapped in their wind shadow. We collectively agreed not to go there.

As we headed south in the steady northerly winds, it looked tempting to sail between the islands and get a boost as the wind was forced between the mountains. Despite all agreeing before the race not to do this, in our naivety we were persuaded by Clive that this was a good course of action.

We peeled off from the leading pack and went for it. Twenty-four hours later we were completely becalmed staring at the islands next to us. The gamble had failed.

In an attempt to find the breeze again, crew were hoisted up the 100' mast to look out for tell-tale signs of wind on the water, however small the puff of air was. It was for one of these excursions that Tony, one of our leggers, was chosen. He was a reluctant volunteer and had been quietly up there for about five minutes when he shouted. Everyone on deck instinctively looked up only to realise - too late - that Tony was being sick. Not good at the time, but we all saw the funny side afterwards.

We emerged from the Canaries in 9th place, a massive 165 miles from the leaders, and immediately set about catching the next boat, *Unisys*. Once back in the trade winds we flew along, taking 32 miles out of their lead in eight hours.

We knew this from the six-hourly schedules (skeds) or position reports we received from the race office. Nicko plotted the statistics on to a computer chart so we knew exactly where the other 11 boats were four times a day. We could also work out how far ahead or behind we were and how much we had made or lost since the previous sked. These reports were tense times on board as it told us how we were performing against the rest of the fleet.

It was great to get a good sked, however it was easy to get complacent if the results were positive. Just because a boat made up distance on another boat 100 miles away, did not necessarily mean it was sailing better; it could mean it had better wind, or the other boat had a problem. The key thing was to keep sailing at maximum possible speed all the time.

15th October 2004, Day 13

200 miles off the coast of Mauritania

The day began with the usual 05:20 wake up call for the off watch. The boat was fairly level, which meant good sailing conditions outside. One by one the off watch emerged from their cocoon-like bunks and went into one of the two 'heads' (toilets) to have a quick wash (which was usually a wipe down with a baby wipe) and to brush their teeth. They then had a breakfast of warm, fresh bread and porridge which had been lovingly - or grudgingly – prepared by the mother. The two Watch Leaders caught up and chatted with both Nicko and Clive as to what had been happening over the last four hours and what the plan was for the next six.

Once dressed the Groaners headed up on deck to take over at 06:00 and immediately noticed that something was different. As dawn broke, the sea was a bright orange colour; more than just the reflection of the sun. On closer inspection it was plain to see the reason. The ocean was covered, as far as the eye could see, with millions upon millions of dead locusts, like a carpet on the water.

It was hard to work out. We were a good day away from land and yet surrounded by locusts. The plot thickened later in the morning when a couple of live ones landed on the boat. One even got below deck and was adopted by Paula who was on mother duty at the time. She fed it bread soaked in milk and sugar and called it 'Larry'.

The following day more arrived and we decided that, due to their destructive power and insatiable appetite, they had to go, which was easier said than done. Larry, with his strength back, proved difficult to catch, eventually flying off, never to be seen again. We later learned that there had been a plague of locusts which had decimated crops in Mauritania. We assume that they were blown 200 miles out to sea by a strong wind and deposited in the ocean where we were.

There was of course more typical wildlife around such as pods of dolphins. These would often come and 'play' around the bow, diving underneath then emerging with a leap in the air and occasionally a complete flip. At night, dolphins sped alongside the boat like torpedoes, creating beautiful trails of phosphorescence.

We also got flying fish. These amazing creatures, up to about a foot long, would leap from the water and glide 30–50 metres through the air. Sometimes, usually during the night, they would get disorientated and land on the boat.

Unfortunately the only way we would find out they were there would be a day or two later when they had started to decompose in the sun and smell.

18th October 2004, (20:23 GMT), Day 16

11°29'.12 N   25°53'.23 W

In was mid-October and we were in the trade winds, experiencing ideal sailing conditions with a steady 15 knot north-easterly wind. The boat barrelled along at 10 knots with the heavy spinnaker up.

One of the characteristics of sailing in the trade winds is the tropical rain squalls. During the day these squalls can be easily seen; massive black clouds, with grey slabs of rain underneath them. As well as the torrential rain, they also produce very powerful gusts of wind ahead of them as they track across the sea. During the night they are much harder to detect, and we had to rely instead on following yellow patches on the radar; sitting below deck at the navigation station, informing the watch on deck where it was heading and how far away it was.

One particular evening there was a large squall to windward of the boat, ominous black clouds were approaching and the wind was picking up and dramatically shifting direction – sure signs of an impending tropical squall. On deck, the crew was debating whether to take down the lightweight race spinnaker which would be torn to shreds in the wrong conditions. Clive came on deck having just woken up and hesitated before deciding. We belatedly took down the race spinnaker and started to haul up the heavier 'flanker' spinnaker.

Paula:

As the squall hit the boat with 38 knots of wind and rain, the flanker broke early out of its 'sock' and we had to try to heave the heavy spinnaker up the mast as it filled with wind. Six metres to go, the wind whipped up, the sail ballooned out and tore away while the 30cm diameter Kevlar and carbon fibre spinnaker pole snapped in half. The power of the wind in the spinnaker knocked the boat right over on its side so the mast was lying flat on the water and it was pandemonium on deck. People were falling over each other as the deck became vertical.

The shredded spinnaker flew like a 30m long, tattered white strip in the water, the boom was submerged and the broken ends of the spinnaker pole jerked dangerously around the foredeck like a mad puppet. It was very dangerous and chaotic on deck, and Clive had to shout out names to check everyone was still on board.

Meanwhile below...

Alex:

I was asleep in my bunk and was aware of a commotion on deck. There was a lot of noise and shouting and then suddenly the boat heeled over until I was almost falling out of my bunk. I decided to go and offer my help. As soon as I stepped out of my bunk I was walking on the walls rather than the floor. I headed for the 'foulie locker' where the waterproofs were hung and where my lifejacket was also hanging up. I noticed that there was water pouring in through the roof vent, indicating that the boat was right over on its side. By the time I got on deck the sail had shredded itself and the (spinnaker) pole was broken and the boat was starting to right itself. Everyone was soaked due to the rain and some had been up to their waists in water. There was confusion as to which hatch to recover the sail through and below decks Flash and others were running from the foredeck hatch to the main hatch and back again. We eventually recovered the remains of the sail and I headed back to my bunk to try to get some sleep as I was due to be back on watch in an hour's time.

The broken spinnaker pole meant that we could no longer carry out certain sail manoeuvres and everyone just hoped that we would not be in a tight scrap with another boat at the end of the leg. The sewing group began in earnest to repair the flanker as we would need it again for certain.

The events of that night shook everyone up and served to reinforce that the sea is a volatile environment and the boat a very powerful one. In hindsight we were lucky to get away with only a torn spinnaker, broken spinnaker pole and several lost ropes. It was amazing that nobody was injured.

23rd October 2004, Day 21

Approaching the Equator

Today was Alex's birthday, so it began with a 02:00 rendition of *Happy Birthday* from the whole crew during the watch changeover. It was also the day when we were due to cross the equator.

There is a very old Navy tradition applicable to 'new' crew sailing across the equator for the first time. In our case this was the entire crew except for Clive who had previously delivered a boat from South to North so making him exempt from the ceremony. The tradition states that crew who have not crossed the equator before (Pollywogs[1]) have to be tried

---

[1] See Wikipedia 'Line-crossing ceremony',

in a mock-up court presided over by 'King Neptune' (the Skipper). They are accused of such heinous crimes as falling asleep on watch, making a poor round of tea and snoring. For their sins, the crew member – who is always found guilty - is doused in a bucketful of old food which has been collected over the previous couple of days, rotting and fermenting in the equatorial heat. Everyone in turn was tried, found guilty and then ceremoniously covered in porridge, marmite, soup, couscous, spaghetti bolognese, etc.

Once King Neptune has served up the punishment to the crew, they then become 'Shellbacks' and have earned the right to cross the equator.

Today was also 'operation' day for Nicko. During the start of the race he had slipped and banged his leg, thinking nothing more of it until a few days later when it began to swell. Dr Ruth had a look and decided it was not broken but kept an eye on it. After some time he developed a haematoma which would need to be drained. We waited a few days for a steady spell of calm weather when the boat would be flat and Ruth could operate more safely.

The saloon table was cleared and covered in paper towel. Nicko's ankle was covered with iodine and he was given a local anaesthetic before Ruth cut open the haematoma to drain it. There were some green-looking crew who quickly left the area for some fresh air. Once drained, a dressing was put on and Nicko was ordered to stay below decks in his bunk for a couple of days.

Later on that eventful day, while Phil was on mother duty, he managed to bake a birthday cake for Alex. But due to the angle of heel of the boat the cake came out rather wedge-shaped; about four inches thick at one end and one inch thick at the other. Even so he did a great job covering it with chocolate spread and smarties. It went down well with the crew as they all sang *Happy Birthday* again at the 18:00 watch changeover.

Alex:

What an amazing day. Just to be sailing was great and to cross the equator the same day was amazing. A birthday to remember forever.

―――――――――――

The sailing was steady and pleasant, with the trade winds helping to keep the temperatures on deck bearable, while below decks it was like a sauna. Living inside a metal box with 17 others in the tropics was becoming most unpleasant. There was no air-conditioning and because of the steady wind we could not open the deck hatches for fear of a wave coming in and soaking everything below decks. This meant sleeping was getting very difficult indeed, especially during the day.

Alex:

Around the equator, the temperature outside was well into the high 30s and below decks it was even hotter, with the humidity sky high. What this meant was that once I got into my bunk I would just lie there and sweat; feeling the sweat pool on my stomach and trickle in rivulets down my sides.

Eventually I would drop off to sleep, only to wake up literally in a puddle of my own sweat. In order to try to cool down you could head off to the galley and make yourself a cold drink. The only problem with that was that the water for drinking was taken from the sea and pumped through a desalination machine to turn it into drinking water. This meant that it was the same temperature as the sea water which was in the high 20s. So even the coldest drink was still lukewarm.

The other option for cooling down was to dowse yourself with a bucket of sea water on deck. Initially cooling, the water would evaporate quickly in the breeze and within minutes you were bone dry again. Also, because it was salt water, the salt would stay on the skin and become an irritant. Some of the crew suffered from bad cases of 'yottie bottie'; a condition where the salt causes sores on the backside from continually getting damp and not drying properly. Several crew were seen at the helm (the only place you could go on deck where no-one could be behind you) with their shorts round their ankles trying to get some fresh air to the affected area to dry it out properly. The only real cure was to have a fresh water shower, a rare luxury.

26th October 2004, Day 24

11°22'.20 S   35°35'.81 W

100 miles off the coast of Brazil

It was very hot both day and night. We managed to get through the doldrums without too many problems or losing too much time. There were frequent shows of dolphins and flying fish. The spinnaker had been up for several days and there was the constant job of keeping it carefully trimmed with someone at the front calling trim and someone else on the winch winding in the sheet.

Twenty-three days into the leg, there was talk of arrival time in Buenos Aires and a sweepstake had begun amongst the crew, even though we were still over 2,500 miles from the finish.

During the radio chat show, Paula managed to get some information from the Save the Children boat that had been seriously lagging behind. They had had a terrible time, with damaged sails, lightning strikes and long delays in the doldrums. Also their water-maker kept breaking down which meant rationed drinks and no showers – hard to bear in the heat. They were now over 600 miles behind.

The tropical storms were still around and everyone had to be prepared for them. During one watch, the Grunters did eight sail changes one after the other as the wind changed in strength and direction.

It was during one of these mad watches that Alex and Wrighty were finishing off packing a spinnaker in the sail locker under the foredeck. This space was laughingly nicknamed the 'Zero G Lounge' due to the fact that the when boat took off on a large wave, it would drop away leaving everything suspended in the air for a split second, much like a fairground ride. This time when the boat hit a wave, the two of them went flying. Wrighty landed on the metal door frame and Alex unfortunately landed on top of him, breaking three ribs. Wrighty was confined to his bunk for a few days as he couldn't move without being in pain.

The oppressive heat began to make tempers flare and everyone had to be that extra bit more tolerant of each other. Not an easy thing to do in a 72' steel box in the tropics. Boredom was becoming an issue with the monotony of the day-to-day routine. This race was bringing out the worst, and best, in people.

4th November 2004, Day 33

35°10'.38 S   54°54'.74 W

Entering the River Plate

We were about to pass our first waypoint in the run up to Buenos Aires. Turning from the Atlantic into the River Plate, the water went from blue-green to a muddy brown. The wind was all over the place and we had been warned of the 'Pampero', a local wind which can suddenly increase to 40 knots.

We were making good progress in the dark under spinnaker when the wind suddenly died away and there was an eerie feeling on board. It was pitch black with no lights around and we slowed down to one knot of boat speed. Thinking this may be the precursor to a Pampero, Alex climbed to the end of the spinnaker pole, ready to release the sail. The rest of the Groaners were busy on the foredeck getting the Number One Yankee ready.

The wind began to stir, but from the opposite direction. The call was given to drop the kite and Alex released the sail from the end of the spinnaker pole as the crew hoisted the yellow foresail. The drop was slick with no foul-ups, which was just as well because the wind dramatically increased, the Yankee One came down to be replaced by the Yankee Two and two reefs were put in the mainsail. It was now blowing 36 knots and we were trucking along again, Alex still hanging from the end of the pole.

At 23:01 ship's time we passed Waypoint Two and Paula radioed Challenge Business to let them know where we were. This reporting was a requirement of the Race Control and continued all the way to the finish.

As dawn broke it was a grey blustery day over the brown muddy waters. There was now almost constant radio reporting by Paula as we neared the finish line. The rain was drizzling down and the whole crew came up on deck for a photo as we crossed the finish line, between an orange buoy and a small committee boat.

We had made it. We crossed the finish at 09:06 boat time on 5th November, having covered 6464 miles in 33 days. We were disappointingly in eighth place.

There was still some way to go before we could relax as we still had another ten miles to go and lots of arrival tasks to complete before we reached the marina and Yacht Club Argentina. The sails were dropped and folded away; the mooring lines and fenders were retrieved from behind the crash bulkhead in the bow where they were stored. All the ropes were coiled and hung up in the sail locker; the ships log was completed, passports were found, customs forms filled in and the race declaration was signed by everyone.

It was time for a cuppa as we motored towards the skyscrapers on the horizon and reflected on the journey. Everyone was tired and in need of some rest, but there was still more work to be done.

As we neared the marina we could hear our song blaring out on the PA system. We rounded the corner and could see hundreds of people lining the walls and the seven other Challenge boats already in. The crew of *SAIC*, who had finished at midnight, also came down to greet us in. They had been partying all night and were still going strong. It was a very emotional moment for everyone and there were a few tears, some of joy, some of relief.

The shore crew from Challenge Business came down with a box of cold beer, five bottles of champagne, beef steaks, fries, fruit and croissants. We ate as if we hadn't had food for weeks; it was good to have something solid to actually chew on.

There were lots of photographers and we sprayed the champagne and posed for team photos. Clive was interviewed by a TV crew. We then all gratefully headed up to the 'Rock the Dock' bar, where our sponsor David was waiting for us with a bar full of drinks. At 10 o'clock in the morning, after over a month at sea, it didn't take long for the alcohol to take effect and we were soon dancing on the tables. We staggered back down to the dock to see *Unisys* and *Me to You* come in and the party started all over again.

Eventually we all headed for our apartments and a well needed night's sleep in a nice bed which would stay still for the whole night. Mind you, we were all so tired and drunk that we could probably have slept anywhere that night.

Buenos Aires Stopover

There was so much to do before we could relax and enjoy our time off. We had to empty the boat of everything, all the unused food and rubbish, sails and kit. The bunks were removed and taken to a local laundry to be cleaned. All the equipment had to be checked and repaired or replaced. Paula had the job of collating all the requisition requests and ordering them from Challenge Business, who had a container of spares shipped to Argentina. Phil would carry out complete checks on the engine, generator, water-maker and all the systems on board. Alex went up the mast to carry out a detailed rig check. The winches were stripped down, cleaned and repaired. The sailmaking team, led by Wrighty, Paul and Rob would check over each sail carefully and carry out any minor repairs needed. Major repairs would be carried out by the sail manufacturers and points deducted from the team. Luckily we had no major damage, except for the storm staysail which was in two pieces. Fortunately for us, the storm sails did not carry a penalty for damage.

However, we were soon to learn of a protest against us and two other boats. We had crossed the Traffic Separation Zone off the coast of France. While not explicit in the rules, we were deemed not to have crossed it correctly at right angles and were subject to a one place penalty, making us joint 9th overall. This protest hearing set a precedent and was to have repercussions in all future round the world yacht races.

The crew also had time to reflect properly on their own performance and that of the team during the first leg. Clive debriefed everyone individually and together as a whole team. We were all given the chance to have our say and then move on without dwelling on the issues or starting witch-hunts. These were crucial to our development as a team. It appeared that things had not been happy on the Grunters watch, which was led by Mike, and he was not pleased with his own performance.

After several days of hard work on the boat we had a few days off to relax and explore the country. Some stayed in Buenos Aires, while others travelled around seeing the sights. It was well needed time away from the boat and each other.

The crew started to gather back in Buenos Aires a week before the race start. This was to be a tough leg; 40 days in the Southern Ocean, including rounding the notorious Cape Horn. We would need to pull together and support each other if we were going to get through it safely.

There was a leaving party for our leggers, Adrian and Tony, to thank them. The jobs on the boat started again, with the arrival of the bunks from the laundrette, clean and fresh-smelling. The food had arrived and it was a massive job to load it back onto the boat. This had to be done in a disciplined manner, with the food for the end of the leg going in first.

To help get the crew working better, Clive arranged a team-building day. We headed out of town into the forests around the city. There, next to a river, was an old cruise ship which was to be our base for the day. One of the new leggers, John (JC), came straight from the airport to join us, while Mike was nowhere to be seen. We all changed into running shoes except JC who only had his leather deck shoes. The challenge for the day was to compete in teams of three in a running, cycling, paddling and swimming endurance event.

The first leg was a ten mile cross-country run with one member of each team on a mountain bike. The terrain was hard going with the temperature around 30 degrees and very high humidity. Quickly the teams spread out. After the run there was a series of rope and plank bridges to cross, then a three-man kayak had to be paddled around an island before the teams dived into the appropriately named Piranha River to swim towards the finish. The final act was a climb and zip-wire across the finish line.

Tired and dreary, soaked in sweat, we headed back to the base for a shower and debrief. JC had massive blisters on his feet from running in his deck shoes, Rich got stung by a bee and a few people had ticks buried under the skin in their legs. In hindsight, we all thought it was too much.

Clive gave the team a talk about the next leg and how we would be facing a tougher time in the Southern Ocean than we had on the team build. After a BBQ we headed back to our hotel.

Once back it was clear that things were not right. Mike was nowhere to be seen and his room was empty except for a note. He had decided to leave the team and fly home, not happy with himself. This was a shock to some and expected by others. The problem now was that it was too short notice for Challenge Business to find a replacement crew member and get them out to Buenos Aires for the start in a couple of days time. We would be doing the tough second leg one crew member short.

Drastic measures were called for and we had an emergency meeting. After extensive talks, Clive asked Alex to change watch and become the new Watch Leader of the Grunters. This meant that the Groaners would be one crew down in one of the toughest legs when every available pair of hands would be needed. Nicko (the Navigator) would have to help out and become a part-time Groaner for the leg when required.

Alex:

The first thing I did as the new Grunter Watch Leader was to have a one-to-one meeting with each of the watch members to find out more about them and how the watch was structured. Without dwelling on it too much, I also needed to know what had gone so wrong on the previous leg. We then had a complete watch meeting where we agreed we couldn't change what had happened but we would move on and learn from it. I also outlined how things were going to work on the next leg and got buy-in from everyone. This was critical if things were going to work and it was also vitally important that we trusted each other. In the Southern Ocean we would literally be looking out for each other's lives.

Paula:

I was on the Grunter watch with Mike. He didn't manage us well during that first leg and the team had fallen apart a little. It was a relief when he left us; it cleared the air. We were completely ready to have someone like Alex come across to our watch. We needed to rebuild and Alex was great; calm and relaxed but practical and professional. It was a good solution and I went into the challenging second leg feeling much happier than if Mike had stayed.

On the Thursday before the start we had the prize-giving ceremony. We knew we were not up for a major prize, but we did win the award for first over the start line and the 'Rubber Chicken' Media Award for the funniest story. (The time when Tony was sick from the top of the mast.)

All the jobs were finished by Friday and the boat was ready to go. Saturday, the day before the start, was becoming a traditional day off for us and this was no exception. A last chance to email friends and family and relax before we headed off into the fury of the Southern Ocean.

Start day. Stelmar first across the line

Beating out past the Needles four hours after the start.
Crossing tacks with *Save the Children*

Phil on the bow

Phil climbing to end of spinnaker pole

Leg 2
Buenos Aires - Wellington
6000 miles, 40 days
Sunday 28th November 2004
Buenos Aires

MANY OF THE TEAM WERE BEGINNING to get itchy feet ashore and wanted to get back on to the boat and go sailing again; even Paula who never thought she would think like that. We would be leaving behind the luxuries of dry land and civilisation; restaurants, parties and warm, dry beds.

There was a quiet, anxious feeling over breakfast as people began to think of the task ahead; cold, stormy weather, huge seas, danger, Cape Horn, wet bunks, lack of sleep. But there were also the positives; the Southern lights, camaraderie, teamwork, New Zealand.

There was a buzz in the marina as all the crews lined up on their boats for the blessing of the fleet. Then a prep talk by Sir Chay followed before the final interviews were given to reporters. We left in reverse order so we were the 5th boat to go. *Praise You* blasted out over the speaker system as we cast off and headed out to the start line. We had plenty of time to get everything shipshape as we sailed the ten miles from the marina to the start. Phil and Alex undid the 24 bolts to remove the cover of the crash bulkhead right at the front of the boat, to store the bulky fenders away for the rest of the leg. The mooring lines were coiled up and placed in heavy-duty black bags and put right in the bottom of the bilge under the floor. We wouldn't be needing those either for at least 37 days.

As we neared the start area we were joined by lots of small spectator craft, all jostling for the best viewing positions and kept back by the Prefecture (Argentine Navy). Everyone knew their jobs for the start, only this time Clive decided to take the helm. The winds were about ten knots and as we made our run for the line we were not in the leading bunch. We crossed the line in 8th place, disappointing but not the end of the world as there was still over 6000 miles to go. Two boats however had crossed the line too early and were given a penalty. They had to wait at a designated point for one hour. Better to be five seconds late than two seconds early.

We had full sail up as we tacked down the muddy waters of the River Plate to the Atlantic. Everything was running smoothly and we broke into the watch system. The Grunters were the first ones off so we headed below decks, grabbed a quick snack of oatcakes and lay down. Most people went straight to sleep. The novelty of start day had worn off and we all knew what lay ahead. We also knew we needed to grab sleep whenever we could.

Our first full watch was from 18:00-22:00. We settled straight back into the routine of the boat, only this time we were going to be much more proactive with trimming the sails and data logging every 15 minutes as agreed in our team debrief. The wind was fairly steady all night and it was hard to make up much distance in such a close fleet. The race became a procession down the River Plate as teams made up a boat length here and there.

The weather was warm and sunny as we entered the Atlantic and began our run down the Tierra del Fuego coast to Cape Horn. The gentle swell rocked the boat as we steadily made our way through the fleet under spinnaker. There was also an abundance of wildlife to watch; dolphins, whales, albatross, sharks and at one point we were joined by a turtle.

Wednesday 1st December 2004, Day 4

40°45'.29 S   56°49'.82 W

It was the first day of December and everyone was focused on the racing, but to brighten things up below decks, Paula decided to turn the boat into a giant Advent calendar. She put numbers on the cupboard doors, drawers and storage boxes using coloured insulation tape, then grabbed some 'goodies' from the snack box and made some cards. She then popped a card and some goodies into a plastic zip-lock bag and put it behind each 'door'. Then during the first watch changeover of the day, someone would pick a name from a hat to find the relevant door and open it. A great idea to help relieve the monotony below decks during the race.

So far on this leg we had damaged two of our spinnakers, but not too badly, and there was a team of 'sewers' busy stitching them back together again. We were hearing reports from the other boats of much more significant damage which would hinder them throughout the rest of the leg. There was a lot of downwind sailing and the fleet had spread out quite a bit, some staying close to the shore and others heading out to sea. We were sitting mid fleet in 6th place.

We were still enjoying good weather although it had begun to get colder as we headed more and more south. It was much easier to settle into a routine in these conditions, a complete contrast to leg one with a storm and a man overboard on the first night and 56 knots of wind. Despite being chilly at night, the sky was clear with amazing sunsets and sunrises. We had already moved the boat time back one hour and it was starting to get light at 02:30.

Monday 6th December 2004, Day 9

54°44'.5 S   65°04'.0 W

Passing Tierra del Fuego

Everyone was beginning to put on more and more clothing as it got colder and colder. Thin thermals, thick thermals, fleecy mid-layer jacket and salopettes, drysuit, hat, inner gloves, fleece-lined diving gloves, thin socks, thick waterproof socks, neoprene lined Le Chammeau boots, ski goggles for the helm and a life jacket. It was taking longer and longer to get ready to go on deck. That meant less and less time sleeping.

We were running down alongside Tierra del Fuego and getting ready to round Cape Horn. It was unbelievably close racing with three other boats right next to us (*BP*, *VAIO* and *Me to You*). Incredible after just over a week. We managed to pass and pull away from all three and set off after the two leaders, *Sark* and *BG*, in the race to be the first round Cape Horn, 100 miles away.

The weather was getting worse and it was starting to rain. We were closing in on the leaders when Clive announced that we had a problem. Karen, our legger, had swollen legs and hands and although she felt OK, we didn't know what was wrong. She had been like this for a couple of days and her symptoms weren't getting any better. Although we had very comprehensive medical kits on board, one of the things we were unable to do was blood testing, and we were worried that the swelling could indicate kidney or liver problems. Without a proper diagnosis and blood tests we couldn't be sure. Ruth consulted the Challenge medic and it was decided to play safe. We were about to enter the most dangerous and isolated waters on the planet. We had no choice but to suspend racing and head for shore to drop Karen off.

The nearest suitable port was Puerto Williams in Chile. The wind was blowing hard and we made good progress towards land. Alex was on the helm, fighting to keep the boat upright, whilst Clive told the crew about what was happening. We tacked, put the 3rd reef in the mainsail and headed for Puerto Williams, surrendering our 3rd place to the boat behind.

Emails traded back and forth between Clive, Ruth, the medical team at Derriford hospital near Plymouth, Challenge Race Control, Vale (Clive's Argentinean wife) and the coastguard. Amazingly both Clive and Nicko had been to Puerto Williams before and Clive called an old friend, 'Wolf', who began to sort things out on shore for us.

We took eight hours to get to Puerto Williams. The scenery was stunning; a cross between a Scottish loch and a fjord. All very barren and desolate. When we arrived there was a small Chilean Navy boat for us to moor alongside. Wolf had also arranged an ambulance to collect Karen and take her to hospital. We had made up a Chilean courtesy flag to fly on the way in as we didn't carry one because it was not a planned stop. Julian handed it over to the Chilean Navy officer who asked us all to sign it and they returned the compliment by giving us theirs. It was quite an occasion – formal, but surreal too.

After the authorities checked all our passports, we said goodbye to a tearful Karen as she headed off in the ambulance and we turned back out to sea. The whole episode took no more than 20 minutes, but we still had to return to the exact spot where we had suspended racing in order to restart. We were now two crew down. Clive gave everyone a pep talk about keeping our heads up and re-evaluating our goals for the leg.

As we motored back out to sea, we re-arranged the watch system for the second time in as many weeks to even them up. It was decided that Rob would move across and become a Groaner. The mood on board was sombre as the adrenaline of the race, 3rd place and Cape Horn had disappeared and everyone had to remind themselves to focus on the race and the challenge ahead.

When we finally restarted racing at exactly the same place that we had suspended racing, we had not only lost 3rd place, but also 19 hours and were now in last place. We all hoped to get some redress from the race committee for the time lost.

After only 24 hours of racing again, we rounded Cape Horn and despite losing 19 hours we had already caught and passed *Pindar* and were only 114 miles from the leaders. Our goal now was to catch as many boats as possible before New Zealand.

Clive came up on deck with more bad news. We were **not** eligible for any redress, either in points or time allowance, for the medical evacuation (medivac) because it was our own 'fault'. If we had gone to help another boat with their problem, then there may have been some redress. This is to prevent boats from cheating.

The wind was steady around 40 knots most of the time. It was freezing cold, often snowing, and the seas were huge, breaking over the boat and sending crew sprawling along the deck. Mother duty was tough in these conditions and we put up a plastic screen between the galley and the saloon table just in case a pot of food went flying across the boat as it lurched off a wave. Paula scalded herself while making hot drinks for the watch on deck. Luckily it wasn't too bad and it was decided anyone cooking should wear 'foulie' trousers in case of spilled hot water or food.

Friday 10th December 2004, Day 13

58°31'.52 S   78°05'.94 W

There was a burning smell coming from the navigation station from time to time which no-one could figure out. Phil had a look behind the computer screens but found nothing.

The good news was that we were up to 8th place and homing in on *Samsung* for 7th place. Within 12 hours we had passed them too. We were working well as a team. We kept ourselves motivated by setting new goals of catching the next boat. We didn't know it at the time but it was during this period that we set the 24-hour distance record for the leg (259.2 miles). We were flying.

The cold was becoming an issue and some people were putting calamine lotion on their faces to soothe them. The salt spray would hit your face so hard it would sting. Frostbite was a concern too, especially at night, and to combat this it was decided that we would rotate the crew at half-hour intervals with only three on deck at a time. This also reduced the risk of more people getting hurt should a wave come crashing over the boat. Below decks everything was at an angle and it took longer than normal to do anything. Even getting dressed would take 25 minutes.

Paula:

During happy hour yesterday we had a bottle of champagne to celebrate going round Cape Horn. Good to all be on deck together and have a drink, but one bottle of champagne doesn't go far with 16 people!

There were five other boats in sight of us and we couldn't believe how much we had made up over the last couple of days. We had now sailed a quarter of the way around the world. Clive issued a statement about the medivac and lack of redress saying: *we support the race rules and are cracking on.* We also had some news on Karen. She was not suffering anything terminal, she had had an allergic reaction to some medication. Even so we couldn't have taken the risk of going into the Southern Ocean not knowing what was wrong and everyone agreed that we had made the right decision.

We were now so far south that it didn't get dark at all during the night, just twilight. When the clouds broke we could sometimes make out the Aurora Australis or Southern Lights which were stunning. There were no injuries or damage to the boat, and we could see five other Challenge yachts around us. Incredible after 2,600 miles of racing.

Monday 13th December 2004, Day 16

56°19'.49 S   97°32'.97 W

Southern Ocean, 1000 miles west of Cape Horn

The Grunters had been up on the 02:00-06:00 watch. It was freezing cold outside with snowstorms and massive seas (a nearby survey ship recorded a 22m wave). The wind was touching 40 knots at times. Black clouds would come scudding across the sky, under them was snow and more wind. We were in a close battle with *Save the Children* for 5th place, having been in last place only one week before. We had been doing incredibly well under the circumstances and with two crew down. As the clouds came over we would lose sight of the other boat and once the visibility came back we would see if we had made or lost distance to them. It was very close and tense racing, we were pushing hard despite the almost survival conditions on deck.

The Grunters came off deck at 06:10 after handing over to the Groaners. We headed down the steps and hung up our lifejackets and drysuits in the foulie locker. There was always a fight to get to the locker as the boat was pitching around and people wanted to get to breakfast and off to bed for some sleep.

Eventually we all sat down around the saloon table and had a bowl of nice hot porridge. Served up in a dog bowl, the technique was to hold the bowl under your chin and scoop the food in. This was the same for almost every meal as the table was at such an angle that anything put on it would go flying across the boat. We became experts at wedging drinks bottles and bowls in our laps. All food was served in bowls and eaten with spoons. It was easier.

The boat hit a large wave and Paula spilled her porridge everywhere. Over herself, the table, seats, floor, cupboard doors and Newton's foot. Everyone else found it funny except Newton. Paula headed off to the heads to clean up while the others went to their bunks to get some rest.

Alex:

I was lying in my bunk trying to get to sleep, listening to the howling of the wind outside and the sound of the water washing along the deck. Every other wave was massive and each time the boat slammed into the next one I wondered how long the mast would be able to stand up to such a pounding and I ran through in my mind the process of cutting it free should it break. As I lay there, despite being strapped in by three bunk straps, I would slide along my bunk until my head banged against the bulkhead at the top of the berth.

07:12

The boat took off on a particularly big wave and came crashing down. After the water rush had gone from the cockpit there was the one sound you never wanted to hear - especially in the freezing Southern Ocean - 'Man overboard!'

Alex:

The first thing to go through my mind was, Did I hear that or did I imagine it? A split second later I thought, Why were they not clipped on to the boat? I sat up in my bunk and heard Julian call out again. Immediately I sprung out of my bunk, grabbed my fleece jacket and headed to the steps to see what we could do to help. On the way I got Ruth up and had her put her drysuit on ready to go on deck if need be.

Phil and Paula were also up, having heard the pandemonium on deck and we all met at the bottom of the steps. I climbed up and asked Julian what was happening. He said that nobody had gone overboard but that Flash was injured on the foredeck.

Paula:

I was in the heads cleaning off the porridge spilt at breakfast when the boat lurched unusually violently and I heard those dreaded two words, 'man overboard'. I immediately felt sick with worry, but also that calculated calmness took over, as it does in crises. I grabbed the boathook just in case we needed it, heard that Flash was seriously hurt and that he was coming down the foredeck hatch. I went to the sail locker to help. The hatch was open, it was raining hard and all I saw were Flash's legs hanging down with his red and blue boots. Clive, Paul, me and Phil helped ease him down onto the sail bags. He was soaked and pale and in a lot of pain but conscious.

Flash had been up at the bow tightening the leach line on the Yankee when the boat nosedived into a huge wave. The force of the water washed Flash off his feet and threw him along the foredeck and into the rigging. He was hurt and in a lot of pain.

The Groaners (on watch) turned the boat away from the wind to reduce the heeling and make it more stable. Ruth went forward to assess Flash while the Grunters began to prepare things below decks and get the kettle on for some warm drinks.

As the boat was now upright it was safe to open the foredeck hatch and get Flash down that way. It was ironic that it was this exact situation we had practised in the training sail all those months before. Flash was gently lowered down to the waiting Grunters.

It soon became apparent that things were not good for Flash. He had smashed his left arm, with his forearm moving completely independently of his upper arm.

It was difficult to carry him along the narrow corridor past the mast and onto the saloon table which had been cleared. He was 6' 4" and must have weighed 14 stone. Plus the boat was still pitching and rolling in the high waves, despite being hove to. He was still in a lot of pain, his face showed it, and he was holding his arm tightly to stop it moving too much.

Once on the saloon table, Alex and Phil began to cut off his drysuit, mid-layers and thermals, while others held him still to stop him falling or bouncing too much. First the drysuit was cut open, then the layers of thermal clothing, until Ruth could properly assess the damage. His arm was certainly broken and in more than one place, but luckily there was nothing else wrong with him.

Ruth administered anaesthetic and with Kate's help (Kate was a physio) very carefully strapped Flash's arm up to immobilise it completely. Three hours later and he was cushioned in his bunk which had been cut up specially to contain him securely and comfortably. The bunk above him had been dismantled completely to allow Ruth access to him. All this took a couple of hours.

Ruth spoke with 'Dr Spike' at Derriford hospital using the satellite phone and told him of the situation. After consultation it was decided that with such a bad fracture, Flash needed to be operated on within seven days, before the bones started to fuse together and he would lose the full use of his arm.

11:22

A quick look at the chart and it was plain to see our predicament. We were in one of the remotest positions on the planet, about as far from civilisation as you could get. There were no fishing fleets around or shipping routes, so a ship-to-ship transfer was not an option. We were also well out of helicopter range so we were effectively on our own and had to deal with this situation ourselves.

The nearest land was Antarctica to the south, but there were no medical facilities there. New Zealand was still over 3,500 miles and three weeks away. To the north, Easter Island was 1,800 miles away, about 12 days.

The nearest port which was suitable was 1,000 miles behind us, back in Chile which we had just left. We decided we had to turn around 180 degrees and start making progress towards South America. This meant that we would probably have to retire from the leg and also that we would have almost no chance of winning the race overall.

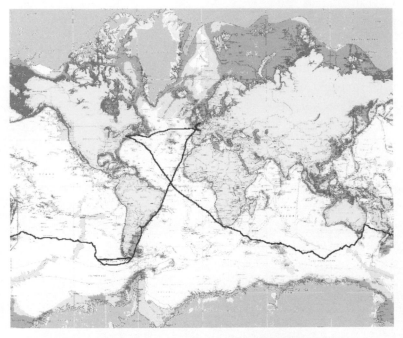

Actual route from the on board computer showing detour west of Cape Horn

There were also logistical obstacles to overcome. We would now be at sea for an extra 2,000 miles and about 12 days. We would need extra food, gas for cooking and fuel to run the generator and heater. Even once we dropped Flash off, things were not going to be straightforward. We would have a 50+ day leg and very little time for rest in New Zealand, arriving ten days after everyone else. Also all the boats were due to be hauled out in Wellington to check for hull damage before the second Southern Ocean leg. The Challenge technical team were worried that we would not get back in time for this.

It was demoralising to sail back past all the boats we had painstakingly caught and passed, but there was no other sensible option.

We had our second communication embargo from the boat while Challenge Business informed everyone's next of kin what was happening. There was frustration and disappointment on board. Flash was angry with himself and felt he had let the team down.

Tuesday 14th December 2004, Day 17

Tuesday 14th December 2004, Day 17

56°10'.3 S   93°27'.5 W

We still had 611 miles before getting to Chile. The Chilean authorities suggested we head for a navy base called Punta Arenas and evacuate Flash there for medical attention. Looking on a chart we were not so sure. Punta Arenas was quite a way inland, behind a very fractured coastline with many rocks. It would be difficult and dangerous to navigate through and we didn't have decent charts on board for this part of the country.

After a discussion, we came up with a second option, Ushuaia, on the Argentinean side of the Beagle Canal. Clive's Argentinean wife Vale could fly to Ushuaia and sort things out prior to our arrival (again!). This was the preferred option for us, not only because of Vale, but the Beagle Canal was a much safer option for both boat and crew. The problem was that the Chilean authorities didn't see it that way. They were still adamant that we use their port and facilities.

Unbeknown to us at the time, emails, faxes and phone calls were going back and forth between the British, Argentinean and Chilean embassies and Challenge Business, trying to sort out the situation. Meanwhile we were still staunchly sailing towards South America as fast as we could.

There was a lot of media interest; the *Daily Telegraph* ran a full page front cover article in their sports section on our predicament and there were requests for interviews when we eventually arrived in New Zealand. All this went over our heads; we were just focusing on getting Flash to safety. There was a huge upwelling of team spirit on the boat.

As we were now not officially racing we were allowed to use the engine to help us, although most of the time it was still quicker to sail. We also allowed the crew to spend more time below decks out of the cold. However, even with the heater on, below decks it was still only about seven degrees. Positively balmy compared to the freezing temperatures on deck.

Thursday 16th December 2004, Day 18

55°52'.6 S   80°34'.5 W

We had expressed our dissatisfaction about sailing to Punta Arenas and the latest plan was to do a ship-to-ship transfer once we were near the coast. A Chilean Navy ship was to meet us and lower a small inflatable RIB to use for the transfer of Flash and Ruth. Initially this sounded like a good compromise, but after some thought it was also deemed to be too dangerous, considering how serious the break was. We would continue to Ushuaia and evacuate Flash in a controlled manner onto firm, dry land.

Clive had been emailing Challenge Business for special dispensation for getting 'outside assistance'. This is not normally allowed during yacht racing except in special circumstances. We believed ours to be 'special circumstances' and Clive got verbal and written consent to dock and collect extra food, fuel and water. Another obstacle surmounted.

However, we were being encouraged by both Challenge Business and Sir Chay Blyth personally, to retire from the leg and motor-sail as quickly as possible to Wellington. We **had** to be in Wellington by 12:00 on the 21st January for our maintenance check. On an email to us Sir Chay Blyth wrote:

The Global Challenge is certainly a challenge. We have seen in the past some major damage to yachts and severe injuries to individuals. What we have also seen is how the crews respond and get over their adversity. You on board Stelmar have certainly had your share of adversity with two medivac situations.

Soon you with Clive will be faced with a choice. The options are to return to where you stopped racing. This has powerful ongoing other potential challenges. For this you will receive 4 points for 12th position. The second option is to discontinue racing, take a more northerly and, in theory at least, a more forgiving route. It will still be hard. For this you will receive 3 points for retiring.

Within this equation and, to my mind, probably more important is the focus for the next and subsequent legs – there is the time factor for the preparation of the yacht in Wellington to consider. The more time spent there preparing the yacht will ensure your competitiveness for Leg 4.

You will have questions and by discussion amongst you the answers will come through. If they don't then contact me.

My personal belief and what I would be doing and expecting if I was to suffer in such a situation would be expecting us all to be on the same team. To concentrate on getting the yacht and its crew to Wellington as fast as reasonably possible. To prepare and focus on the remainder of the race.

You cannot win the Global Challenge Race now but you certainly have the potential to win legs. This was evident when you were catching up the fleet after you dropped off Karen.

Good luck and safe berthing to get Tim off.

Chay

We were advised to head further north, along the Chilean coast, once we left the Beagle Canal rather than head back south into the Southern Ocean. The reasoning behind this was that we were now a lone yacht and didn't have the safety net of the other eleven boats should we encounter a problem. Also, at latitudes of around 40° south, we were more likely to be nearer shipping and fishing fleets should we need help, and not alone in the cold desolate, iceberg-strewn wastes further south. The down side was that we would have to retire from the leg which meant that we would receive points equivalent to last place plus one, or 13th place.

There were debates on the boat as to what to do. Were we still eligible to compete in the whole race, bearing in mind that we wouldn't be completing this leg? Could we race again from where we had stopped racing (from Waypoint Flash) as we did with Karen, although this would mean going against the wishes of the race organisers?

We had many team meetings to discuss the options and generally decided that our desire was to continue racing. It was important to us. However, it was also the most dangerous option and safety was our first value. The odds were stacked against us and unless we had total agreement from everyone it was decided we should retire. Most of the crew wanted to continue racing and go back to the Southern Ocean, there were, however, some who expressed concern.

Clive, as the Skipper responsible for our safety, was understandably leaning towards the decision to retire, but decided he would not notify Challenge Business until after we had dropped Flash and started to head back west.

Another consideration for the crew was, if we were to retire, should we sail back to Wellington or motor-sail? For the purists among us it was the difference between 'sailing' around the world or not if some of it was under engine. Also if we were then just delivering the boat to Wellington, could some of the crew get off in Ushuaia, go home for Christmas and then fly out to rejoin the boat again in Wellington? Or quit altogether? We had already lost three people, we couldn't afford to lose any more. Plus, for those that stayed on the boat for another month under-crewed in the Southern

Ocean, it would be very tough to think about the ones who had left and were home at Christmas in front of log fires and eating Christmas dinner. Would we ever have been one team again after that? Unlikely.

Paul couldn't make up his mind what to do. He wasn't a sailing purist; in fact he had hardly done any sailing before the race. He was in it more for the experience of sailing round the world. He was also experiencing great agony because of a recurring pain in his elbow. He teetered and teetered on making a decision. He phoned his wife Karen on the satellite phone and said he would probably be home for Christmas. Initially she agreed, but after thinking about it for a while, sent him an email explaining that this was his dream and if he left he would probably regret it for the rest of his life. To make sure he didn't leave, and to emphasise her point, she cancelled his credit card so he couldn't buy a ticket home from Ushuaia. Fantastic.

During this difficult time we occasionally played the 'Sunscreen Song' by Baz Lurhman. The words were very poignant for us, one line reads;

"Sometimes you're ahead, sometimes you're behind,

But the race is long

And in the end it is only with yourself."

We were all very reflective over what had happened, but knew we still had a long way to go and needed to stick together and help each other through.

Meanwhile the Chilean authorities saga continued. They were still insistent on us going to Punta Arenas and once we told them we were going to Argentinean Ushuaia, they threatened to arrest the crew and impound the boat as soon as we entered Chilean waters. They claimed that they didn't believe we had an injured crew member onboard, otherwise we would have accepted their help. We carried on regardless.

The priorities to us were Flash's safety and looking after the boat and crew. Also, by now we were used to facing up to tough situations and we wouldn't be bowed.

Eventually we reached the safety and shelter of a large bay at the western end of the Beagle Canal. We dropped the sails and began the long journey under engine to Ushuaia, still almost 100 miles away. We continued with the watch system and began to collect Flash's belongings together ready for him to leave.

Just after midnight on 18th December a bright white searchlight lit up the boat and we were ordered to stop motoring. A large Chilean Navy vessel was blocking our way. They lowered a small boat over the side with three officials on board, heavily armed with machine-guns. We sat there in the dark and watched them motor across to us.

As they climbed on board they were greeted by Clive and escorted below. The crew stood by nervously. They asked to see the injured crew member and everyone's passports. One by one they checked the crew against their passport and woke the off watch to check theirs. It was quite daunting to be woken up by an armed guard shining a torch in your face.

Once they were satisfied that we did have an injured crew member, they left and returned to their boat, but not before they ordered us to travel on to clear Chilean customs in Puerto Williams - the same place we had dropped Karen off 11 days earlier. This just inconvenienced us more as we had to motor a further 30 miles in the wrong direction, clear customs, then motor back 30 miles past Ushuaia again and along the Beagle Canal.

Saturday 18th December 2004, Day 20

54°48'.56 S   68°18'.1 W

Ushuaia, Argentina

We finally tied up, alongside two other boats, in Ushuaia at 06:30 boat time. It was grey and murky and very cold. Ushuaia was set up for dealing with Antarctic cruise liners and icebreaker ships which docked there, rather than a relatively small sailing boat. The grey concrete town was set against a dramatic backdrop of snow-capped mountains. Luckily for us it was the middle of the summer and the temperature was around freezing, although without the wind it felt warmer.

There were two ambulances waiting for us and after we tied the boat up a couple of paramedics came on board with a stretcher. Ruth spoke to them about Flash. We gathered his belongings and he walked up the steps into the cockpit, where the paramedics strapped him to the stretcher to be carried over the other two boats to the ambulances.

It was an emotional moment as he sat in the back of the ambulance. We said goodbye and the doors closed on him and Ruth. The other ambulance took Paul away who had been suffering with a painful elbow, to have a hydrocortisone injection.

Vale had flown down to Ushuaia a few days earlier to sort out the arrangements and had managed to find a local hotel (The Albatross) to host us while we were there. They gave us two rooms to use for the day; the four remaining girls had one room and the eleven surviving guys the other. Very soon the radiators were covered with drying socks and gloves and there was a queue for the hot showers, our first for almost three weeks.

Everyone gathered for lunch in the hotel restaurant and discussed what needed to be done. Vale, who had competed in the previous Global Challenge race, had organised for us to take on 1,770 litres of fuel plus some full jerry cans and to have our gas bottles refilled. For the water tanks we had to use the fire hose on the pontoon. The crew who remained jobless were sent out to restock with whatever food they could find...

Even though we had full tanks and five extra jerry cans of fuel, it was only enough for about 2,000 miles of motoring; Wellington was still over 5,000 miles away. We would need to sail the majority of the distance whether we retired or not.

We packed the food away and tied down the new gas bottles under the cockpit. Everyone was back on board but we were not allowed to leave. The harbour authority decided that we came under the classification of a commercial ship, and as such would have to pay for a pilot to escort us the 200m out of the harbour. For this privilege he wanted $1,000. We managed to barter the price down to $500, but still thought it unnecessary and too much for five minutes work. However, they would not let us leave without him and we had to wait until he was ready.

We waited and waited and at 01:20, after five hours, he finally arrived to take us the 200m out of the harbour before stepping off onto a following boat to return to shore. We, however, carried on towards Puerto Williams for our meeting with the Chilean customs.

Three hours later we were back alongside the same navy ship where we had dropped off Karen, to sign the customs forms. We departed again - hoping that this was the last time we would visit Puerto Williams - headed west and three hours later motor-sailed past Ushuaia.

After ten hours of motoring past the stunning glaciers, which flowed down from the mountains to the Beagle Canal, we reached open water. While in the last bit of shelter provided by the mountains, we hoisted our mainsail and began sailing again. Rather poignantly a dolphin escorted us back to the open sea.

We now needed to maintain an average speed of seven knots in order to arrive on our deadline date of the 21st. If we averaged eight knots we would arrive four days earlier on the 17th.

During the journey from Ushuaia, we discussed whether to retire or whether to return to where the accident had occurred and continue racing, even though we would not make up the 2,000 miles to the other boats. Despite pressure from the race organisers, Sir Chay Blyth and Clive, we decided to return to the Southern Ocean and continue racing. We were determined not to give up, despite everything that had happened. We owed it to ourselves and to Flash.

Clive emailed Challenge Business our intention, but with the concession that we would head north once we reached the incident waypoint.

Once the news of our plans got out, we were inundated with supportive messages from family and friends and the other boats, as well as their supporters - people we had never met. Many people seemed to be getting inspiration from what we were going through.

There was also another front page article in the *Daily Telegraph* by Brendan Gallagher:

Battling Brits turn and turn again

In the best tradition of Brits fighting the elements in remote parts of the world at Christmas, Team Stelmar were heading back out into the treacherous Southern Ocean for a third time in two weeks yesterday after a second medical emergency threatened to end their participation in the Global Challenge...

The crew, skippered by professional yachtsman Clive Cosby, ...confounded yachting experts by opting to continue the second, and hardest, leg of the race from Buenos Aires to Wellington.

They now face a daunting 5,000 mile race against time to arrive in Wellington before Jan 23, the organisers' cut-off date if they wish to continue the race on Feb 6...

"There is almost no room for error and they are now three crew members light, but don't write them off yet. They have already shown themselves to be an incredibly durable and close crew. To turn around yet again and retrace all those hard-earned miles takes some doing."

By way of compromise with the organisers, ...Stelmar will head first for waymark alpha – which at 52 degrees south, 120 west is reckoned to be the most remote spot on Earth, some 2,000 miles from the nearest land – but then have agreed not to sail below 52 degrees. They will take a more northerly but marginally safer route than they would otherwise prefer if wishing to maximise boat speed...

Monday 20th December 2004, Day 22

55°25'.7 S   74°07'.3 W

We were now back in the Southern Ocean proper and the weather was there to greet us; freezing spray and 25-30 knots of wind. Everyone soon got back to the rhythm of life at sea; sailing, eating and sleeping, though with three less crew.

In contrast to the fresh air on deck, the burning smell had returned to the navigation station and this time Phil completely dismantled the area behind the computer. The bulkhead was wet and the salt water had been corroding the terminals, causing them to short out and burn. We had at least found the cause, fixing it would be a bit trickier. Luckily Phil was a fixer and never let a problem defeat him. With Alex 100 foot up the mast for over two hours, the masthead light in bits and an ammeter to test the current, Phil managed to get everything back working again.

Ruth decided to put a poem up on the bulkhead by the foulie locker which summed up the feeling on board:

Don't Quit;
Don't quit when the tide is lowest,
For it's just about to turn.
Don't quit over doubts and questions,
For there's something you may learn.
Don't quit when the night is darkest,
For it's just a while 'til dawn.
Don't quit when you've run the farthest,
For the race is almost won.
Don't quit when the hill is steepest,
For your goal is almost nigh.
Don't quit, for you're not a failure,
Until you fail to try.

Thursday 23rd December 2004, Day 25

56°10'.4 S   93°26'.2 W

We reached the place close to waypoint 'Flash' where we had suspended racing and started our engine. We had been told by the International Jury for the race that we didn't have to go back to where the incident happened, only to the point when we started our engine. This saved us a few hours motoring and we were able to get back to sailing our own race once more.

It was just before midnight in the UK and we decided to call Flash on the satellite phone to find out how he was and let him know how we were getting on. His parents answered the phone and were surprised to hear Clive's voice. Flash had had his arm operated on in Buenos Aires and after recovering for a few days, flew back home just in time for Christmas. His parents woke Flash up and he was amazed that we had called. Everyone individually got the chance to wish him Happy Christmas and he wished us luck in getting to Wellington on time.

The following day was Christmas Eve, and for us it was very cold, wet, windy and rough. Everyone was pretty much in 'survival mode'; eat – sleep – stay warm – go on watch. The night watches were bitterly cold on deck, with only three people up at any one time and rotating crew every half-hour to reduce the risk of frostbite.

Saturday 25th December 2004, Day 27

54°54'.5 S   99°23'.6 W

Christmas Day

The Grunters were woken at 05:20 for breakfast. Despite it being Christmas morning, it was business as usual on board. The weather hadn't changed for several days. It was still cold, wet and windy. After a warm breakfast it was up on deck to put the third reef in the mainsail as the wind was now over 30 knots. The sky was grey and it was raining. The salt spray stung as it lashed people's faces. Nicko popped his head up from the computer screens at the navigation station with the good news that the weather was expected to deteriorate over the following six hours.

Paula:

What a bleak start to Christmas. I remember being fed up with our situation, depressed about the number of watches still to come and generally miserable and cold. It was Christmas Day and to top it all when Nicko saw how glum I looked he said, "Cheer up, there's worse weather on the way".

Conversation on deck was difficult with that much wind and spray and with faces hidden behind face protectors and hoods. The crew would just sit on the cold steel deck, in the cockpit trying to keep warm; huddling with hoods up. Eating chocolate bars and drinking tea for comfort was impossible too as there was the ever-present risk of a wave coming over and snatching them away, even at the back of the boat.

At 12:00 the whole crew, except Alex and Wrighty, had Christmas lunch below decks. The two Watch Leaders nobly stayed on deck to keep the boat going. Conditions below decks were more festive, with a dinner of tinned turkey, powdered mash, tinned new potatoes, freeze-dried vegetables and gravy. A real Christmas feast, followed by tinned Christmas pudding and a spattering of custard.

There was a two hour 'happy hour' while everyone had lunch, then the clocks were reset at 14:00 back to 12:00 and the watch changed with the Groaners going on deck and the Grunters hitting their bunks.

With all the festivities over it was back to the same old routine of sailing the boat as quickly as possible to New Zealand. Some people hit an emotional low at this point, none more so than Ruth. She had done a marvellous job with the medical evacuations but had taken it out of her and she now spent more and more time in her bunk, refusing to come up on deck when the weather was particularly bad. This caused some friction on the Grunter watch, which was carefully managed by Alex, Clive and Wrighty to prevent it from escalating.

We were literally all in the same boat, the more we all pulled our weight the quicker we would get to Wellington.

It was decided that we would spend the extra time at sea educating everyone on the finer points of weather and sail trim, as well as working on fitness. It was easy to sit back and let others get on with the work, but we were all proactive and wanted to make up for our loss by doing better on future legs. We tried out different ways of sailing the boat and different sail combinations, to see what worked and what didn't. As we were not close racing other boats it didn't matter too much if we tried something that didn't work; at least we knew for the future.

We kept our spirits up by keeping busy and staying focused on the final goal of reaching New Zealand by our deadline. We were getting very slick at running the boat shorthanded.

Friday 31st December 2004, New Year's Eve

44°52'.7 S   117°30'.8 W

2000 miles from Cape Horn

Paula woke up and had an interview on the Satellite phone with Brendan Gallagher of the *Daily Telegraph*. There was to be an article in the New Year's Day edition about how things had been on board since the accident.

We also found out that there had been a huge earthquake and tsunami in south-east Asia which had reportedly killed many thousands of people. We held a two minutes silence during the next watch.

Also we had news about another medical evacuation on one of the other boats, *Unisys*. One of the crew had become seriously ill and they diverted to the nearby Chatham Islands. Once within range, a helicopter was despatched and the crew member was lifted off the boat and taken to hospital.

Life on deck in the southern ocean from left to right: Phil, Alex (helm), Ruth, Newton

Survival conditions

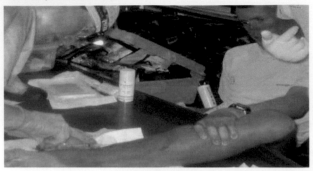

Nicko's
operation

20 minutes
after
Flash's accident

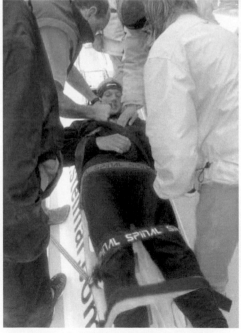

Flash being stretchered off in Ushuaia   Flash's x-ray

Arriving in Sydney

Leaving Cape Town

Proudly living our new sponsors brand

Hooning along from Boston to La Rochelle. In the lead, on the way to setting a new record.
From left to right: Adrian, Alex, Paula

Spontaneous on deck celebrations as we cross the finish line
From left to right: Rob H, Flash, Julian, Phil (with headcam),
Alex, Clive, Wrighty and Paula in foreground

Winning Leg six

From left to right: Rich, Primrose, Kate, Paul, Flash, Clive,
Julian, Alex (with trophy), Wrighty, Mike T, Ruth, Sue, Rob H,
Adrian, Newton, Phil, Paula

Before

After

Despite being only 400 miles from the finish, they decided to retire from the leg and motor-sail the two days to Wellington.

This was good news for us, as it now meant that by not retiring we were going to finish 11th (as long as we made it in time), and therefore saving another point. Had we retired, both boats would have been given points for 13th place.

At this point in the race, the lead boats were only two days away from the finish; we still had three weeks to go before we reached dry land.

Friday 7th January 2005, Day 40

42°58'.6 S   141°40'.6 W

The other eleven boats had finished and were safely in Wellington. We still had over 2200 miles to go.

We were doing our best to avoid the worst of the Southern Ocean storms and tried to skirt around the edges where the winds reached 'only' 40 knots. If we had still been racing with the fleet then we would have been more aggressive with our approach and punched through them. Instead we tended to head in a more northerly direction as this put us closer to the shipping lanes should anything else happen and we needed help. Also, we couldn't afford to lose any more crew or damage the boat unnecessarily. Our stay in Wellington would be short; there would be little time to repair any serious damage to the boat, so we were being cautious. It was now a case of getting to Wellington safely and in one piece.

The weather was not so bad between the storms and the further north we headed, the more bearable it became. The biting cold and sleet of the Southern Ocean gave way to grey skies and rain.

The watch routine continued. We couldn't afford to let up physically or emotionally as we still had a deadline to make and would be penalised with retirement if we didn't, which would mean all our hard work and efforts would have been in vain.

Thursday 20th January 2005, Day 52

Cook Strait

The wind had suddenly increased from drifting conditions to a full storm in a very short time and we had to take the mainsail down completely. Our ETA was looking good for early afternoon and we had been advised by Challenge Business to arrive in daylight if possible to make the most of the TV coverage. All was going to plan but then the weather played its final hand. We were struggling to make headway against the 50 knot winds and building seas. Our afternoon ETA came and went and we were still no nearer the entrance to Wellington harbour. We were desperate to get there.

Watches changed and darkness fell. Many of the crew were staying awake for the finish, but wary of getting in the way on deck, they waited in the saloon which was getting busy with people sitting around.

A police boat came out to escort us in to the harbour entrance. It seemed to take an eternity, as we had to continually tack back and forth. We were still theoretically racing and unable to switch our motor on.

Eventually the wind died enough for us to rehoist our mainsail and head over the finish line. The time was 23:05 when the gun eventually fired. We had sailed for 52 days and covered over 9700 miles in what was supposed to be a 6000 mile, 40 day leg of the race.

There were the usual formalities on board to sort out; folding the sails, sorting out the paperwork, getting the fenders from behind the crash bulkhead and the mooring lines from the bilges.

There was just enough time for a quick team hug before we entered the marina. The other eleven challenge boats had already been lifted out of the water for their damage surveys and the marina was empty, except for the crowds who had come to see us in. As well as family and friends, there were many local supporters who had been following the race along with press and TV crews.

We were mobbed once the boat was tied up. Champagne was sprayed everywhere and there were tears of joy and relief at actually finishing the leg. Reporters were interviewing any of the crew they could get hold of. TV cameras captured the event and we all became instant stars. Wherever we went in New Zealand after that we were recognised and people wanted to hear our story.

Amazingly and emotionally, Flash was there to meet us. He had flown out especially with his parents to see us in with David Chapman from Stelmar. We were all hustled to the Dockside bar where we had our very own welcome reception which had been put on by Flash's parents as a thank you for looking after him.

We all stayed in the Intercontinental Hotel for the first couple of nights courtesy of Stelmar and after a couple of days work everyone had some well deserved rest and took the opportunity to travel and explore New Zealand before returning to Wellington to prepare for the next leg.

Leg 3
Wellington - Sydney
1400 miles, 7 days
Monday 31stJanuary 2005
Wellington Harbour

AFTER A WELL-EARNED BREAK the crew got back together in Wellington to begin preparing for the next leg to Sydney.

Sails were collected from the sailmakers and checked over before being folded back into their sail bags, food was sorted and loaded and the rigging was checked.

There were training sails and corporate entertainment days to fit in as well. Clive, Nicko, Alex and Wrighty had meetings to discuss the weather and tactics for the next leg. The new leggers, Rona, Adrian, Karen and Nigel were integrated into the team. Adrian had done the first leg and Karen had done some of the second leg before she was dropped off in Puerto Williams. Rona had done much of the previous race four years earlier and Nigel had helped out before the start, so they already knew the crew and the boats. We were lucky to have them, but we had twice as many new people as the other boats due to our two losses (Mike and Flash) which put us at a slight disadvantage.

Alex and Wrighty had meetings with their relative watches to make sure everyone was focused and to deal with any issues, as well as to discuss the plan for the next leg. This was a much shorter leg and the focus would be on trimming all the time for maximum boat speed. It was less about endurance and more of a straight line drag-race from A to B. We would not be having showers as we would only be carrying water for drinking and cooking and the clothes we wore were the clothes we took. All weight was reduced to an absolute minimum; it would take every bit of effort to beat the competition on such a short leg.

Sunday 6th February 2005, Start Day

Wellington Harbour

After a final hearty breakfast on the dockside everybody made their way down to the boats in front of the assembled masses. With such a short, sunny leg to come and after such an arduous Southern Ocean leg, everyone was in good spirits and looking forward to racing again. There was a great atmosphere with huge crowds clamouring for a view of the boats as they left one by one to their own theme tunes. *Team Stelmar* was the last boat to leave from their side of the marina and after a group hug on the bow they began preparations to depart. Flash was there to wave a tearful goodbye, his arm was still not strong enough for him to rejoin the race. As soon as *Team Stelmar* left, he was mobbed by reporters asking how he felt watching his boat leave without him – he was of course gutted not to be on board. His plan was to stay in Wellington for a few days then fly to Sydney to meet the team again seven days later.

On *Team Stelmar* the mood was calm and focused. The start area was quite tight. Our policy of 'best for boat' meant that the watches were mixed up at each start, with the best crew doing their specific jobs. Phil was number one bowman, looking out for the other boats and 'calling' the start line by estimating the distance from it as we approached. Paula ran the snake-pit behind the mast, relaying messages between Phil and the cockpit as well as being ready to hoist the spinnaker. Wrighty was up by the mast helping co-ordinate the foredeck action and calling trim on the headsails. Dutch Rob was on the mainsheet trimming. Nicko was working out the best way to proceed after the start. Rich was in charge of rules and helping out with tactics. Alex was helming and coaxing exactly the right speed out of the boat as necessary and Clive was keeping an overall eye on things and deciding when to make the run for the line.

Everything went like clockwork. It was the best start of a leg for the team and the most decisive. *Team Stelmar* charged across the start line first and in no time at all was over 100m ahead of the other boats. The lead stretched even further after the first mark as slick teamwork kicked in. The tough 52 days of the previous leg had served us well, we were now more confident than the other teams.

By the time the boats reached the mouth of Wellington harbour, *Samsung* had managed to creep up the inside along the shore and steal the lead. Rich was adamant that we should have stood our ground and not let the other boat through as we did have right of way, but Clive decided not to get involved in a battle this early in the leg.

During the first few days, there was constant activity with trimming and sail changes and data logging every 15 minutes. The pace was quick and the entire fleet were only separated by a few miles. Most boats were in sight of each other and the six-hourly skeds really showed who was sailing best. *Team Stelmar* managed to drop to 12th place within the first 24 hours by heading further offshore, but remained only a few miles from the leaders and within the next 36 hours had steadily progressed up the rankings back to first place.

The racing was very tight and with only a slender lead of less than a mile, the front runners changed positions on a regular basis. The slightest lapse of concentration and drop in boat speed left the door open for other boats to make up distance and sneak in.

Friday 11th February 2005, Day 6

36°40'.4 S   157°36'.7 E

The winds had been frustratingly light and it was hard to keep the boat moving, but *Team Stelmar* remained one of the front runners. There was a high pressure system between us and Sydney and we had two options: either stay to the north of the fleet with a slightly better wind angle and shorter distance but potentially less wind, or head further south with a less favourable angle and greater distance but more wind. Clive and Nicko pored over the weather charts and decided to take the shorter, more northerly route.

The crew worked hard at extracting everything from the boat and their hard work was rewarded with a small buffer created back to second placed *Sark* and a further two miles back to *Samsung* in third place.

With about 24 hours to the finish things were looking good; the shorter route was paying off. Those further south like *BG*, although sailing faster, were losing ground as the greater distance was costing them dearly.

However, the race was not over. We had taken our eye off the ball and not paid enough attention to the East Australian Current which runs south towards Sydney then turns north-eastwards out to sea. We got caught up with the current and it started to push us towards the centre of the high pressure system. The wind got lighter and lighter and the boat slowed.

With less speed to carry the boat against the current, its effect on pushing the boat north was increasing. Within a few hours *Team Stelmar* had dropped from first to ninth place as the boats behind saw the predicament and headed south to avoid the trap.

The team were distraught but the race was still not over. The race office issued hourly skeds as the fleet closed on the finish in Sydney harbour. *BG* had taken the lead and were now revelling in the stronger winds. Eventually *Team Stelmar* too picked up the strong wind and the race to the finish was on. *Samsung* in sixth place was 11.8 miles ahead with about 80 miles to go. They were the target now.

With the stronger winds and the heavy spinnaker set, *Team Stelmar* began to reel in the boats ahead. It wasn't long before they caught and passed *Barclays*, quickly pulling away from them, then worked on reducing the ten miles to *Sark* and *Samsung*.

An hour or so later and the other two boats were in sight, but so was Sydney. *Samsung* entered the harbour first with *Sark* about a mile of so behind them. *Team Stelmar* was only one more mile behind *Sark*.

By sailing harder and better we managed to close right up to *Samsung* and *Sark*, but it was too late. *Sark* crossed the finish less than a minute ahead of us. Had the race gone on for another mile the team believed they would have had the place, but there was no point in wishing what might have been. *Team Stelmar* was eighth and that was that.

Disappointed with the result and annoyed we had not paid more attention to the current, we sailed under the famous bridge with our full spinnaker still up. It was quite a moment. After tying up in Darling Harbour, the team made their way to the nearest bar to drown their sorrows. A lesson learnt the hard way. Sailing the boat fast was not the issue for the team; it was keeping the focus.

The third leg of the race had taken us just over seven days and 1345 miles.

Alex:

It was all rather surreal entering Sydney harbour through the Heads. Everyone was working really hard to try to reel in Sark who were only a couple of hundred metres ahead. Unfortunately they just pipped us to the line and Samsung were only a few hundred metres ahead of them.

Despite spending almost a hundred days racing and being away from home for over four months, it wasn't until we rounded Bradley's Head and the bridge and opera house came into view that it suddenly dawned on me what we had achieved. Here we were in Sydney Harbour, on the opposite side of the world, and we had sailed there under our own power. It was quite an amazing moment.

Paula:

We had a fantastic finish; it was at 17:30 local time under blue skies. We sailed through the Heads and then passed the opera house and under the Sydney Harbour bridge – all with our promotional spinnaker up. I remember looking upwards as we went under the bridge to soak in the moment. Dutch Rob's wife Peggy was out on a supporter's boat to greet us and as it was her birthday we all sang Happy Birthday to her and she cried. It was another emotional time for everyone.

Nicko's parents generously put on a party for the team at their house in Sydney. It was a chance for everyone to let their hair down and relax. Nicko's father had created a fantastic video montage set to music about our achievements so far, right from the early days of team building, which now seemed so distant. We had already been through a lot together as a team and come through it stronger than ever. It was easy to forget what had happened over the previous months, but watching the video made everyone reflect on the past and we were all very proud of what we had achieved. We realised that the challenges we had faced, and dealt with, had made us stronger and better people.

In fact it was not the actual challenges that had made us better; it was the way that we had dealt with them. Nobody ever said, "It's not fair". We were the ones in each situation and what happened had happened; no amount of moaning was going to change that fact. We were all literally in the same boat and together worked out a solution for the best.

There was time for sightseeing as we were all given a few days off. Most of the crews stayed around Sydney and just took the opportunity to relax and go surfing at Bondi beach. It was good for everyone to spend some time apart although there were the inevitable get-togethers most evenings in a bar somewhere.

There were all the usual jobs to do on the boat, cleaning and repairing, stripping down the bunks and removing all the unused food. We had corporate entertainment days and training days. Some of the storm sails had been modified and we needed to check that they fitted and worked.

The prize-giving ceremony was held at Star City Hotel and Casino and after a photo call on the steps outside there was a buffet followed by the prize-giving itself. Although we were not up for a leg-winning prize, we did win the prize for being first over the start line after our fantastic get away in Wellington. So far, after three legs, we had won a prize on each leg, but we were still looking for our first podium finish.

Wednesday 23rd February 2005

Sydney

Our four new leggers had arrived and Paula and Flash went to the airport to meet them. These four had flown in to join us on our next leg, adventurously choosing to do the Southern Ocean leg to Cape Town. They were Rob, Ben, James and Sarah. They were soon introduced to the others in the team and it was important to quickly integrate them and make them feel at ease on the boat. Sarah and Rob became Grunters while Ben and James were assigned to the Groaners watch. It soon became apparent that Ben was keen on photography and very quickly he amassed an impressive archive of footage for the team. James earned himself the nickname 'Ducky' after playing with a yellow plastic duck while entertaining Clive's young daughter Delphi.

The last couple of days in Sydney were boat preparation days; getting all the food on board for the next leg took a while as we would be at sea for another long spell of over 40 days. Winches were stripped and greased and all the moving parts on deck were checked and lubricated. The boat was as ready as we could get it. Weather was checked, watches were briefed and we were ready.

There was one last chance for the crew to have some proper food and China Town was very popular on the last night ashore, although there was little or no alcohol drunk that night.

There is nothing worse than heading out to sea with a hangover.

Leg 4
Sydney – Cape Town
6200 miles, 40 days
Sunday 27thFebruary 2005 Start Day
Sydney Harbour

ALL THE CREW MET AT 09:00 for breakfast at Yots Café on the waterfront. Everyone was in team T-shirts, shorts and deck shoes. The whole team looked very smart and professional. The new leggers were excited, but a little nervous and daunted compared with the hardened core crew.

One by one the boats left to their theme tunes. *Team Stelmar* headed out and the sound of *Praise You* rang out over Darling Harbour. We made our way under the bridge and past the opera house for the last time and headed towards the start box near Shark Island.

The start was not until 15:00 so we had plenty of time to get ready. There were supporters' boats everywhere and helicopters circling overhead filming the action. There were also three other races going on in the harbour so the water was quite crowded and everyone had to keep a sharp eye out for other boats.

We discovered we had a problem with our fresh water pump and Paul quickly had the pump disconnected and a replacement was bought out to us by a RIB. Better to have the pump fail now rather than three weeks into the Southern Ocean.

The twelve Challenge boats circled round the start box impatiently. There was a good 20 knot breeze blowing under grey skies. *Team Stelmar* decided to go for a spinnaker start, although it was marginal as to whether we could hold it for long, but we hoped it would give us clear air before reaching the Sydney Heads.

The ten minute gun fired and everyone set their watches for the countdown. We ran exactly the same set up as we did in Wellington and everything went smoothly. The gun fired and once again we were first across the line. Three out of four, we just need to be first over the finish line.

It was very exciting and once again we pulled away from the fleet, only this time *BP* came with us under spinnaker. Just before the first mark we dropped the spinnaker and hoisted the headsail; frantic work on the foredeck and in the snake-pit to get the massive sail safely down and below decks.

Once again we slipped down the leader board as we headed offshore in search of better winds and the East Australian Current which had been so cruel to us on the way in to Sydney. Now it would be running south and on our side.

The first night watch was quiet with smooth seas and pleasant sailing. Everyone was quickly into the routine of watch on, watch off, and the miles slipped away as we raced south towards Tasmania across the Bass Strait.

Sunday 6th March 2005, Day 8

48°30'.7 S   138°07'.8 E

500 miles south of Tasmania

The weather for the first week had been variable with some calm patches and some stormy weather in the Bass Strait between Australia and Tasmania. It was during one of these storms at night that *Save the Children* was hit by a large wave and one of the crew members, who was below decks and off watch at the time, was thrown out of his bunk and severely hurt. So bad were his injuries that they had to stop racing and have him evacuated to Hobart for medical treatment. This only served as a warning to everyone that we were once again entering dangerous territory.

Team Stelmar made the most of the heavy weather and had been steadily reeling in the leaders, moving up to sixth place. We had already covered 1000 miles towards Cape Town. The weather was getting more wet and wild the further south we headed. It was cold on deck but not freezing yet. We had already recorded wind speeds of 47 knots but now we would leave the mainsail up rather than dropping it, having discovered during leg two that we could handle the boat for short periods with three reefs and our smallest headsails up in these winds.

Waves were now starting to come across the decks during the storms and we found three shrimps in the snake-pit after one particularly large wave broke over the boat.

Both the new Grunters, Rob and Sarah, were coping well with the extreme conditions. The new Groaners were also getting on well, with Ducky constantly smiling and Ben taking pictures. They had integrated well into the team.

We were now far enough south to begin seeing the Aurora Australis or Southern Lights. An amazing light display caused by solar radiation and only visible a long way south towards Antarctica. The night sky would be lit up with shimmering curtains of green and red, almost ghostly in appearance. This was an indication that we were now quite a way south and the weather would be getting considerably colder, especially when the wind came from the south, blowing off the Antarctic ice sheets.

Just one day later, on the 7th March, the weather changed completely. It was suddenly freezing cold with snow on deck, huge waves and storm force winds. Nicko was the bearer of the news that this weather was set for a few days and the pattern Southern Ocean storms began once again...

The pattern would last about three days then be repeated. We would be headed further and further south, tack and get lifted, then as the weather system passed, the wind swung right round and the whole process continued again. It became routine and we would check the computer showing the weather to see where we were in the pattern before going on deck to ready ourselves for the sail changes on the next watch.

We were back to having only three crew on deck every 30 minutes during the night watches; one helming, one riding 'shotgun' to grab the wheel in case the helm got knocked over, and the third ready to ease the mainsheet in gusts of wind and call below for help if needed. The others on watch huddled below decks trying to keep warm and dry.

Saturday 12th March 2005, Day 14

56°21'.1 S   113°20'.3 E

500 miles north of Antarctica

The water temperature was four degrees centigrade and the air temperature well below freezing. Exposed skin would freeze if left exposed to the elements for long. Everyone was wearing all their clothes just to try to keep warm. Drysuits were the order of the day and safety harnesses were clipped on at all times, even before leaving the safety of the companionway and going on deck.

Although we were well below the ice limit, meaning that we were within iceberg territory, we had not seen any. This was a relief to us. Although beautiful to look at from afar, the large bergs have many smaller 'growlers' which drift downwind. Even the smaller ones, about one metre across, could do serious damage to the boat and would be floating only about 10cm above the water, so making them very hard to spot, especially at night. We were glad not to see any.

We had crossed 56° south and were now the furthest south we would go on this leg (we reached 58°44' S on leg two just before Flash broke his arm). The race office had set up a waypoint seven miles north of the Kerguelen Islands. This was done for safety reasons and to keep the boats from going too far south on the shorter great circle route to Cape Town. This meant that the fleet would dive south into the stronger winds of the Southern Ocean, then loop up to the waypoint before dipping back south again on the shortest route to the finish.

We had already covered several thousand miles and were in third place. We had scratched our way up the leader board once again, showing that we could sail the boat fast. This was a familiar pattern for us as we had managed it on every leg so far; from Portsmouth to the Canaries we went from 12th place to 3rd; from Buenos Aires to the first medivac 12th to 4th, from the first medivac to the second medivac 12th to 4th, from Wellington to Sydney 12th to 1st, and on this leg 11th to 3rd. We could sail fast; it was 'just' a few simple navigational or tactical errors which were costing us good finishes. Most of the other boats tended to be more consistent in their positioning in the fleet, whereas we tended to have brilliant starts then in the first 24 hours drop to the back of the fleet, only to climb back up the table towards the front. This seemed to show that we were motivated by catching the competition and passing them.

The Sunday Happy Hours were continuing every week and we were changing the ship's clock to keep up with our westerly progress; we were now only seven hours ahead of GMT. We tacked to begin our loop northwards towards the Kerguelen waypoint. This was a psychological waypoint as well as a physical one as it meant an end to the Southern Ocean pounding, plus the weather should begin to get warmer.

However, we were still in the Southern Ocean and the conditions were extreme; freezing cold, snow and sleet and lots of water on deck from the massive waves. It was tough; just getting around the boat was difficult. Sail changes were few as we had the smallest sails up most of the time and three reefs in the mainsail. It was tough, but some of the crew revelled in it, particularly the more experienced sailors like Alex, Rich, Phil and Wrighty. These were extreme conditions, but exhilarating and the only place on the planet where they could be found. The downside was that even with the best equipment and clothing that was available, hands and feet were still cold to the point of hurting.

Monday 21st March 2005, Day 23

47°42'.1 S   74°46'.1 E

Nearing the Kerguelen Islands Waypoint

Despite heading north, the weather was still rough. Paula was on mother duty and cooked up some pasta with pizza topping. High in carbohydrate but, just as important, it was hot.

The Grunters had just had a trio of very tough watches. It was freezing cold and the wind was blowing at over 40 knots. Fingers hurt so much that it almost brought tears to your eyes. Problems took hours to sort and even Nicko and Clive were called upon to help out. Each time, in 40 knots of wind and often in darkness, working under pressure on the low side of the boat, it was dangerous work and Clive was constantly calling out people's names to check they were all right and still on the boat.

The first problem happened during a tack and the new working sheet (sail control line) wasn't pulled in quickly enough. As the Yankee flogged in the wind, the excess rope became wrapped up with itself and formed a massive knot. The only way to sort it out was by dropping the sail onto the deck and untying the sheets before they broke, then attempting to sort it out below decks in the relative safety of the saloon. Meanwhile, Alex and Nicko replaced the two sheets with spares from below and then had to re-lead them along the side decks.

Paula:

I was on mother duty for the day and Clive shouted for everyone to help on deck. The Yankee sheets had become tangled and the foredeck crew had dropped the sail to untie them. Alex and Nicko were busy leading the new sheets on the low side, which was often under water. As I was based in the snake-pit I clipped on to the high side, and leant across holding onto Alex and Nicko while they worked. Rough seas meant that huge amounts of water were coming over the boat all the time despite Clive's best efforts to keep the boat steady.

Afterwards we ended up with sodden drysuits and poured water out of our boots, with frozen hands, face and feet.

Once the sail was back up again, the Grunters piled below for dinner one hour late and very tired. Two hours on, it was time to go up again and get ready for the next watch. Once there, Phil found the leach line on the Yankee had broken. Again, we had to drop the sail on deck, only this time we had to remove the whole sail and carry it below for repairs. We sailed on with just the storm staysail up which compromised our speed until the Yankee was fixed.

Another hard watch, dropping sails and working on the low side of the boat; the Grunters finished the watch cold, wet and spent.

Wrighty, although on the off watch, was awake and set about repairing the sail. Two hours later it was fixed and the Groaners then had the task of carrying it back on deck, up to the foredeck, clipping it on and hoisting it back up the mast. We were back to full speed again.

Paula:

All things considered we did well: Kate head-butted a winch, cutting her head and getting slight concussion; Rob hurt his ribs and Nicko's got a cold. It just keeps getting tougher and tougher. I'm no longer scared so much by the environment, I just get tired and cold. I actually love the adrenaline of the situation. Now that I understand the boat and the way it reacts to the water, I feel safer, but when a wave hits you from behind and it's a surprise one, it's like someone very angry has run up and shoved you in the back with both hands, enough to shock you with the force of it and even wind you.

Sunday 27th March 2005, Day 29

44°51'.4 S   51°37'.8 E

Easter Sunday

Since passing the Kerguelen waypoint the weather had certainly been kinder, and warmer. The spinnaker was flying and speed towards Cape Town was good. We were in fourth place very close to *Pindar*, swapping places with them regularly. This was an issue for Clive as his younger brother, Nigel, was sailing on *Pindar* for this leg of the race and it had become personal; we had to beat them.

The finish was now 1400 miles away, about eight or nine days sailing. The closest we had managed to get to the leader was 26 miles, any more was proving elusive. We were currently 54.8 miles away from *Unisys* who were the surprise leader, not having shown that kind of performance at all so far in the race. *Sark* were second, 14 miles behind *Unisys* then *BP* a further 11 miles back. Then it was us and *Pindar*, neck and neck. It was amazing that the fleet was still this close after several thousand miles of racing through the Southern Ocean.

We were trying everything to get back to the leaders and get the podium place we so badly wanted.

As it was Easter, to relieve the tension on board, it was decided to have an Easter quiz with chocolate mini eggs as the prizes. Paula had bought a pair of fluffy ears in Sydney and was now the Easter bunny quizmaster, giving out chocolate to the best confessions and correct answers to the quiz. She also teamed up with Ducky on the other watch and they hid chocolates around the boat for people to find. This plan backfired after they put a couple of mini eggs in Rich's bunk. He didn't find them and fell asleep, only to wake up with molten chocolate everywhere. He wasn't impressed.

Monday 4th April 2005, Day 37

35°24'.6 S   21°46'.0 E

60 miles off the coast of South Africa

What a difference a week makes in yacht racing. We made the decision to split from *Pindar* and take a more northerly route, hoping to catch the Agulhas current to help us to Cape Town. The move proved to be the right one. We were now closing fast on the leading trio and had left *Pindar* behind; they were now over 74 miles back.

The wind was coming from behind us and the weather was much warmer. No more snow or hailstones for the rest of the race we hoped. *Unisys* were now only 32 miles ahead; we had just had the six hourly sked and we had done exceptionally well as the table below shows. We were the fastest boat by some margin, taking many miles out of the whole fleet in just six hours.

Position	Boat	Distance Run	+/-	Ave speed
1	Unisys	55.2	25	9.21
2	Sark	59.7	20.5	9.94
3	BP	66.0	14.9	11.00
4	Stelmar	77.2	-	12.86
5	Pindar	61.0	14.1	10.17
6	SAIC	71.0	10.1	11.83
7	Barclays	53.6	26.3	8.93
8	Me to You	57.0	23.0	9.51
9	Samsung	63.2	17.5	10.53
10	BG	60.8	19.8	10.13
11	Save the Children	55.2	25.1	9.20
12	VAIO	40.3	38.2	6.72

Our 77.2 miles was a new record for the Challenge boats in a six hour period – we were flying - but the official records (and awards) were for 24-hour runs.

The wind was too strong even for the heavyweight spinnaker so we used the spinnaker pole to hold out the Yankee 1 to maximise our sail area. The main was eased right out and we were surfing down waves at almost 20 knots.

At one particular time while Alex was helming, the boat shot down the front of a wave and smashed straight into the back of the wave ahead; the boom hit the water and there was an almighty bang, like a gun going off, and the mainsail shook.

Alex:

The boat accelerated down the wave and the boom hit the water. There was a huge bang and my first thought was the mast was about to come down. I looked up and saw it was still there, but the mainsail was luffing. It was then that I realised we had broken the preventer[2]. The boom was moving around, so to avoid an accidental gybe, I headed slightly more into the wind while we sorted it out.

The force of the exploding rope had bent one of the pulley blocks on the foredeck and it was a difficult job to extract it and replace it with a spare one. Alex then respliced the rope together and made up a new preventer. We were then able to bear away back on course and continue chasing the leaders.

There was a large area of light wind ahead of the fleet which would cause compression amongst the boats. Close to the shore was the wind shadow of the land and Table Mountain. We all knew that there would be more wind further offshore, but we were in a procession led by *Unisys*.

---

[2] An 18mm diameter rope from the outboard end of the boom to the foredeck, used to stop the boom coming across the boat accidentally.

During the morning watch, the Grunters sighted another boat on the horizon ahead. From the last position reports we worked out that it was probably *BP*. They were in very light winds and we caught up to them quite quickly before we too slowed down. They were less than a mile away and closer inshore. It was very tense as the finish was only about 20 miles away. Further inshore, right under the cliffs, was *Unisys*, completely becalmed and going nowhere. They had sailed into the wind shadow of the land and lost a solid lead and certain victory. They were now in 4th place and off the podium.

The last few hours were like playing cat and mouse in the light winds and shifting fog, with *Team Stelmar* and *BP* constantly changing positions, under the watchful eye of a media helicopter. *Sark* crossed the line first, followed half an hour later by *BP* and then us less than an hour later. We had done it! We had a podium finish at last through determination, good tactics and a sure-fire will to succeed. It was great coming into the marina and joining just two other boats on the pontoons.

Unisys came in a few hours later, totally distraught for not winning the leg after leading for the last three weeks. It just proved to us that we should never become complacent and had to fight for every inch, right up to the finish line.

Our finish time was 01:52:29 on the 6th April after having sailed 7225 miles.

The drinks flowed that night as the four crews talked about their adventures on the last trip in the Southern Ocean. Champagne, beers, chips and burgers were the order of the day along with the celebration of a podium finish.

Despite it being early morning, the local bar, Bayfront Blu, stayed open 24 hours a day for five days while all the boats came in. The crews from *Sark*, *BP* and *Team Stelmar* stayed in the bar for the remainder of the night celebrating. At 08:00

most of the *Team Stelmar* crew left to get some breakfast on the way to their apartments, which had been arranged for us by our sponsors.

After several hours of well needed sleep, many of the crew returned to the bar to welcome in *Pindar* and *Samsung* and the party carried on for another night. There was an advantage to coming in at the front of the fleet.

After two days of hard partying and celebrating, it was back to work on the boat with the usual list of jobs; rig check, safety check, sails off, bunks cleaned, food and rubbish off, etc.

Apart from the problems we had with the number three Yankee, we suffered very little sail damage on this leg, but we did however manage to snap four stainless steel stanchions on the foredeck, just by crashing through the waves day after day.

There was a chance to debrief the whole leg and we talked through lots of small points for improvement. There were one-to-ones with Clive and the Watch Leaders as well as individual watch meetings.

We had five days allocated to boat work and then the whole crew were on leave from the 12th to the 22nd. Most people took the time to leave Cape Town and explore the region, especially the many vineyards and the Garden Route.

It was during the stopover in Cape Town that the announcement was made that Stelmar, our sponsor, had been taken over by an American shipping company called OSG (Overseas Shipholding Group). It had been a turbulent time for the old Stelmar board and they had drawn a lot of strength from our trials and tribulations; while they were battling away in the boardroom, we were battling our way through the Southern Ocean and coming out the other side in one piece. They were all inspired by what we were going through thousands of miles away, in a small boat, in the middle of the ocean on the other side of the world.

The good news was that we still had the charismatic David Chapman as our main contact and in a show of solidarity we decided to have a team haircut. This was no ordinary trim though. In Wellington, Phil had had his hair dyed blue and green, Stelmar's colours. On our arrival in Cape Town, Flash, who was back to rejoin the boat for the remainder of the race, 'rebranded' and had a crew cut which was bleached white with a neon blue Mohican (OSG colours). It set the tone and the next day Alex and Wrighty went to the salon and had their hair cut and dyed the same. On their return to the boat they then encouraged the rest of the crew to have theirs done too.

Fourteen out of the eighteen crew had their hair bleached and dyed, with Mohicans for the boys. Ruth and Sue had blue and white feathers in theirs. All in all we were a striking sight and had the photographers snapping away. It not only showed our support and commitment to our new sponsors, but our support for each other. It was a bold statement.

The prize-giving ceremony was held at the Rickety Bridge Vineyard in Franschhoek. All the teams were bussed there with family and friends for the evening. Team Stelmar had won three prizes; first over the start line again, the rubber chicken media prize for the funniest daily log and of course the podium place finish. There was a huge cheer as the team went up to collect the 3rd place trophy.

After the meal and prize-giving, most of the crews returned to Cape Town and the favoured Bayfront Blu bar which had promised to stay open again for the night.

Leg 5
Cape Town - Boston
6775 miles, 36 days
Sunday 1st May 2005, Start Day
Victoria and Albert Waterfront, Cape Town

THE FORECAST FOR THE START had been for strong winds, but on start day we awoke to clear skies and very little wind. At least it was warm. Our shore bags had already been packed and handed in to be shipped to Boston. All we had with us was what we would be taking on the boat for the next leg to Boston.

All the team lined up on the back of the cockpit for the blessing of the fleet. We looked good with our blue and white hair and certainly stood out. There were the usual 'Safe Happy Fast' banners everywhere.

One by one the boats left to head out for the start. *Team Stelmar* was the eighth boat to leave to our theme tune of *Praise You*. Once outside the marina it was back into race mode and time to hoist the mainsail.

There were fewer supporter boats out than at previous starts and it gave us the chance to manoeuvre easily towards the start line. The wind was light and fluky and constantly shifting. The start would be as much about luck as judgment. Some of the other Global Challenge boats were following us around as we now had a reputation for good starts.

The leg was to begin with a short run along the coast to a mark before heading out past Robben Island (where Nelson Mandela had been imprisoned) and on to Boston. With little wind we just did what we could to keep the boat moving and maintain steerage. If the boat was to stop then it would be impossible to keep it in a straight line, so momentum was all important.

We would only have one chance to get the start right and we made our move. We headed for the line and managed to cross in second place just behind *VAIO*. We aimed straight for the first mark and got past *VAIO* before we reached it and were the first boat round. Over the VHF radio we heard the Race Control announce that *VAIO* went over the line too early and had to do two complete turns (720°) as a penalty. That meant that once again we were the first boat 'officially' across the start line.

We hoisted our spinnaker and headed towards Robben Island, leading the fleet by some margin. As we got further away from Table Mountain, the wind increased and this only served to increase our lead even more.

The weather was set to be stable and we were on a straight course, so we broke into watches and got back into the routine of ocean racing; eat, sleep, sail.

The first three days gave the new leggers a chance to settle in and by 20:00 on the 4th May we had already covered 800 miles and were only 78 hours into the leg. This worked out at an average of 246 miles in 24 hours. The conditions had been ideal; sunny, windy and warm.

Generally everyone was more upbeat than in the previous leg. It was easier to be happy wearing a T-shirt and shorts compared with a drysuit with freezing water washing over you all the time. It also meant that the crew could be up and dressed in five minutes, rather than the twenty-odd minutes it took in the Southern Ocean. The sea was also generally flatter which meant moving around below was easier, and the sun was shining; good for now but we knew it would get hotter and hotter as we headed north.

Our new leggers were turning out well. Sharon (Shazza) had been learning the snake-pit with Paula while David was foredeck 'fodder', there to help out Phil, Rich and Newton with the sail changes. Both also learned how to trim the spinnaker, which was crucial because it was flying for 90% of the time as we charged towards the equator.

During the chat show it became apparent that not everyone had been revelling in the conditions. There were many reports of torn sails and broken kit; not a good sign so near to the beginning of the leg.

Wednesday 4th May 2005, Day 4

25°18'.6 S   7°21'.4 E

The six-hourly skeds showed us constantly in the top three and we were currently in first place ahead of *BP*, leading the charge north. The fleet had split into three groups: *Team Stelmar*, *BP*, *Sark*, *Barclays* and *VAIO* in the leading group. Then *SAIC*, *Me to You*, *Samsung*, *Pindar* and *Save the Children* further south. *BG* and *Unisys* had taken a flyer and stayed further inshore to the east of us.

The race organisers had placed a waypoint on this leg at the islands of Peter and Paul, which the fleet had to leave to port to keep the boats away from the Brazilian coast and the very real possibility of meeting pirates there. In fact we would have preferred to have passed to the west of them because the doldrums tend to be narrower the further west one goes.

For this leg we had three small bottles of champagne on board because we would be crossing our outbound track and thereby completing a circumnavigation of the globe. We would also cross the equator again, only this time we had three pollywogs to initiate; Sharon, Rob and David.

The food was going down well amongst the crew. The kind of food we ate varied from leg to leg, but on this one we typically ate:

Breakfast

- Porridge or Muesli

- Fresh bread made from powdered mix, jam, peanut butter, etc.

- Powdered scrambled egg once a week

Lunch

- Pasta and pesto with pine nuts

- Oatcakes and tuna

- Packet soup

- Couscous

- Pasta and parmesan

Dinner

- Corned beef hash (a favourite with everyone)

- Boil-in-the-bag stew and powdered mash

- Packet noodles

- Pasta and powdered cheese sauce, tinned ham and peas

- Packet lentil dhal

- Boil-in-the-bag beans and sausage

- Risotto

The meals were rotated each day, so one day we would have noodles, the next we would have risotto and so on over a ten day rotation before it started again.

There were also a lot of snacks to eat between meals:

- Snack bars, such as high five energy bars

- Sesame seed snacks

- Twix, Mars, Snickers, Kit Kat, Dairy Milk, Yorkie, etc.

- Fruit Pastilles and Wine Gums

- Nuts

These snacks were handed out every day to each watch for them to graze on.

On the colder Southern Ocean legs each crew member ate their way through 5000 calories a day and still managed to lose weight. During the warmer tropic legs, there tended to be fewer calories consumed and less hot meals like pasta.

Sunday 8th May 2005, Day 8

Sunday 8th May 2005, Day 8

18°39'.0 S   2°34'.2 W

200 miles south east of St Helena

We had already covered over 1500 miles, averaging 200 miles a day. We had been flying the spinnakers almost constantly since the start; this was trade wind sailing at its best. We were swapping the lead with *Barclays* and sailing well. Teamwork was working well too; we were making very few mistakes and had no significant damage to our sails, except for three small holes in one of the spinnakers. *Save the Children* were already 120 miles behind us and we later found out they had some problems with blown out spinnakers.

Happy hour from 18:00 gave everyone the chance to get together on deck. This was the first time we had all been together for a long while. Happy hour in the Southern Ocean meant changing watch at 18:30 rather than chatting together. This time it was nice and sunny and warm. Beef stew and herb mash was served up in foil pouches.

Rich did a short presentation on St Helena as we were due to pass the South Atlantic island later that evening. Clive and Nicko had been looking at the weather and our position, trying to decide when to gybe and cross the doldrums; a crucial decision. If we got it right then we could pull clear of the chasing pack; get it wrong and the others could close right up. Despite having weather information, it was still a bit of a lottery.

We were gybing frequently, making the most of every change in wind direction. Gybing big ocean racing yachts, with several thousand square feet of spinnaker, is a labour-intensive job.

Paula describes the process from the snake-pit point of view:

Once the decision has been made to gybe, everyone takes their positions. Phil goes to the foredeck ready to release the old Spinnaker pole and help with the setting of the new one. The cockpit trimming team prepares the sheets and guys, and Alex takes the helm and gives the command to start. This is the sequence of events in the snake-pit:

1. *Jam off the spinnaker halyard*

2. *Prepare the mini/temporary preventer*

3. *Put the new staysail halyard on the winch (to act as topping lift for the new pole)*

4. *Release the old preventer and free up the rope to become the new foreguy*

5. *Hoist the new pole using the new staysail halyard*

6. *Put working staysail halyard on a winch ready to drop the old pole*

7. *Release the mini preventer and gybe the sails*

8. *Quickly lower the old pole to the deck*

9. *Pull in and tighten the new foreguy*

10. *Adjust the new pole as necessary*

11. *Set up the new preventer (old foreguy)*

12. *Put the spinnaker halyard back on a winch and open the jammer*

13. *Set up the 'take down guy' through the letter box (gap between mainsail and the boom) and clip it on*

14. Tidy up and prepare spinnaker halyard in case a drop is called for.

This and putting the third reef in the mainsail were the two busiest manoeuvres, requiring dexterity and multi-tasking. It was a good feeling to get it right though.

Friday 13ᵗʰ May 2005, Day 13

4°47'.8 S   21°44'.2 W

Friday 13ᵗʰ; the day didn't start too well. During the 02:00–06:00 watch, whilst gybing, the 1.5oz spinnaker completely blew out for no apparent reason. The wind was only 14 knots and the sea relatively calm, but during the gybe the sail ripped all along the foot and right up one side. It seemed that the spinnaker was just getting worn out and had become fragile. The sail was dropped quickly and the heavier 2.2oz flanker hoisted instead. Although not the ideal sail, at least we could keep sailing at a reasonable speed and not lose out too much to the rest of the fleet.

All available hands were put to work repairing it. Over 130 feet of edge tape (hem) had to be unstitched, repacked, stuck together and then hand sewn with double row stitching. Wrighty and the sail repair team also took the opportunity to reinforce some areas of the sail with some thicker sail material.

In all it took the team 40 hours to repair the sail, working round the clock, with only four crew on deck sailing the boat and the other four below deck sewing.

Later that day, while sailing fast in flat water, there was a loud bang from the top of the mast. It shuddered, but nothing else appeared to happen, all the sails were still pulling and the mast was intact. It then became apparent that the top of the spinnaker was flying about ten feet from the mast.

The shackle holding it up had broken and it was now flying directly from the exit slot in the mast where the halyard came out. The entire load was now on the wall of the mast, rather than the reinforced bracket at the top. Very quickly the crew de-powered the sail and dropped it in order to save the mast from being damaged.

The spinnaker was taken below deck and packed very quickly before being hoisted up again on the spare halyard. At least we were back up to speed again.

On closer inspection it appeared that a 10mm stainless steel shackle had bent and broken under the load from the sail. It served to reinforce with everyone the huge power of these sails and the possibility for disaster.

During the daily chat show with the other boats on the radio, we discovered that *Save the Children* had had some problems and destroyed two spinnakers which had hampered their performance as they limped along in 12th place.

They say disasters come in threes and within 24 hours we had our third incident.

With the Groaners on deck, *Team Stelmar* was making good progress towards the equator. The spinnaker was flying and we were regularly recording 10-12 mile runs every hour. The sea was relatively flat and the stars shone in a cloudless sky.

At just after midnight on the 14th May a squall came over. Although typical in the tropics, sometimes at night they are hard to spot and we had to rely on the radar to see the heavy rain underneath them. This one got through without being spotted as there was little rain associated with it, just strong gusts of wind.

The Groaners, caught unexpectedly, fought to drop the spinnaker before it was damaged and the boat went out of control.

The wind was gusting well over 30 knots and as the spinnaker came down it fell into the water. With the boat travelling at over 12 knots it soon got dragged along the side of the boat. Unfortunately Julian's safety harness got caught up with it and he was dragged along too, through the snake-pit until his harness stopped him going any further.

The spinnaker guy was wrapped around his waist and he was now bearing the load of the sail as it trawled behind us. He was in a very dangerous predicament as the rope was crushing his body. The only way to release him was to cut his harness. With two crew holding on to him, his harness was sliced through and he was free, but badly bruised.

Ruth took him below and checked him over. Although badly bruised and shaken, nothing appeared to be broken.

The remainder of the on-deck crew, now with the help of the Grunters who had come up off watch, very slowly pulled in the spinnaker. It took everyone's effort, like a giant tug-of-war between the crew and the sail in the water. Eventually the heavy, wet spinnaker was in the cockpit and taken below to check for damage before being packed away ready to be re-hoisted.

During the tidy-up on deck, the full extent of what had happened came to light. During the drop, the spinnaker halyard had been eased, causing it to run over the Yankee halyard. The halyard jammed and the only way to release it was to cut it, but as it was released it literally cut through the Yankee halyard as it shot out. We found the ends of the rope had melted with the friction. The spinnaker had escaped without major damage, only a dozen or so small rips.

Julian's harness had suffered serious damage. The stainless steel hook had almost worn right through with the friction as it ran along the stainless steel wire it was attached to. Had it broken then Julian would have been flung overboard into the water and it could have been a very different story.

Dutch Rob and Paul had been caught up in the mayhem too and also suffered bruising.

Monday 16th May 2005, Day 16

0°03'.2 N   27°01'.3 W

Crossing the Equator

We finally crossed back into the Northern Hemisphere at 20:31. The weather was hot but with a cooling breeze and progress was steady around 9 knots.

It was Sharon's birthday, but as she was one of the leggers and had not crossed the equator with us on the first leg, she had to endure the court of King Neptune along with Rob Packham and David Hulf.

Food had been stored up after each meal before the equator crossing and then ceremoniously poured over the victims, much to the amusement of the rest of the crew who had endured it seven months earlier.

Twenty-four hours later we crossed our outbound track at 21:46 at position 3°42'.6 N and 29°01'.5 W. We had now officially sailed around the world, no mean feat in itself, but the race was far from finished. We still had 3,500 miles to sail on this leg alone.

BG had taken a different route to the rest of the fleet in an attempt to avoid the large high pressure system ahead. The weather information we had showed the light winds heading east, so along with the other ten boats we took the western option and stayed in the down wind conditions.

Several days later the high pressure system stopped tracking east and turned around and moved back west. This meant that the entire fleet slowed right down, while *BG* leapt ahead and took off in the stronger winds. Luck or judgment? We didn't know, and as there was nothing we could do about it, we set about being the leader of our pack; sticking to our rule of controlling the controllables – doing the best with what we had and not worrying about the things we had no control over.

The weather was typical for the tropics, with generally light winds. The clear azure-blue sky was occasionally punctuated with towering black thunder clouds that reached right down to the sea. Heavy rain and strong gusty winds were under each of these clouds and we had to be careful not to get caught out again as we had been on the first leg when we blew our flanker and broke our spinnaker pole.

During the day the squalls were easily spotted and the radar watch was constant throughout the night, as we looked out for the large yellow blobs on the screen indicating rain.

Lightning was spotted to starboard, far away on the horizon. The humidity was very high, despite it being the middle of the night. The wind was a steady 14 knots and the 1.5oz spinnaker was flying.

More lightning was spotted to port and closer. Some people reported feeling a few spots of rain. The radar was still clear up to 24 miles.

Everyone was in a state of readiness. Prepared to drop the spinnaker at a moment's notice and hoist the Yankee up in its place.

There was a feeling of tenseness on board. It was very quiet, save for the sound of the water passing the hull. Outside the boat, everything was inky black; you couldn't even make out the horizon.

Then the rain suddenly increased in intensity and the wind picked up. Like clockwork, the on watch sprang to their positions for the drop. Phil free-climbed to the end of the spinnaker pole and released the sail as everyone else pulled it down and over the boom before passing it down the companionway hatch. The Yankee was straight up and before long we were blasting along in 30 knots of wind and torrential rain into the blackness beyond the bow.

Saturday 21st May 2005, Day 21

15°33'.6 N   37°40'.0 W

Mid-Atlantic

The repair on the race spinnaker was finished and we had our saloon back. It was nice to be able to sit down and eat, rather than stand around propped up wherever we could, as the sail took up most of the seating area.

We had headed up slightly a couple of days earlier to get into better wind conditions. We also spotted *VAIO* and *BP* on the horizon. The skeds and position reports had them both a couple of miles behind us. Still very close after three weeks of racing.

They both had their spinnakers up and Clive decided that we needed to have ours up as well in order not to lose out to them.

The Groaners, on watch at the time, prepared the flanker and hoisted it cleanly. Kate in the snake-pit co-ordinated with Flash on the foredeck and dropped the Yankee and staysail.

The boat heeled over with the extra power now available and the boat sped up.

It was a very fine wind angle to be flying a spinnaker in and it wasn't long before the flanker blew out with a loud bang. The boat came upright and slowed down. There was a scramble on deck to drop the tattered sail and get the Yankee and staysail back up again. The flanker had been up for less than 30 minutes, and trying to sail with an 18 knot wind blowing 70° from the bow, the strain was just too much and it ripped all the way down one side and along the foot.

The saloon had been clear of spinnaker for 24 hours and was now full with shredded sailcloth. The repairs began again in earnest.

The other two boats dropped their spinnakers as they drew closer and got into the same wind pattern as us. Another lesson learned the hard way – keep your eyes in the boat; concentrating on what is happening to us, not the others.

The flanker took five days to repair. If a job was worth doing then it was worth doing properly. This was a critical sail in our inventory and we would certainly need it again.

No sooner had one task been completed – repairing the flanker – than something else cropped up. This time it was the water-maker which refused to start. The unit had a high pressure electric pump which would pass the sea water through a semi-permeable membrane to extract fresh water. We had four water tanks; two were reserve tanks which were only to be used after getting permission from the race office, the other two were 'working' tanks which were filled from the water-maker for our day-to-day use. We could only 'make' fresh water when the boat was fairly upright, so we would top up the tanks if there was heavy weather expected.

This time however the water-maker refused to start. The motor had broken. Although not a critical situation as we had emergency supplies, it was still crucial that we fixed it and got it working again.

There was a backup system which could be used in the event of a motor failure, but it required removing the large pump from the water-maker and connecting it directly onto the boat's main engine.

Phil struggled with the unit for a few hours and eventually had it coupled up. With the engine in neutral, we started it up. There was a small leak from the high pressure hose connection but at least it was working; we were producing fresh water and as the conditions were calm we decided to top up the tanks.

After a couple of hours we switched it off. Lifting the engine cover, Phil noticed that the aluminium engine was now coated in a very fine covering of white salt. It looked like it had been snowing, but it was just the fine mist from the high pressure hose which had settled and evaporated on the hot engine, leaving the salt. There was nothing we could do until we reached Boston; we weren't going to waste fresh water cleaning it.

Sunday 29th May 2005, Day 29

40°58'.6 N   65°49'.0 W

East of Bermuda

As it was a Sunday, during the 18:00 watch change we had another Happy Hour and all the crew gathered on deck. Because the weather was warm and not very windy it was decided to have fancy dress; the theme was 'tarts and vicars'. Once again the crew showed their ingenuity with duck tape and black bags to create their costumes. There was a good atmosphere onboard under the clear blue skies. The wind was light at only seven knots.

Suddenly on the horizon ahead someone spotted a thin line of wispy cloud reaching down to the water. Sharon pointed out that it was a waterspout; a tornado that reaches down from the clouds and sucks up the water, spinning at speeds in excess of 80 mph. We would do well to avoid it.

As Sharon scanned the horizon she spotted a couple more under the distant clouds ahead, and just as a precaution Paula got on the radio to notify the other boats near us that there were waterspouts in the vicinity.

Alex:

As everyone was watching the horizon I suddenly noticed a disturbance on the water about 100m away to starboard. It looked like fish feeding as the water was getting more and more disturbed. Sharon then said to look up, and there under the cloud right above us was a funnel forming and reaching down to the water. A waterspout was forming right next to us...

Quickly everyone went to drop the spinnaker. It all seemed rather surreal with all the crew still in their fancy dress, especially Phil as he climbed to the end of the spinnaker pole. The sail came down smoothly and was stuffed below decks. As the waterspout tracked towards us we decided to drop the mainsail completely and lash it to the boom. We also lashed the headsails down and removed anything loose on deck. The one thing we didn't want was debris flying around. Once we had tidied everything away, all but a couple of crew waited below decks for the tornado to hit.

It was a tense time as the boat bobbed up and down and everyone waited quietly. Luckily for us the waterspout veered away before it reached the boat and then disappeared as quickly as it had arrived.

Sunday 5th June 2005, Day 36

40°58'.5 N   65°49'.5 W

200 miles to Boston

Visibility was down to 50m in the thick fog and the wind was about ten knots. Sailing was pleasant in flat water, albeit quite damp and cool. Ahead lay a smooth area of water and clear skies. As we sailed towards the calm patch, we noticed that there was a definite line on the water between the rippled area we were sailing in and the glassy sea ahead. As the boat crossed from one to the other, we slowed down to almost zero knots and the sails fell limp. The sky cleared and the water temperature changed sharply. We had just found the edge of the Gulf Stream. Immediately we tacked and headed back south to find the wind again. As soon as we crossed the line on the water it was like someone turning on a fan. The wind picked up again. We would have to cross the Gulf Stream at some time in order to get to Boston, but here was not the place. We would wait until we had better breeze in order to get across as quickly as possible without being pushed too far eastwards.

The radar was monitored constantly for other vessels as the visibility was very poor and we were making about eight knots. Occasionally we would pick up a target or two and watch them slip past, unseen in the thick fog.

The sails were trimmed frequently and the crew had other sails ready to go at a moment's notice should the wind direction or strength change. There was constant changing from Yankee 1 to Yankee 2 and back again. Spinnaker up, Yankee down, spinnaker peel to a different size, spinnaker drop, Yankee up; it was non-stop as everyone tried to get the maximum from the boat.

By now *BG* had a huge lead of over 100 miles on the second placed boat *Barclays*. We were languishing mid-fleet, struggling to cross the Gulf Stream and on to Boston. The wind was shifting often and Nicko and Clive had their work cut out trying to make the most of the shifts.

Twenty-four hours later and we were within 50 miles of the finish. We had not done well with the wind shifts and were in 8th place. The wind was still infuriatingly light and behind us we could make out a set of yellow sails from another Challenge boat – *Me to You*. As we sailed into ever lighter wind, they closed up on us, to within a couple of miles.

It was very tense right up into the harbour and the finish line, as we trimmed constantly. Eventually we crossed the line, holding on to 8th place and even pulling away again from *Me to You*.

The leg had taken us 38 days and another 7088 miles had been clocked up.

We tied the boat up just before two in the morning with the help of the Challenge shore crew and our dedicated team of supporters. We feasted on burgers and fries and champagne before heading off to our waterfront apartments which had been arranged by Stelmar/OSG. Everyone was totally exhausted and there was no place open to party; that would have to wait until the following day...

Leg 6
Boston – La Rochelle
1600 miles, 16 days
Sunday 19th June 2005, Start Day
Boston Harbour Hotel

THE ENTIRE CREW MET AT THE BOSTON Harbour hotel for breakfast. The new leggers, Primrose Keenan, Mike True and Adrian Stafford-Jones (again) were there with us. Clive, Nicko, Alex and Wrighty looked over the weather routing information they had bought from *Commanders' Weather* regarding the next leg across the Atlantic. A strategy was decided upon and conveyed to the rest of the crew over breakfast.

The plan was to head out of Boston harbour and stay to the north of the fleet. Initially this might mean we lost ground to those further south, but if we held our nerve then we should begin to pick up the stronger westerly winds and the Gulf Stream current which hopefully would propel us to La Rochelle.

We knew we could sail the boat quickly, having already collected a couple of 24-hour distance trophies, we needed to back it up now with sound decision making and tactics.

After breakfast there was the usual ceremony of boarding the yachts, followed by the blessing of the fleet. Then one by one the boats left the dock to their theme tunes. Because of the way the boats were arranged *Team Stelmar* was the 10th boat to depart. *Praise You* bellowed out from the PA system as we slowly motored out into Boston Harbour. Mooring lines and fenders were packed and stowed away. The sails were prepared and brought up on deck. It was time for everyone to settle back down for the sixth time and get into race mode.

We motored out to the start line and got our bearings. There was still plenty of time before the start and we ate a light lunch of bagels and muffins as we discussed the plan for the start. The line was biased towards one end and it was decided that we would either have to be at the front and aggressive, or more conservative and cross the line further down. As we knew we had good boat speed and handling skills, we decided to go for the first approach.

The wind was fairly light at ten knots so we hoisted the full mainsail with the No 1 Yankee and staysail. Ten minutes to go and we were starting to get ourselves into position to begin our run for the line. The start area was quite tight and with 12 large, powerful yachts charging around everyone needed to keep their wits about them, as well as keeping an eye out for the competition.

We began our run and were side by side with *BP*. Both the yachts were neck and neck charging for the line. Just as we crossed the line the gun fired, followed by a second gun. We were over the line early by three seconds. This meant that we had to take a penalty once outside the harbour in clear water.

All we could do initially was keep the boat powering along and stay at the head of the fleet. The harbour was congested with spectator boats and cruise ships as we short-tacked our way between the buoys, gaining on one tack and losing out on the other.

We were the fourth boat to exit the harbour and joined the procession along the narrow shipping channel, staying between the buoys. The wind was dropping all the time as we headed out to sea. The Grunters headed off watch at 15:00 and managed to get a couple of hours sleep before coming back on watch at 18:00. By now the wind was down to three knots and the boats were just ghosting along.

It was decided that we could now complete our penalty turns to exonerate ourselves from our starting penalty. We had to complete two 360° turns. Because the wind was so light, we very slowly crept round through two tacks and gybes. Luckily for us it didn't really cost much in time as most of the boats around us were becalmed anyway. It had been a wise decision to hold. At least we were now back racing with the others.

Throughout the first night, the masthead lights of the other 11 boats could be seen close by. Nobody had managed to get away and the whole fleet was tightly bunched, slowly creeping eastwards.

The first 24 hours involved a lot of crew work, constantly changing sails between the spinnakers and the Yankee 1/staysail as the wind fluctuated in strength and direction.

Tuesday 21st June 2005, Day 3

Tuesday 21st June 2005, Day 3

42°59'.27 N   66°47'.34 W

50 miles south-west of Nova Scotia

By the third day, the wind had settled, blowing steadily from the west at between 15 and 20 knots. *Team Stelmar* established her position as the northernmost boat in the fleet as they headed out into the Atlantic. The weather began to get colder and the fog closed in. Visibility was down to a couple of hundred metres. The days were clear and pleasant, but the starry nights were cold.

There was no drama or problems on board *Team Stelmar*, just good slick crew work. Sail changes were completed without fuss and there was no damage to equipment or crew to report. We had initially dropped down to tenth place, but were not too concerned as we had expected this. *Samsung* had taken the early lead, but they were the southernmost boat of the fleet and initially had more favourable conditions. As the leg progressed, the stronger wind in the north would help the northern boats, while the more southerly boats would be closer to the North Atlantic high pressure system and be influenced by the lighter winds. A short-term gain but a longer-term loss.

The crew had already seen pilot whales and dolphins, along with fishing boats and lobster pots. These had to be avoided as they could become entangled with the rudder, keel or propeller under the boat and slow the boat down. There was also a large ship displaying the lights for 'vessel not under command'. A very unusual sight to see.

There were also three transatlantic rowers fairly close by, two teams of four rowers and one solo attempt, all heading the same way as us. We decided to keep an eye out for them and contact them on the radio to wish them luck if we saw them.

The food for this leg was different to the other legs. There were fewer snack bars. We were still eating freeze-dried food and making our own bread each day. Coffee was in ample supply along with energy drinks and caffeine tablets to help the on-watch crew stay alert during the night watches.

Team Stelmar was now sitting in eighth place, only eight miles from the leaders, *SAIC* and *Samsung*. We were very much in touch with the rest of the fleet and still the most northerly boat.

We were only two days away from reaching waypoint Charlie. A waypoint placed by the race organisers to stop the boats heading too far north and meeting icebergs coming down the Labrador Current from Iceland and Canada. The larger icebergs are tracked by satellite and their positions reported. We had to sail to the south of waypoint Charlie to comply with the race regulations.

The nights were now really cold, with everyone wearing full thermals, hats and gloves. Memories of the Southern Ocean came flooding back, but the sea state was different. This time we were sailing downwind in moderate seas; not experiencing the blasting icy headwinds and massive waves of the Southern Ocean.

We stuck with our strategy of staying north, rather than settling into the safety of the rest of the fleet. We believed in ourselves and the information we had. It was tempting at times to head south as we lost miles to the others, but our decision was soon to be vindicated.

Wednesday 29th June 2005, Day 11

Wednesday 29th June 2005, Day 11

47°07'.9 N   29°39'.7 W

1200 miles west of La Rochelle

We had been leading the race for two days and pulled out a comfortable lead on the chasing boats. After the stalemate of the first week, *Team Stelmar* made the break and held it. The wind was constantly over 20 knots, and very often over 30 knots. We were regularly changing from the heavy spinnaker to the Yankee 1 as the wind increased. The seas had been building for several days and the boat was beginning to surf down some of the larger waves. Our plan to head north was paying off and despite sailing more miles than the others we were now enjoying fast and exhilarating sailing, day after day after day. Our hourly runs were in double figures, every hour, and the forecast was for more to come. The next boat was ten miles behind us and we were pulling away all the time. Things were looking promising, but there was still over 1000 miles to go.

Life on board had taken on a new dynamic. Everyone was trimming that bit harder and being more proactive, motivated by our success. When on deck, all the crew gathered at the back of the boat around the helmsman, in order to get the weight at the stern. This would stop the bow from digging in and help the boat go faster.

Due to the constant load on the sails, we were starting to experience some problems with the Yankee. The large metal hanks which clip the sail to the wire forestay had started to come undone as the sail collapsed and filled again. We would need to reconnect them or the sail would be damaged and perhaps even rip.

Thanks to our new found confidence and aggressive sailing style, we decided that rather than drop the Yankee down to the deck and slow down, Phil would climb the forestay and then re-attach each hank one by one. It was a team effort to hoist Phil up the forestay to each hank where he clipped himself onto the stay to stop himself being thrown back into the mast. Once safely clipped on, he then used a short length of rope to pull the sail back in line and get the hank clipped back onto the forestay. Once re-attached, Phil was then hoisted up to the next errant hank and repeated the process again.

All in all, Phil spent well over an hour up the rig sorting out the five disconnected hanks. All the while *Team Stelmar* was surfing down waves while the rest of the crew concentrated on getting maximum boat speed. If we were going to get a result on this leg then this was how to do it.

We were still leading the fleet and were determined to stay there.

Sunday 3rd July 2005, Day 15

46°33'.5 N   05°02'.6 W

With only about 100 miles to go to the finish line in La Rochelle, the atmosphere on board *Team Stelmar* was electric. We were still in first place but the weather file was showing light winds ahead and continuing strong winds behind. This meant that *Team Stelmar* would slow down first, while all those behind would theoretically close up with the help of continuing strong winds.

It was tense waiting for the 22:00 sked to come in from the race office. The previous sked, six hours earlier, showed us 21 miles ahead of *BG* in second place, a very comfortable lead with only 100 miles to go.

One by one the boats' positions came in and Nicko plotted them onto the computer and fed the data in to the spreadsheet to work out the distance to go for each boat.

Up on deck, things were just as tense.

Alex:

It was a glorious summer afternoon and everyone was in T-shirts and shorts. The wind was light and we were trimming the lightweight 0.75oz spinnaker in 5.5 knots of wind. I was walking back towards the helm and thought I saw something on the horizon. I grabbed the binoculars and couldn't believe what I saw. There were now several large spinnakers on the horizon. At first I didn't believe that they were our fleet, the last sked showed the next boat over 20 miles away.

I stood up on the pushpit at the back of the boat and was amazed to see that they were indeed Challenge boats and they were all flying their Flankers, indicating that they had around 20 knots of wind and lots of boat speed, compared to our 5 ½ knots of wind and 3 ½ knots of boat speed. Surely we couldn't let victory slip away this close to the finish.

There was nothing we could do about the boats behind us. We just had to 'control the controllables'; **our** boat and **our** sails with the wind **we** had.

Nicko popped his head up and announced that *BG* was now a mere six miles behind us and in no uncertain terms he was told that we knew as we could see them. We had lost 15 miles in the last six hours!

We knew however that they too would either slow down as they entered our area of wind, or they would bring the stronger wind with them which we would also benefit from. We were still six miles ahead; it just meant that the finish would be closer than we all thought 24 hours earlier.

One by one the heavy spinnakers behind were replaced with lighter 1.5oz race spinnakers. At last, the charge from behind slowed down and we were back on even terms. We just had to make sure we stayed between the competition and the finish line and ideally pulled away again. We knew we could sail the boat fast.

Slowly but surely the wind began to fill in again as the chasing pack drew closer. We peeled from the lightweight spinnaker to our race spinnaker; a slick manoeuvre. Within a couple of hours the wind strength was back up to 20 knots and we dropped the spinnaker in favour of the Yankee 1 and staysail. Fifty miles to go and Julian sent a message to Race Control using the satellite communications to let them know we were 50 miles from the finish.

It was important that everyone kept focused on their tasks and keep their 'eyes in the boat' and not spend time watching the others behind. Everyone was concentrating on keeping up maximum effort right to the finish. Our lead was now down to just over five miles from *BG*, both watches were awake and alert.

There was a magnificent electrical storm over the land ahead and Nicko and Clive were wondering if and how it might affect the boat, or if we could take advantage of any wind shifts. The sky would light up with every flash and we could see the outline of the land below. We were now only 25 miles from finishing.

By now it was 03:00 and Julian sent another message to Race Control to tell them we were 25 miles away and had sighted two lighthouses which we had to pass. The wind was now steadily over 25 knots and gusting to over 30. We held on to the Yankee 1 and full mainsail for the final close reach.

An hour later and we passed the Ile d'Oléron and the Ile de Ré, the two islands near La Rochelle. The finish line was in sight, but so were *BG* behind us, albeit five miles behind. We powered towards the finish, spray everywhere. Nobody dared celebrate until we crossed the line.

At 05:33 on the 5th July 2005 *Team Stelmar* crossed the finish line in first place. We had done it! As soon as we were over the line there was a huge crew bundle on the side deck. We were over the moon.

Our emotions were soon subdued however as we had to wait for the lock gate into the marina to open before we could get in. As this only happened a couple of hours either side of high water, and we had just missed it, we had to wait for nine hours.

As we motored around in a large circle we had a grandstand view for watching the other boats finish.

Behind *BG* was *Unisys*, followed by *BP*, *Me to You*, *Barclays*, *Pindar*, *Save the Children*, *VAIO*, *SAIC* and finally *Samsung*, who had led in the early days of the leg.

The waiting around gave us time to get on with the jobs we would normally do in port, such as rig and safety checks. The more we could get completed now the more time we would have free when we got in.

Eventually, at 14:00, we began to lead the procession into the marina. There were crowds lining the route, shouting and cheering. We could make out 'Safe Happy Fast' banners amongst them. We all lined the deck waving madly. FIRST PLACE.

As we entered the empty marina, with no other Global Challenge boats before us, *Praise You* rang out once again over the PA system. The Challenge Business shore team were waiting on the pontoon to take our lines, along with many family, friends and supporters. All smiling and clapping.

Once we were tied up, the champagne corks popped and everyone was liberally sprayed. Alex, Phil, Clive, Wrighty and Julian spontaneously jumped in the marina, much to the delight of the crowds.

Once the initial celebrations died down we were presented with the trophy for the leg win. A large stainless steel yacht which stood almost three feet tall.

We all posed for photos with big grins on our faces and then headed for the bar to party. It was the best party of the whole race.

At the prize-giving, as Team Stelmar climbed onto the stage there was a cheer and standing ovation from all the other crews. We were held in high regard by the others. We were a very close-knit team with a lot of trust in each other, we had been through a lot. The other teams didn't have this so much and they commented on it with grudging respect.

As well as winning the leg, we also picked up another 24-hour distance trophy. This time we had covered 276.4 miles in 24 hours, a new record for the Global Challenge Race, and for the boats themselves.

Leg 7
La Rochelle - Portsmouth
500 miles, 4 days
Wednesday 13th July 2005, Start Day
La Rochelle

THE STOPOVER IN LA ROCHELLE was only short, and one week after the elation and parties of the previous leg victory, it was back to business.

The leggers from the previous leg stayed on for the final dash to the finish in Portsmouth. All that is except Mike True, who left to fly home. We were joined by Adrian McMahon from Stelmar, who went on the Groaners watch for the remaining few days of the race.

We had agreed some changes for the final sprint leg. In keeping with our best-for-boat policy and doing everything we could for maximum boat speed, it was decided that key crew members would be excused from mother duty for the leg. For the Grunters, that meant Phil, Paula and Rich wouldn't be on mother duty, but would be on deck instead for every watch. We would also be carrying much less kit. Many of the crew left their drysuits ashore to save weight. Our Curver boxes, which contained all our personal kit, were virtually empty, save for a toothbrush and thin thermals. We would be wearing the same clothes from the start right through to the finish.

We had two podium finishes now and wanted to push ourselves up the leader board as far as we could. Every place counted, right up to the finish line. The final results were still up for grabs.

This leg was different to all the others, in that the actual finish time was choreographed by the race organisers to coincide with TV broadcasting times. Unusually, the leg started on a Wednesday and we knew that it would finish around midday on the following Saturday which would best suit the media, sponsors and supporters. In order for this to happen, there was a series of marks to pass round in the English Channel. If the boats were going to finish ahead of time, then they would be asked to round all the marks; if the winds were light and time was running out, the course would be shortened. This would be communicated to the entire fleet well before the lead boat reached them, so as not to disadvantage anyone.

We were leaving on a high. There was the usual Challenge shore team to see the fleet off and having been the first boat in, we were the last boat to leave. After the blessing of the fleet and three cheers for the town from everyone, the boats left one by one.

It was an earlier start than the other legs in order to make the lock gate and the first boats began to leave at 08:15. We were set to leave at 09:15 and motor out to the open sea and the start area.

The wind was light, less than ten knots, but it was a beautiful, clear summer's day with a blue sky.

The drill was now very standard to everyone as the boat prepared for racing and everything was stowed away. Although a familiar routine we couldn't be complacent and did everything methodically and carefully as if it was for the first time. We had much less food on board and everything pretty much fitted in the galley without us having to put anything under the floor in plastic bags. This meant it was much easier for the mother to sort out and organise the food for the day.

Once out in the bay, we had about three hours before the start, so everyone sat in the cockpit and had a briefing about the intended route and the expected weather. Clive and

Nicko took some last minute weather advice over the phone. Under the race rules we were not allowed any external weather information, other than that approved and supplied by Challenge, once each leg had started. This was the last chance to get advice on the route.

We practised the start a few times to make sure we could time it right. It was going to be tricky. Like the start in Cape Town, this was also going to be down wind with spinnakers. The trick was to time the hoist just right; too soon and the extra power and speed could carry you over the line early, too late and you potentially lose ground to the other boats.

The wind was very light by the time the gun fired and everybody drifted across the line with limp spinnakers hanging from the masthead. It was difficult to tell who was in the lead as positions changed constantly as the zephyrs of wind blew in.

There were a couple of marks to round before heading up the coast towards Brest and the Raz de Seine. Each mark was logged as it was passed. The fleet began to string out in a long procession. The lead group of boats managed to pick up the wind offshore before the others and made a break of a couple of miles on the chasing pack.

As darkness fell, there was talk of one of the boats missing a mark. It was *BP* and they had to turn back to round it. Although only a detour of a few miles, in the light winds and fighting the current, it was a long and slow struggle for them. To make matters worse, once they managed to get there the tide had turned again so was against them for a further six hours.

BP's problems had been compounded and the short detour had cost them many miles to the rest of the fleet who were now sailing in better wind conditions and pulling away still further. This was a short leg and any mistakes were going to be very costly.

Since the start, the wind had varied from 5.8 knots to 19.1 knots, all in the space of 12 hours. We were continually trimming the sails, and spinnaker peels and repacks were common.

Flash was very happy when the snack box came up during one night watch, pleased to find full-size chocolate bars and not the mini bars we had before. He was a chocoholic.

By 16:00 on the second day we had peeled to the 0.75oz lightweight spinnaker as the wind dropped again. We were just approaching the Raz waypoint near Brest. The tide race there is vicious but luckily it was with us and helped push us along at a healthy 7.8 knots. Good speed with only 8.5 knots of wind. However, by the time *BP* reached this 'tide gate' the tide would have turned and they would have to wait for it to turn back before they could proceed again.

We were now heading north, across the English Channel and towards the UK. The wind was still infuriatingly light and progress was frustratingly slow, but at 13:40 on the 15th July, we spotted first the Eddystone lighthouse and then the land beyond. This was our first sight of England since October, ten months previously.

As we rounded the lighthouse it was an emotional time on board. We all knew that we had only a day left in the Challenge; only one more sunset, one last sunrise.

However, we couldn't relax yet and had to put emotion to one side until after the finish. It was very close with the lead four boats still very much in sight.

As the weather had been so light on the way up from La Rochelle, it was decided by the organisers to miss the rest of the marks allowing everyone to sail straight into the Solent and the finish line off Portsmouth.

Slowly, steadily, mile by mile we made our way along the South Coast, passing recognisable landmarks and towns. Some of the crew had done a lot of sailing around this coast.

At 07:28 on Saturday 16th July, we passed the Needles off the western tip of the Isle of Wight and entered the Solent. It was amazingly close with five challenge boats all within 100m and drifting along together. Eyes were peeled looking for any signs of wind on the water and looking out for any other sailing boats to see if they had any wind. It was tight racing as the group passed Cowes. There were crowds of people watching and cheering, but we had to remain focused.

BG had already crossed the finish line in first place when the wind began to fill in. Having already dispatched *Unisys* and *Pindar*, we were now in a straight fight with *Me to You* to the finish. They were ahead and had the advantage, all they had to do was stay between us and the finish, but at the very last mark they made a mistake which allowed *Team Stelmar*, with excellent and slick crew work, to slip inside them as they rounded the mark. A huge cheer went up from the Stelmar support boat which had followed us down the Solent, once again full of family, friends, supporters and well-wishers.

We managed to quickly hoist the spinnaker and crossed the line in 6th place at 14:22 on 16th July 2005 after sailing over 35,000 miles and spending 184 days racing at sea.

Once across the line, we dropped the sail and with the engine ticking over, there was time for a quick team hug on the side deck. Everyone congratulated each other and the supporters' boat gave three cheers.

However, there was still work to be done before we could go into the marina at Gunwharf Quays in Portsmouth, the same marina we had left ten months earlier.

The mainsail was dropped and folded for the last time and the cover was put on. The fenders and mooring lines were retrieved from their storage places and set up ready.

We waited our turn outside the harbour before we were escorted in by a Navy warship. As we rounded the corner of the harbour we could see masses of cheering people, waving flags and shouting. Balloons were released and confetti cannons fired. Above the noise we could still make out our boat theme tune.

We motored into the marina and passed our lines to the waiting Challenge shore crew and moored up *Team Stelmar* for the very last time.

Some family and friends were allowed down onto the pontoon to welcome us in. They passed champagne on board and we exuberantly sprayed it everywhere. Several of the crew spontaneously jumped into the water, as they had in La Rochelle.

We had done it. We had raced all the way around the world. We were all very proud of what we had achieved, but it was also very sad. Over the previous year and a half, we had formed great, lifelong friendships. We had been through thick and thin, seen each other at our best, and our worst. For the last ten months we had lived and breathed the yacht race, it was our life.

Some had set out as adventurers with little or no sailing experience and for them it was just enough to complete the challenge. For others, it was a race through and through, and the 6th place result overall was satisfying bearing in mind what we had been through. By the end, even the 'adventurers' were willing the boat faster and enjoying the spirit of the racing. We were **one** team.

We had all changed and grown; not only physically fitter, but mentally fitter too. We were now able to look at life in a different light. What had been perceived as difficult or impossible tasks at work or with life now seemed possible. Things seen as problems were really insignificant, priorities were clearer; the race enabled us to put things into perspective and work out what was really important. We had taken on the challenge and succeeded. It was indeed a life changing experience.

Very soon there were 11 Challenge boats moored up in the marina, all except *BP* who were still a long way away in the English Channel after missing the mark right at the start of the leg. Hundreds of BP employees had come down the previous day to see their boat in, and were disappointed to learn that they would not be finishing until the next day and were too far away to see. Many BP supporters turned to support *Team Stelmar* instead as their 'second preferred boat' having witnessed and appreciated our traumas on leg two.

The following day was the final prize-giving, to be held outside on the waterfront overlooking the marina. *BP* were still to finish, but just as we were all getting ready news came through that they had just finished. They literally motored into the marina, moored up and then came straight from the boat to the prize-giving ceremony.

There were hugs from well-wishers as we left the ceremony to be with family and friends. Everyone fought through the crowds to try to get some space and peace in a quiet bar somewhere, but every bar was packed. There was no peace and quiet, quite a contrast to the life on the boat.

Alex:

*It was very emotional at the finish, and for me it was **the** hardest day of the whole experience. The huge waves and cold of the Southern Ocean, the searing heat and frustration of the Tropics, all paled into insignificance compared to the last day. We had lived together, 24 hours a day, seven days a week, without a break. At least with family you get a break when you go to work, and you get a break from work colleagues at weekends. This group of people, who had lived so close together, and been through so much together, were now just a group of individuals again.*

Paula:

I was quite emotional at the end. My family and friends probably thought I was crying with happiness, but, to be honest, it was sadness. Sadness that the most amazing experience of my life was over. I had leapt blindly into participating in the challenge, having hardly any sailing experience and with only three months notice. I then persevered through the hardest ten months of my life; half loving it and half wondering what on earth I was doing out there. But at the end, it was such a wrench to break away from the feeling of ultimate fitness, unity and focus. Life seemed pretty ordinary in comparison.

Despite finishing in 6th place overall, Team Stelmar were happy with what they had achieved. They went through more than any other boat with two Southern Ocean medical evacuations. They set four 24-hour records out of the seven legs and hold the outright distance record for the race. They sailed over 2000 miles more than the others. They were more often first over the start line and were revered for their boat speed. Overall they won more prizes than any other team, 14 in all.

But more than anything else, Team Stelmar were regarded by everyone - competitors, Challenge staff and supporters - as being the closest team of all.

BOAT to BOARDROOM
The Business Chapters

Chapter 1. Leadership

Definition

THE CONCEPT OF LEADERSHIP is hard to define. Warren Beatty used a great - but imprecise - definition when he compared it to the concept of beauty: *"It's hard to define but you know it when you see it"*. This is true, you do know leadership when you see it (even in children), but it is also true that it eludes precise, consensual definition.

Leadership is about *influencing* others through style, charisma, communication, visionary thinking, inspiration, self-awareness, integrity, clarity of direction and strength of purpose; compared with management which is about influencing others from being in a position of authority.

Peter Drucker, author of nearly 40 books on leadership and management describes the difference between management and leadership as follows:

Management is doing things right; Leadership is doing the right things.

Once you see past the concise wording, this short phrase unlocks a broader definition, along the lines of: *once a leader decides on the right course of action, management is in making sure that it is carried out properly.*

Leading eighteen people on a boat in the freezing Southern Ocean, 2000 miles from anywhere, means deciding on the right course of action **and** doing the right thing; for the sake of the race, the crew and the very survival of the team. Great leadership on the Global Challenge was a critical and lonely position to be in. A skipper held ultimate responsibility, with very little support and no time off, often in life-threatening conditions.

Leadership in the Global Challenge

In the 2004/5 Global Challenge there was a broad range of leadership ability among the twelve skippers selected. However, this was probably an improvement on the ten chosen for the first 'British Steel' race in 1992/3, where the main selection criterion was the amount of sea miles candidates had clocked up; no matter that these were often on **solo** voyages. These 'salty old sea dog' characters, strong in their solo handling of yachts, were less used to leading a crew of amateur sailors in dangerous conditions. This resulted in several personnel issues and change of skippers during that first race. (Admittedly some real master mariners were skippers of this race, such as Pete Goss[3], Mike Golding[4] and the winning Skipper of *Nuclear Electric*, John Chittenden, who went on to win the 2001 Yachtsman of the Year Award.)

How could a single-handed sailor, used to surviving – and actually often thriving - in a harsh environment be expected to care for and lead thirteen raw recruits? It was a big leap. So taking on board their lessons from 1992/3, Sir Chay Blyth and the Challenge Business concentrated more on recruiting skippers with people management skills and gave leadership training in the build-up to departure. Skippers were invited to apply for the 2004/5 race back in 2002, following a global recruitment campaign. Forty were selected to go through to

---

[3] Pete Goss, MBE, received the *Légion d'honneur* for saving fellow sailor Raphael Dinelli in the 1996 Vendée Globe solo round the world yacht race during a severe storm in the Southern Ocean.

[4] Mike Golding, one of the few yachtsmen to have raced round the world non-stop in both directions, holds the solo record for sailing round the world westwards between 1994 and 2000. He was 2nd in the British Steel Challenge 1992/3 and 1st in the next race in 1996/7.

the next stage - a selection weekend at Calshot Activity Centre, in Southampton, UK. None of the activities during this intense weekend took place on the water. Instead, candidates were tested on their personal, management and leadership skills. Simon Walker, MD of the Challenge Business, justifies this decision as follows:

Our initial lack of focus on sailing skills may sound strange... but our skippers have one of the toughest jobs in sailing. It's not just sailing a boat around the world with seventeen strangers. It's about personnel management and leadership skills and juggling the expectations of crew, sponsors, media and Challenge Business as well as their own objectives.[5]

Selection for the 2004/5 skippers was certainly competitive (nearly 400 people applied globally), and out of the final twelve chosen, only two had sailed around the world before, one in the 1989/90 Whitbread and one in a previous Global Challenge. This man was Duggie Gillespie who had been a crew member of the British Steel race in 1992/3 on the sixth-placed boat *Interspray*. As Skipper of *Sark* in 2004/5 he came in fourth, and then went on to win the only other amateur round the world yacht race two years later, the 2007/8 'Clipper Race.'[6]

The emphasis on leadership changed from mileage clocked up, to the ability to lead a team; perhaps a reflection of the leadership qualities sought these days compared to the 'job is for life' mentality in the past. The point being, rather than recruit leaders solely on their technical knowledge and length of service, talent is required to inspire individuals and teams towards achieving great and extra-ordinary things.

---

[5] Quote from the Official Race Guide.
[6] The Clipper Race also sails every four years, but sails eastwards, following the prevailing winds and currents. It does not go around Cape Horn, unlike the Global Challenge.

Race Results 2004/5 Global Challenge

Position	Yacht	Leg 1	Leg 2	Leg 3	Leg 4	Leg 5	Leg 6	Leg 7	Total
1	BG SPIRIT (Andy)	5=	3	1	9	1	2	1	90
2	Barclays Adventurer (Stuart)	1	9	9	7	2	6	2	76
3	BP Explorer (David)	5=	2	5	2	8=	4	12	74
4	Spirit of Sark (Duggie)	7=	1	7	1	6	7	10	73
5	SAIC La Jolla (Eero)	7=	8	2	5	4	11	4	71
6	Team Stelmar (Clive)	9=	11	8	3	8=	1	6	66
7=	Me to You (James)	10	7	3	8	9	5	7	63
7=	VAIO (Amadeo)	2	5	12=	RET	3	10	3	63
9	Samsung (Matt)	3	4	6=	10	10	12	9	58
10	Imagine It. Done (Dee)	9=	RET	12=	4	7	3	8	56
11	Pindar (Loz)	11	10	6=	6	12	8	5	54
12	Save the Children (Paul)	12	6	11	11	11	9	11	41

N.B. RET = retired

The winning Skipper of the 2004/5 Global Challenge Race – Andy Forbes of *BG* – was a case in point where leadership is *"hard to define but you know it when you see it"*. Andy was a strong personality, with a clear strategy, whom his crew liked and respected. In *Yachting World* magazine, just before race start, they listed the 'runners and riders': *"Who's hot and who's not? The 12 Challenge skippers, their teams and a pre-*

start form guide from 'The Tipster'." Andy was described with having 'masses of self-belief':

Masses of self-belief and has a lot of maturity. Maybe a lack of ocean racing experience, but probably in top 5.[7]

There is that lack of sailing experience again. If you were to compile a list of leadership skills and traits – or even just look up the extensive and fairly comprehensive list under 'Leadership' in Wikipedia – then two (connected) qualities in particular stand out for the Global Challenge skippers: confidence and strength of personality, and Australian Andy Forbes had plenty of both. Confidence was needed because skippers had to make and communicate strategic decisions in a tough and life-threatening environment; an environment that was 72' long, with 18 people who were competitively racing for 24 hours a day. It was a pressure-cooker situation leaving no room for doubt or navel-gazing. Strength of personality was needed because those seventeen fee-paying crew members were highly-committed extreme adventurers, full of spirit, opinion, passion and personality. They were the ultimate stakeholders. Somehow the skippers had to shine stronger and brighter than their incredible crews, earning their respect and therefore their commitment. Mutiny was the alternative.

In general, the diverse leadership styles affected each crew differently. The 'shadow you cast' as a leader is bigger and more powerful than the one you cast as an employee or crew member. What a leader says and how they say it; what they sanction, choose to ignore or focus on; how they behave socially; their body language with certain people; their reaction to bad news; and so on, are all magnified and given greater significance because they are leaders. Certainly some boats took on the 'personalities' of their skippers. One boat was very professional and hard-working, but had a serious, heads-down approach which bordered on being aggressive at times; contrastingly another boat was 'the party boat' and

---

[7] *Yachting World*, October 2004

expectations of them winning the race were low. One crew were almost permanently dissatisfied with their leader, whilst one crew adored their young skipper – often coming in last but happy! The crews evolved and shaped-up under the influence of their skippers, and the most successful teamwork was a result of Andy Forbes' leadership of his crew to achieve first place.

There were two particular methods Andy used that stood out from the other skippers, and these helped him to win the 2004/5 race by 14 points (see race results above).

In small races during one or two days out sailing, there are often races 'around the cans'. The 'cans' are buoys that are used to mark the course, and when there are a hundred yachts all competing for position in a two-hour race, the action is understandably intense. The skipper and crew give it 100% for every second of the race, knowing that in such a short time, every centimetre gained is a centimetre towards beating all the others. In comparison, the Global Challenge is a ten-month race covering 35,000 miles. To maintain 100% of effort by 100% of the crew for 100% of the time is impossible... or is it? As a leader, Andy Forbes raced as if each day was a 'race around the cans', thus intensifying the effort and concentration required from his crew, and altering their mindset towards the long-drawn-out race.

The second thing that Andy did was he raced his own race. On each boat is a Navigation Station including two computers and communication tools: VHF; HF and GMDSS (Global Marine Distress Safety System) radio, satellite phone and email. Every six hours the latitude and longitude of each of the twelve boats is sent out by email from the Global Challenge office which is staffed 24 hours a day. This six-hourly update was called the 'sked', short for schedule. The atmosphere on the boats would become more intense just before each sked and then change, often dramatically, according to the statistics and how well or badly each boat had performed over the other eleven in the fleet. On *Team*

Stelmar, we then plotted all twelve positions onto a computer chart using a program called MaxSea. The on watch would be told the results on deck and when they had a chance to go below deck, look at the overall picture of where we had all been six hours earlier and where we all were now. This – and the weather reports - then informed the Skipper's tactical choices as to what to do next. Often skippers would choose to navigate tactically to 'cover' the other boats.

For instance, if a boat was lying in first place towards the end of a leg, it sailed so that the focus was on keeping itself between the port and all the other boats behind. Not being overtaken is 'all' that it would take to win the leg. Another example: if the results showed that some yachts were gaining a strong advantage from riding a certain wind system or current, the skipper may decide to go their way too. The decisions a skipper took were often influenced by what the rest of the fleet were doing.

However, Andy sailed his own race. He made his own decisions based on his predetermined strategy. This meant that he could often be seen heading off 'doing his own thing' like a rogue boat; an orange blip on the computer graphic miles from the other coloured blips. And although this would not always be to his advantage, it sometimes shot him days ahead of everyone else. In one leg, from Cape Town to Boston, he came in days before the second placed boat.

As a result of this strategy he won three legs, came second in one and third in another. Five podiums out of the seven legs.

Leadership from Boat to Boardroom

Skippers for the Global Challenge are faced with a specific and unique situation in that they are the only paid, officially employed people on an otherwise 'amateur' and voluntary crew. They therefore have to tread quite gently in managing the seventeen individuals on their boat who have each paid £26,750 and effectively lost a year's wages to take part. This situation, and the fact that they are in charge of competitively sailing a racing yacht 35,000 miles for 24 hours a day, are the fundamental differences between boat and boardroom. Otherwise, they are facing very similar leadership situations: communicating vision and values; getting buy-in to decisions and change; running management meetings; setting goals and revisiting objectives; planning strategies and tactics; preparing for and reacting to crises; managing, coaching and motivating teams; keeping stakeholders, sponsors and media informed; competing in a tough environment; adapting to changing climate and conditions; and so on.

Leading a crew in the Global Challenge round the world yacht race holds many parallels with leading a team in business - the situations and lessons are often just more black and white, which is why it is useful to take experiences, tips and mindsets from sport or extreme adventure into business. Organisations, leaders and teams can learn from extreme worlds which are explicit and concise and one step removed from the internal complicated, complex, compact, business life. The beauty of the Global Challenge is that it intensifies and simplifies the situations. The sole focus is *to sail as fast as possible* for almost a year. The simple objective is to win.

Here are some specific areas in which leadership parallels are drawn from the boat to the boardroom.

Pre Race Start – a New Team, a New Project

The skippers and their teams were announced at the London Excel Boat Show in January 2004. On October 3rd this collection of disparate individuals sailed off as twelve working teams for the challenge of a lifetime. For the ten months in between, the skippers' work was cut out.

Each Skipper had fifteen core crew and two 'leggers' who joined the race for each leg. The fifteen were unlikely to have met before, except perhaps on a training sail and so they really were starting from scratch. There was also a huge range of ability, experience and motivation. Some had been sailing since they were children, and others had never sailed before. Some were in it to win, and some just for the adventure. People came from all walks of life. The 2004/5 race had a software engineer, ballerina, GP, Board Director, truck driver, accountant and funeral director among others – and that was just on our boat! Ages ranged from 18 to 60. The Skipper had somehow to lead this group of strangers (while still in full-time jobs) from January to October and get them race-fit.

The challenge had begun.

The single, most effective action a skipper took in those ten months was to hold as many face-to-face gatherings as possible. On *Team Stelmar*, with one crew member living in Holland, one Australian living on the boat in Southampton and everyone else working full-time, this was not easy. However, these team meetings were crucial to success and so were held on weekends or during the week when as many team members as possible could book time off work. In addition to this, Team Stelmar held a weekly conference call every Monday night to discuss logistics and project management issues such as kit, food packing, fundraising, etc. The team also had a website and dispatched a newsletter to supporters at least once a month. Communication was critical, but none more so than face-to-face.

These meetings were the opportunity for the skippers to get to know their teams thoroughly; their individual strengths, weaknesses, pressure points and motivations. As in business, to effectively lead and motivate employees, leaders and managers must know their people **very** well to get the best out of them, manage their performance and be able to keep the right people in the right roles. Through close observation and genuine in-depth conversations, skippers learnt what made their crew tick, who was best for certain jobs, and which eight people would be a winning combination to make up each of the two watches.

These meetings also helped the crew to bond and get to know each other better, and in the early 'forming' stages of the team development, the whole crew worked together to generate their team vision, values, goals, brand, rules and strategies. Creating these mutually agreed principles helped to break down barriers, build trust, and progress the group from naïvety to maturity; from being eighteen individuals to a cohesive and collaborative working unit. The fact that the teams had vision, values and goals was important, but the journey they went through to get to them was just as useful to the team's growth. At these times, it was also important that the skippers allowed democratic involvement in the decision-making processes to ensure buy-in and commitment from the whole team.

In addition to workshop sessions to discuss and agree principles and rules, most skippers put their teams through some tough scenarios and physical training exercises. Leaders will get one view of their team as they function normally in comfortable circumstances, and another when they are 'up against it' – discovering who keeps a cool head under pressure, who can be relied upon as a team player and who collapses inwardly in a crisis. These challenges helped the skippers see who was who, but also helped to prepare the crew themselves for the bigger challenges ahead; every crisis experienced generally makes every crisis thereafter slightly less daunting and more manageable. Certainly in business, if a leader is fortunate to have a team who have 'been there, done that', then they are more battle-prepared and experienced for successfully tackling future difficulties. It's about crisis preparation.

On *Team Stelmar* there were two particularly tough team challenges which the Skipper chose to put us through. One was the 'sinking ship' scenario set up at *HMS Excellent* in the Royal Naval Docks, Portsmouth (see pp 19-20).

The second tough team build was in Buenos Aires after the first leg of the race. Here the crew were bussed off into the humid tropics outside the city, generally expecting a pleasant day team building, with a picnic, possibly a team talk and some touch rugby. However, as they arrived at a dirty, rusty old cruise ship, the crew were briefed on that day's endurance challenge: in teams of three, to run ten miles cross-country, over an obstacle course including climbing nets and walls, across plank and rope bridges, kayak twice round an island and swim three miles in the filthy river before finishing on a zip-wire – the only enjoyable bit of the day. Five hours later we were very sweaty and exhausted and not in the best of moods. 'JC', having literally just flown in from the UK and come straight from the airport, had done the whole thing in his deck shoes so had bloody, blistered feet. Richard was stung on his head, five people ended up with ticks burrowing under their skin, Paula had hit Rob over the head with a paddle and everyone was filthy and disappointed that the 'jolly' had turned out to be so 'un-jolly'. However, in the debrief the point was made that if you needed to develop a team who were about to face the Southern Ocean and Cape Horn, then it is best to test the team first in a tough, controlled situation.

So pre race start, the skippers worked hard to pull their teams together and accelerate their development into a high performance unit, able to race competitively, live together in a 72' box for 24 hours a day, seven days a week for up to eight weeks at a time, and face the Southern Ocean. Face-to-face meetings, tough team builds and sailing drills were the answer.

Start Day – Kick-Off

The skippers had a particularly demanding time leading their crews at the start and end of each leg. Firstly, both watches are on deck to experience the thrill of leaving or arriving in a port; this is like having two shifts of employees working the same shift in a tight space. What was a slick working unit of nine people for a month becomes a chaotic, confused mess of eighteen. Communication and role delineation deteriorates. Not least, everyone physically gets in each other's way. Then there is the fact that individuals who had been focused on helming to within one degree of calculation, or checking the trim of the sails every minute, or proactively pumping the bilges each hour, become distracted by the sight of land and the thoughts of friends, family, food and beer. So the past perfection of a smooth-running racing yacht becomes an amateur, embarrassing mess in full view of supporters, media, the race office, friends and family. There is the added pressure that at the start and end of each leg, the fleet inevitably group together and close racing within eyesight is not uncommon for three or four days. The Skipper then has to somehow keep tight control of a crew who were Team Stelmar and are now temporarily Nicko, Paul, Kate, Rob, etc. - excited, distracted, nervous and emotional individuals with lives beyond the boat.

On Sunday 3rd October 2004 at 13:50, all this is exacerbated. There is a force 8 gale in the Solent, 100s of supporter boats are charging around the racing fleet, helicopters with camera crews are whirring overhead, Princess Anne and Sir Chay Blyth are ready to fire the start gun, 1000s of friends and family line the shore at Southsea and wave and shout from the supporter boats, and the Challenge fleet shuffle for position along the start line, their sails fully blown and their steel hulls surging 10' up and down in the gale force waves. The crews are excited, nervous and sick. The skippers are excited, nervous and under incredible pressure. The possibility of a major accident is high – it's happened before. The race of a lifetime is about to start after four years of preparation...

From a boardroom point of view, there will be times when there are distractions (start day) from the day-to-day running of the business (racing the boat). Perhaps a new product launch, a significant pitch or even a take-over. These are demanding times for everyone – but especially the leader who must keep one eye on the ball and one on the 'distraction' whilst maintaining discipline. Clive, as leader of his 'company' Team Stelmar, did what he could to prepare for this critical time.

First, we practised the start of the race at exactly the same location in training sails beforehand. We did timed dry runs again and again, ensuring that everyone knew exactly what was expected of them in different sea states and weather conditions, and if anyone didn't have a job, then they knew exactly where to be. So in business this would be like rehearsing a pitch, preparing for a launch in meticulous detail, or future scenario planning. 'Being prepared'.

Secondly, on the day before the start, Clive gave us the freedom to do whatever we wished with nothing on the agenda. This was an unusual liberty at a time when every minute of the last three weeks had been busy for the sake of the boat, from six in the morning until midnight. We were given 'me' time. This really helped everyone get to grips with what they were about to do and compose themselves in the calm before the storm; to have some space away from the hustle, to say quality goodbyes or just to relax and generally do whatever they wanted to do. 'Breathing space'.

Thirdly, on the morning of the race, which was due to start at 14:00, we all met for a calm, considered team breakfast and Clive talked through the charts and strategy for the first leg. We did this at the start of each leg and it became a pleasant routine which focused the minds and brought the team together. 'Anchoring routine'.

The final important thing Clive did was to let go. He allowed us to do what we had trained to do; having delegated all the jobs he then trusted us to get on with it. No extra management, no extra communication, no extra fuss. This was true professionalism in action. 'Let go'.

Leading Through Time – a Maturing Team

There is a theory about team development which suggests that teams progress through four stages as they mature. The first stage is 'forming'; as the team comes together at the start it is underdeveloped and still finding its feet. Team members are polite to each other in fairly superficial interactions and the leader does a lot of the talking and decision making. At the second 'storming' phase, internal conflict starts to develop as team members test their relationships and boundaries and experiment with feelings and hierarchies. The team is still not functioning well, and the leader has to maintain concentration on the task whilst allowing the team elbow room to find their places. From here, teams settle and consolidate within the 'norming' phase, communicating well, agreeing work practices and clarifying roles and processes. At this point the leader can start to back off and take a less dominant role. Finally, the team matures and enters the 'performing' stage where they work effectively together, team development and success is a high priority, but individuals feel valued too. Theoretically the leader could go on a long holiday at this point and come back to the same or even higher level of performance. Leaders can now concentrate on supporting and coaching their functioning team.

The Global Challenge is a ten-month intensive 'project', but one that happens for 24 hours a day – three times the length of a normal working day - so in relative terms it is 'live' for 30 months, with a planning stage of a further ten months beforehand. In this time, Team Stelmar definitely progressed through forming to storming to norming, to very much high-performing, and the Skipper's role changed as a result.

In the first week, Clive got very little sleep as he was on deck and on duty much of the time. This was perfectly understandable bearing in mind he was responsible for 18 people's lives and some of his crew had little sailing experience. In that first week the whole fleet suffered in storm force weather across the Bay of Biscay with winds of over 50 knots. Storm sails were torn to shreds, equipment and bones were broken, crew members were swept off deck and life was harsh above and below decks. Combining this ghastly October weather with the fact that the crews were 'green' (literally and metaphorically!) then the leaders had no real choice but to stay as present, accessible, decisive and strong as possible. In the beginning, skippers had to adopt a very dominant and directive leadership style.

By the end of the race however, the skippers were almost in the way. Each watch was functioning so perfectly – in calm seas but in crises also – that they didn't even have to talk as they anticipated each other's moves, and if the Skipper did get involved it would throw the teamwork. This felt like poetry in motion. (It **really** did). Even though in the first month we thought we were giving it 100% and working very well together, by the end we knew there was a pivotal 1% difference and we had in fact only been giving it 99%. On the last legs from Boston to La Rochelle and La Rochelle to Portsmouth, Clive was on deck to soak up the atmosphere more than anything. We had made him redundant. If a leader has done an excellent job and the team has shaped up beneath their direction, then this 'redundancy' must be the ultimate sign of a mature team.

Situational Leadership[8]: the style of leadership changes to suit the situation. At first our Skipper was directive and authoritarian which gave us confidence to work within the realms of his guidance and decision making. Once we had settled down, Clive supported and worked alongside us, asking the Watch Leaders for their opinions on sail changes and tactics, and helping out during times of trouble. Towards the end, Clive took a step back and delegated fully to his team under the management of the two Watch Leaders, knowing that his trust and faith in us was justified.

---

[8] See Paul Hersey 'Situational Leader' and his joint authorship with Ken Blanchard on 'Management of Organisational Behaviour' which includes the model for situational leadership.

The Management Team and Decision Making

A quick word about the management team on the boats. A typical structure on each Challenge yacht was that out of the 18 people on board, there was a Skipper, a first mate/Navigator and two watches of seven people, each managed by a Watch Leader. Two 'new' people (leggers) joined the boat for each leg and they were usually placed one to each watch. Every day, out of the seven people who weren't on the 'management team' one person would stay below decks and do 'Mother Duties' such as cooking and cleaning. This mother role rotated every day for a week, so in effect on every leg there were always new people to bring up to speed (leggers) and someone missing from each watch (on mother duty) which required a reshuffling of jobs every day.

The Skipper was the only paid professional and ultimately responsible 24 hours a day. On *Team Stelmar*, Clive would be actively in charge while awake and the Navigator covered for him when he was off watch, only waking him in times of crisis. Between them, Clive and Nicko (our Navigator) were on duty for different times than the watches to ensure consistency during the changeovers. Our watches changed five times a day and once the new watch was briefed, the off watch would then go below deck to eat and sleep. It was then up to the Skipper or Navigator to ensure that the current situation such as the weather or sail plan (the sails that were up) was known and assimilated by the new watch. This was especially critical at night, in poor weather conditions, or during tight racing, though sometimes the new watch took a while to get adjusted purely because they had been fast asleep five minutes before! Often one watch would go below deck during a beautiful sunny day and then come back up six hours later into a stormy night. The lightweight spinnaker sail that was up would have been replaced by heavy duty foresails and there would be no way of knowing that unless you clipped on and crawled 72' along the deck and looked up at the sails with a torch.

The management team, then, was composed of Skipper, Navigator and two Watch Leaders. Before the start of each leg these four would discuss the course, climate, past Challenge routes and agree a strategy. This was then communicated broadly to the crew on start day during the team breakfast. All good in theory but in practice the management structure did not go to plan initially – as many management teams will experience in business, elegant theory and calm planning can go awry when reality kicks in.

There were two very noticeable occasions on the first leg from Portsmouth to Buenos Aires (36 days) when the management structure broke down and the Skipper was left high and dry.

Before the race start, Team Stelmar bought in consultancy advice from the previous winning Navigator – Cian Macarthy (LG Flatron). Part of the advice given was that no matter how enticing it looked to sail through the Canary Islands – don't. There is a large wind shadow effect caused by Mount Teide on Tenerife. The weather systems, currents and 'as the crow flies' route all point towards cutting through the islands, but in practice it is best to sail around them, leaving at least a 50 mile clearance. This advice was taken on board by the management team and discussed with a wider tactical team and it was agreed that *Team Stelmar* would **not** sail through the Canaries.

However, ten days into the race, *Team Stelmar* was just approaching the Canaries, and Clive was looking at a chart of the islands and meteorological data and thinking how advantageous it looked to cut through the middle. He was tempted. We were in the leading pack and it would have given us a boost to shoot through, popping out the other side potentially in first place for the run down to the equator. Despite pre-agreed strategy Clive decided to take this route. No-one challenged him strongly enough to make him change his mind. Disaster. The next day we were sitting in dead calm, with zero knots of boat speed, staring at our reflections in the glassy water. We sat and sweated, hot and listless, day and night, for 48 hours. Meanwhile the other boats sailed past.

The wind came back on the 14th October and we were off again, steaming along at 9–10 knots. But we had missed a big opportunity and were now in 9th place, 165 miles from the lead boat.

Five days later, people again were too faint-hearted to question the Skipper's decision. A squall was approaching and we should have quickly taken down our lightweight spinnaker sail. However, Clive came on deck, having just woken up, and hesitated before deciding. Too late. The squall hit us hard, knocked down the boat, tore the sail to shreds and snapped the Kevlar spinnaker pole in two.

So what? In yacht racing as in business, wrong decisions **are** sometimes made by leaders. Skippers, directors and management teams are not infallible human beings. The lessons come afterwards. What could have been done differently? What checks can we put into place to prevent this happening again? What does this mean about our leader? What does this mean about the way we are willing to be lead? What can the leader do to recover the situation?

Interestingly both of these situations happened in the first three weeks at a time when we were still 'forming' as a team. Had these decisions been made towards the end of the race, I think the wider management team would have been strong enough to challenge the decision, and the Skipper would have been strong enough to trust the judgment of his team. This demonstrates the power shift in a team's development. And although leaders are fallible, it's what they do next that's important.

The Ups

We've come a long, long way together,
Through the hard times and the good,
I have to celebrate you baby,

I have to praise you like I should...[9]

Each boat in the race had their own team song which was played at parties, award ceremonies and as they arrived at or left each port. The twelve tracks were very popular and we all enjoyed jumping around to: *You're a Superstar* by Love Inc. and *Ready to Go* by Republica. Ours was *Praise You* by Fatboy Slim; it was popular, upbeat, and the lyrics were quite appropriate - we **had** come a long, long way together, through both the hard times and the good, and deserved to celebrate and be praised.

Although not a 'party' boat, we certainly had a lot of fun (whilst racing), and one of our three values was to be happy (safe, happy, fast). Happiness came from racing well, being proud of doing a good job, and from creating our own fun. Likewise, at work happiness may come from job satisfaction, especially rather paradoxically from a *difficult* job well done, but also through good humour, and as leaders know (to adapt a slogan) 'you don't have to be happy to work here, but if you are it helps'. Happiness improves the well-being of the organisation and reduces 'sickies' and staff turnover. A happy boat for us meant a motivated boat.

Clive, our Skipper, was only 28 and had a good sense of humour. Although competitive he was perfectly at ease with us having fun at appropriate times. One concept he introduced was 'Happy Hour'. While sailing around the world, the boat maintains 'local time' which gained us an hour every week - although we then lost a day when we crossed the International Date Line on the 18th January 2005. So every Sunday, at 18:00 hours, we had Happy Hour at watch changeover. Both watches would stay on deck for an hour, after which it would be back to six o'clock and the start of a new watch. This was the only time during perhaps a seven week leg, when the two watches would have quality time together, a chance to catch up on a professional basis - swapping tips and best practices - but also to socialise. The

---

[9] *Praise You* lyrics by Fatboy Slim; Team Stelmar's theme song.

two watches, together, sailed the boat 24 hours a day, but if it wasn't for the enforced Happy Hour they would only talk for three minutes at watch changeover when one watch was tired and the other still waking up. This can be compared to departments or shifts working in silos; their combined work is essential to achieving the overall company goal, but they may never or rarely see each other. As a leader of an organisation with departments, shifts or geographically dispersed staff, face-to-face meetings unite the workforces, enabling a smoother operation and better communication across the divides.

During Happy Hour the two watches would eat together, mull over recent events, share best practices and have some fun. Three times the Happy Hour was themed – we had a school disco, a 'vicars and tarts' tea party and a Greek night with 'fancy dress' made out of whatever we had on the boat such as empty food bags, insulation tape, sailcloth material and cutlery. We also started 'Sunday lectures' relevant to where we were in the world. These began with an impromptu talk on the Cape Verde Islands as we passed through, but then we also covered the Battle of the River Plate, the Bermuda Triangle and Albatross among other subjects. Team Stelmar's Happy Hour was a great invention, creating a positive, united atmosphere plus it was good for boat speed giving us the opportunity to discuss and solve problems and share best practice. The face-to-face communication again between the team, was crucial.

We also had more 'natural' fun which arose out of the fact we were a close-knit team living in each other's pockets and having no alternative entertainment to occupy us. No TV, no music, no computers, no games – just sailing and conversation. Again, it was important that the leader – Clive – encouraged and allowed this to happen for the good of the soul, the boat and the crew.

(One bit of nonsense was centred on Newton, our oldest crew mate at 60, who had the critical job of tying the two sheets (ropes) onto the clew of a new sail. He took a little longer at this than we would have liked and often the rest of the watch had completed their jobs and were waiting for him to finish. One day, knowing this was about to happen, we sneakily made a cup of tea and as he was concentrating on tying his knots, we sat down, got out our mugs and started sipping tea and chatting as if we had all the time in the world. It made us laugh and he got the message!)

The Downs

We've come a long, long way together,
Through the hard times and the good,
I have to celebrate you baby,
I have to praise you like I should...

There were certainly plenty of hard times as well as good ones as you would expect sailing around the world, including spending over two months in the Southern Ocean, and it was during these hard times that the leaders really had to stand up and be counted. *(The crew obviously also rose to the occasion and performed brilliantly – see the Teamwork Chapters.)*

As mentioned previously, situational leadership was a style used, consciously or not, throughout the race, and during the tough, dangerous, extra-challenging situations on board, the leadership style had to be strong, decisive and directive; cutting through the 'noise' and uncertainty and providing structure and security in the chaos. Often the crew would be fighting against danger in dark, stormy conditions, and Clive had to shout commands to gain control and maintain safety. Unlike many workplaces where employees would not be in a physically threatening environment, there can still be a lot of 'noise' generated in times of crisis, and it is the responsibility of the leader to cut through and command. Leaders also need to take a step back and understand the whole state of affairs rather than divert to the most obvious (noisy) disturbance.

This can be compared to the system of triage in first aid where on-site medics have to immediately assess the need of multiple casualties in a still hazardous environment and then direct or take action to achieve the best results.

The ability to do this can determine who is an authentic leader compared with who is a reactionary manager. 'Natural' leaders can also come to the fore in these times – people on the staff or crew who are not officially management but who have a natural talent for perspective, decision making and directing in times of crises.

One instance of Clive's leadership has already been mentioned as an example of a leadership situation when the wrong decision was made. In reality, many situations have both positive and negative sides and it is important to review and learn from them both. In this case, Clive, as leader and as a fallible human being, had made a wrong decision. This would become a lesson for the future, but in the immediate moment Clive recovered and took control – saving the situation and saving his reputation. Crew or employees can forgive occasional mistakes and resume respect afterwards for a job well done. Clive recovered, took control and brought us back to a steady and safe state. He then had the wherewithal to call a temporary halt to the racing (for 15 minutes), and sit down with everyone to talk it through, allowing emotions to come out whilst reinstating a sense of calm and capability. It was important for our racing confidence to 'get back on the bike'. Classic post-trauma management, and very well done. In a race where every minute mattered, it was actually worth spending fifteen on sorting everyone out and debriefing, otherwise more time might have been lost in future repercussions.

Interestingly, another 'hard time' that required skilful leadership was when everything was going well. Towards the end of the race, the crews were on the edge of complacency, experts at sailing their particular boat having successfully raced through two Southern Ocean legs and sailed 30,000 miles. There was no doubt that everyone was still racing 100% and getting ever more competitive, but racing got 'easier' because the crews really knew what they were doing, the weather was pleasant and the waves weren't 50' high any more. On a hot, still day, near the equator and in first place, what was there to stimulate and energise the crews? Eighteen people were stuck in the same steel box that they had been living in for seven months, it was extremely hot and oppressive, the competitors were not in sight and there was nothing in particular to focus on. There was *nothing* going on, no noise, no wind, no sail change, no bad weather, and in contrast to the high-adrenaline racing in the past, this depressed the spirit.

There was the potential at this time for complacency at best and at worst, tempers erupting. Skippers somehow had to introduce new motivations to keep their crews sharp, and focusing on boat speed not each other. Clive was proactive about this. He knew that discipline could break down at these times and involved us all in discussing the issue and coming up with solutions. He raised our emotional awareness in doing this but also got our commitment through involving us in the resolution. This in itself gave us something to concentrate on, but we also devised various schemes to keep our minds sharp, including small competitions and targets to beat.

In business, it isn't always the obviously tough times that are tough. Sometimes, when all is peaceful on the surface, trouble can brew from 'nowhere' which is harder to detect, tricky in nature and difficult to deal with. A leader needs to be alert to early warning signs and proactively work out a strategy for heading off conflict at the pass before it has a chance to take hold. There are many ways to handle this, and we dealt with it head-on as a crew, but by then we were a highly-performing team and understood the dynamics. It took a leader though, to take responsibility for doing something about it and rise above the melancholy to reignite the team.

One Big Down

'One big down' was leg two for us (see pp 61-87). In summary this was a Southern Ocean leg, with Cape Horn, two medical evacuations and two detours adding an extra 2500 miles to an already long leg, and losing our chance of winning the race. Very depressing stuff. Clive was good at 'state of the nation' speeches though, and here is the one he wrote shortly after all this trouble:

The Team Stelmar Plan

The task ahead is a big one, the greatest challenge yet. But I have no doubts at all that this will bring us closer together than ever before and will make us an even greater force to be reckoned with on the race course in future legs.

None of us deserved or expected this; no-one can explain the reason or circumstances. As ever things happen in life, I believe for a reason and it is not what happens but how we react and handle it that makes us what we are. We achieved the impossible before and have touched the lives of thousands with our determination and fighting spirit, the only way we know is to continue.

We have to cover the 5,000 miles to Wellington safely and quickly, maintaining our happy boat and close team. We should not underestimate the journey ahead however in this new challenge lie many opportunities; it is the attitude you choose that will affect how we approach it. We will all need new positive goals and objectives.

Along with the resolve that each of you has shown individually we will need strength and determination from each other to endure. No doubt there will be times of frustration and despair for us all, when Wellington will seem further away than ever and when the last place we want to be is where we are, we will all share these emotions. Our strength has been and will be our united approach.

One day New Zealand will appear on the horizon and together we will have achieved something extraordinary.

Friends old and new will be united and we will be proud of what we achieved.

Despite this being written by a 28-year-old Skipper, on a freezing, lonely Global Challenge yacht which was crashing up and down 50' waves after two medical evacuations in the Southern Ocean, it was potent stuff; written with a depth and strength of leadership that was admired and embraced by a struggling crew.

Lessons on Leadership from the Boat to the Boardroom

Race your own Race

A 'leader' is just that, not a follower. When you lead, you decide on where you want to go and how to get there. Race your own race – not someone else's.

Be Aware of the Shadow you Cast

The 'shadow' you cast as a leader is bigger and more powerful than the one cast by others. Be aware of the impact you have. Your words and actions will be magnified because of the position you hold. You must always role model the right behaviours according to your organisation's values and your own ethics.

Immediate and Visible dealings with Issues

Be seen to deal with issues and deal with them immediately; otherwise they may escalate and others will doubt your leadership courage.

Give State of the Nation Addresses

A rousing, passionate speech is a visible sign of great leadership. It will inspire and engage your team but also visibly demonstrate why you are their leader.

Lead Accordingly

Temper your leadership style to suit the situation. Review your natural style and stretch your repertoire by experimenting with other styles fitting to the circumstances or people. Move from directive to supportive as your team matures.

Let Go

When you have briefed, or directed, or coached to a place that is satisfactory – let go.

A Leader is not always Right

Sometimes a leader will make a mistake or a wrong decision. Admit mistakes. Learn from them. Move on.

Share Responsibility, Listen to your Best People

Build the strength of the team and rely on and listen to your best people (who are not necessarily the management). As leader, allow others to lead sometimes, or share responsibility, or be the motivators.

Breathing Space

Give your people breathing space to process their thinking and just 'be'. Give yourself breathing space every now and again, especially before major decisions or demanding times.

Have Fun

Deep Understanding

Get to know the individuals in your team. Engage with them face-to-face.

In Difficult Times

Be prepared. Allow breathing space. Introduce anchoring routine. Let go.

Leadership Exercises

Leadership Scenario 1: Arrest or Authorities

Position:

- Leg two: Buenos Aires to Wellington, Southern Ocean
- Friday 13 December
- 56°19'.14 S/97°32'.97 W
- 4000 miles east of Wellington, 1033 miles west of Cape Horn, 1000 miles north of Antarctica, 2000 miles south of Easter Islands
- Southern Ocean, storms, 40+ knot winds, 40'+ waves

Situation:

- A medical evacuation is needed for 'Flash' who has a spiral fracture in his left arm
- You are advised that we have one week to get him medical attention before his bones fuse and he loses full use of his arm
- There is no shipping, helicopters, Navy or aircraft where we are. No chance of sea rescue
- There are two choices - to drop him at Punta Arenas in Chile or Ushuaia in Argentina
- Punta Arenas has a dangerous lee shore and we have no up-to-date charts on board for that area
- Ushuaia is closer, easier and a known port to us
- The Skipper's wife is Argentinean and would be able to ease our way and meet us if we went to Argentina

But...

To get to Ushuaia, you have to sail through Chilean waters and for petty, political reasons the Chilean authorities want us to use their port – Punta Arenas

- They threaten to arrest us and impound the boat if we go to Ushuaia

- It is about five days sailing to get to either port

Exercise:

1. *What do you decide to do as Leader (Skipper)?*

2. *Write a bullet point list of leadership actions and considerations*

3. *What can you apply from this to your workplace?*

Leadership Scenario 2: Mount Teide and the Wind Shadow

- You had planned all along to sail around the Canaries, as per the advice bought in and received from other skippers and tacticians from previous races because of the 'wind shadow' caused by high mountains on the islands such as Mt Teide on Tenerife

- As a team you decided not to sail through them but to sail around by at least 50 miles

- The Skipper decides to sail through the islands when you got there - it is such a tempting short cut

- You get stuck in a 'wind hole' alongside the island of El Hierro for two days, not moving, going from the leading pack to 9th position

Exercise:

1. *As Leader (Skipper) what do you do once it is clear that the decision was wrong?*

2. *Write a bullet point list of leadership actions and considerations*

3. *What can you apply from this to your workplace?*

Leadership Scenario 3: Ineffective Watch Leader

- You are the Skipper in Buenos Aires for three weeks

- There are two watches of eight people including the Watch Leaders

- For the first leg of 37 days, one of the Watch Leaders has proved to be ineffective and has demotivated his watch, so much so that the watch are hardly communicating with each other and it is affecting race performance

The ineffective Watch Leader:

- Has been brilliant in his contributions and work in the build-up to the race

- Is a very strong and capable member of the team

- Has wanted to do the race for years – it's a lifetime goal for him

- He knows that he has not led as well as he had hoped

- Is a one-way communicator

- Has upset four members of his watch

- Gets on relatively well with the other three members of his watch

- Has a 'do what I say, but not as I do' approach

- Has a 'ceiling' as to his sailing ability

Exercise:

1. What do you decide to do as Leader (Skipper)?

2. Write a bullet point list of leadership actions and considerations

3. What can you apply from this to your workplace?

Leadership Scenario 4: Tough Team Build

You set your team an extremely challenging, tough team-build which actually antagonises them and creates some falling out between team members.

1. Exercise: Should you have done it? Discuss

2. What can you apply from this to your workplace?

Actual Events

Here is what Team Stelmar actually did in the scenarios – not necessarily the right course of action, just the action we took in the circumstances.

Leadership Scenario 1: Arrest or Authorities

- Consideration for Flash was paramount
- We had one week maximum to get him somewhere
- We had at least five days sailing ahead of us to reach land
- **Safety** always came first, but Happy and Fast were our values too
- We turned the boat to generally head towards South America
- Continued long and laborious negotiations with the two authorities
- Global Challenge and Sir Chay also helped from shore
- The Skipper's wife, Valeria flew out to Argentina
- We reviewed the charts for other ports and programmed into our computers the charts and weather for that area
- Took advice from RORC (Royal Ocean Racing Club)
- Decided to head for Ushuaia despite threat of arrest
- Motored up Beagle Canal towards Ushuaia and through Chilean waters
- At midnight, Chilean authorities came out on a boat to meet us
- We were boarded at gun point
- They insisted on a boat-to-boat transfer to take Flash

- We refused because of the unsteadiness of such a transfer when firm land was a few hours away

- They inspected all our paperwork and woke everyone up in torchlight for passport inspection

- Finally they agreed to let us evacuate Flash at Ushuaia on the condition that we then sailed on (eastwards) to Puerto Williams, a Chilean Port further up the Beagle Canal, to clear Chilean customs

Leadership Scenario 2: Mount Teide and the Wind Shadow

- Cursory reference from the Skipper for the bad decision

- Cracked on with racing as fast as possible

- Re-evaluated our race position

- Determined to overtake at least one boat before Buenos Aires (which we did)

- Debriefed in Buenos Aires on how to achieve a better leg finish result next time (we had come in 8th but after a Traffic Separation Scheme misdemeanour got a penalty point which put us down into joint 9th place)

Leadership Scenario 3: Ineffective Watch Leader

- Skipper has one-to-one discussions with everyone about the situation

- Skipper talks with the Watch Leader at great length

- Skipper and Navigator share their views with each other (being the only ones not part of a watch and therefore having a more objective opinion about how each watch was performing against the other) and discuss potential solutions

- A decision is made and communicated to him: a very capable member of the other watch (Alex) is brought over as Watch Leader, and the ineffective Watch

Leader is transferred to their position (number one bowman) on the other watch

- Alex – the new Watch Leader - holds immediate talks with his new watch to re-establish their trust and confidence

- He debriefs their issues and works with them to agree on how they are best being lead in the future

- He also lightens the mood and has some fun with them – relieving a lot of the tension that has built up

- He also holds one-to-ones with all his team and the new legger (JC)

- The ex-Watch Leader finds himself unable to accept these new terms and quits the team two days before the start of the next leg and flies home

- (He re-applies to be part of the team later in the race, but is refused by the race committee)

Chapter 2. High Performance

Definition

HIGH PERFORMANCE CAN BE described as *running at altitude*. Standard performance is normal running - requiring some stamina and fitness, whereas high performance is running at altitude requiring extra stamina (endurance) and extra fitness (peak state), as well as the expertise, specialist skills, focus, mental toughness and winning attitude required for peak performance in very demanding conditions.

The word 'high' does not do justice to the phrase 'high performance'; it falls short of the extra-ordinary attitudes and behaviours it is labelling. High performance is so much more. It is about being at the pinnacle of one's game; in peak state for peak performance; in ultimate mental, emotional and physical fitness for the task, with such a mental toughness and tenacity that nothing (or very little) will prevent achievement. It is about determination; resilience; exemplary effort; professionalism; consummate attention to detail; useful and appropriate knowledge and experience; strong drive; self-motivation; emotional intelligence.

In a team, high performance is demonstrated through consistently over-achieving with complete synergy. In business it is about achieving incredible results. On the boat it was about working perfectly together to generate maximum boat speed 24/7 for weeks on end.

High performance is challenging, and rare. Plenty of people and teams are able to 'run' – to perform in an average or better than expected way; achieving fairly good production with reasonable standards of output. Not many can 'run a marathon at altitude'; to be fit enough to maintain pace in a demanding environment. High Performance should be called Extra-Ordinary Performance, because it is not common, and far from ordinary.

High Performance in the Global Challenge

On the boat a typical high-performing scenario would be as follows:

It is stormy, the rain is lashing down, the wind is howling through the rigging, it is 03:15 and almost pitch black with dark, heavy clouds blocking the moon and starlight. The on-watch team are attune with the weather and 'feel in their gut' that it is about to get worse. They proactively decide to put a third reef in the mainsail whilst they have 5–10 knots less wind to contend with. The Skipper and Navigator are not consulted and remain below deck, trusting the Watch Leader to make the right decisions. Once the decision has been communicated, the whole on-deck crew of seven people spring into action, moving straight into their positions, and start their tasks. One vital crew member is below deck on mother duty but it does not matter. The team adjust and bridge the gap.

Once everyone is ready, they make eye contact and hand signal a co-ordinated reef-in. The Watch Leader does not manage them, he trusts each person to do their job, but he does still keep an overall look-out, especially on safety. The mainsheet is released to de-power the mainsail, slowing and stabilising the boat. The crew know that boat speed will be lost by doing this but in the long run, the manoeuvre will be quicker and safer. The rest of the crew perform the difficult and complicated task efficiently, with safety the primary concern and speed secondary. Verbal communications are impossible, but unnecessary anyway. The crew know exactly what they are doing and also the impact their actions have on each other. At one point, the Cunningham[10] jams. The two at the mast immediately move to fix it and the other five pause their work because they have all seen it happen and can only continue once it is safe. Everyone keeps an eye on the bigger picture, knowing that their actions have an effect on those around them.

The task is achieved in difficult and terrible conditions. Everyone is relieved when it is over. The crew return to the safety of the cockpit and praise each other on a job well done. They then debrief, talking it through to check if there is new learning to come from it.

Several high-performing behaviours are present in this scenario. First of all, the weather is atrocious and putting a third reef in at three o'clock in the morning is perhaps one of the most unpleasant jobs of all, yet everyone is present on deck. No-one is 'busy' down below with a potentially quite legitimate and believable excuse about checking the computers or pumping the bilges or even going to the toilet. It is very tempting in those conditions to go below for some respite and warmth, but each team member is self-responsible; knowing that they are each dependable and accountable.

Secondly, the on-watch 'feel in their gut' that the weather is about to change for the worse. In the book *Blink* by Malcolm Gladwell, he puts this 'rapid cognition' or 'the power of thinking without thinking' as follows:

...your mind takes about two seconds to jump to a series of conclusions. 'Blink' is... about those two seconds, because I think those instant conclusions that we reach are really powerful and really important and, occasionally, really good.

...Intuition strikes me as a concept we use to describe emotional reactions, gut feelings - thoughts and impressions that don't seem entirely rational. But I think that what goes

---

[10] The Cunningham on the Global Challenge boats is a device that clips into the cringle to pull down and secure a section or slab of the mainsail during a reef.

on in that first two seconds is perfectly rational. It's thinking - it's just thinking that moves a little faster and operates a little more mysteriously than the kind of deliberate, conscious decision making that we usually associate with 'thinking.'

There was a valid place for number crunching on the boat and the Navigator's time was spent mainly in doing this *below deck*. Interpreting the weather forecasts and working out the numbers in relation to wind speed, wind direction and boat speed, boat direction. Using computers, charts, data and software programs. But there was also a place for 'gut feel'. Rapid cognition *on deck* through an amalgamation of experience, physical feel, observations, knowledge and a 'sixth sense'. Who knows how many 'blink' factors contributed to this 'gut feel', but in high-performing teams, the 'gut' can be as useful a point of reference as long, slow deliberated evaluation. The 'blink' ability is strong in experienced, established, high-performing teams and individuals. Intuition is more informed, and listening and responding to it, more practised and respected.

The Watch Leader was the one to make the call, but everyone on the watch would have felt the imminence of the decision and been mentally ready to go; running through in their head a 'perfect video' of the actions they were about to take in preparation. Visualising success and reminding themselves of the smaller nuances and accumulated learning of their jobs. In fact, often the snake-pit crew would anticipate most next steps in advance and set up winches and ropes ready for the next change to come.

The third illustration of high performance is around the two management situations. In ordinary 'performing' teams, the team leader would normally consult the 'boss' for a decision such as this. On *Team Stelmar* the Skipper trusted and delegated to the Watch Leaders for on-deck management and making the right decisions. The 'upper ranks' had no need to mess with the middle management. Similarly, the Watch Leader trusted his individual crew members to execute the task without close management or interference. However, he delegated rather than abdicated. He still maintained an eagle-eye view of the whole task, as so many things can go wrong on a boat in stormy conditions. Trust and delegation.

Fourth point, the team *proactively* decide to reduce the sail area before the stronger winds hit the boat. They avert greater difficulty or disaster by being alert, on the ball and proactive. Their decision making is timely rather than reactive and slow.

Fifth, a critical team member is missing – on mother duty (which was a compulsory and time-consuming role). Efficiency was not affected by this however, because the team had worked out in advance how they would cover for each person missing. Another proactive action that diverted a potential crisis (see Crisis Prevention and Management Chapter p.222).

Sixth, communication was effective. Whether verbal, written or physical, communicating in noisy and dangerous conditions needs to be concise and clear. Communications were minimal because team members knew their jobs so well, and knew each other so well; nothing much was left to be said. Words were superfluous because needs were predicted, next steps were anticipated, body language was correctly interpreted... teamwork was slick.

Seventh, long-term thinking was present in the decision to de-power the mainsail. A fairly high-performing decision in a race situation would be to carry on at full boat speed during every manoeuvre; it was possible to change a sail or reef-in in these conditions. Team Stelmar did this initially in the first leg. However, with the long view in mind, it was better to reduce boat speed temporarily, especially for sail changes, by taking some of the wind out of the sails (de-powering) and turning slightly from the wind and waves. This was safer, but in more benign conditions it took less time to complete the task and fewer things were likely to go wrong. (Towards the latter end of the race, winning was more about not making mistakes because all the boats were performing so well.) If the boat was 'powered up' in full wind strength, then the sails were harder to pull up or take down, which took more time. Slowing the boat down felt wrong but was the right thing to do in the long run.

The Cunningham jamming was a 'typical' problem faced by the team during a reef; an unforeseeable and unavoidable problem but requiring fixing nonetheless. Because every member of the team kept their eye on the bigger picture, especially the specific areas which their work impacted, they saw the Cunningham jam and stopped what they were doing, preventing greater disaster, damage or injury.

Finally, even after this energy-sapping, dangerous task, when the crew were exhausted and just wanting a hot cup of tea to recuperate, they (genuinely and respectfully) praised each other, and then had the discipline and desire for detail to hold a quick debrief before allowing themselves to 'relax'.

Compared with a 'norming' or just 'performing' crew - even in a racing situation – this short scenario contains about ten high-performing behaviours and attitudes that would probably not be evident in other teams. That's the difference between running and running at altitude.

High Performance from Boat to Boardroom

In a team driven to win a yacht race, high performance is a prerequisite. After all the training, and planning, team building and practising, consulting and coaching, each team member knows what high performance looks like; it is then up to them to determine their attitude.

On *Team Stelmar*, we did not have a perfect team of 18 high performers on every leg. Some people – just one or two - perhaps gave 70-80% for much of the race. Some people were leggers and it took them a while to adjust from their 'soft' corporate lives to the maximum performance required for ocean yacht racing before they went back to their desk jobs. Some, such as Paula, realised more and more throughout the race what high performance **really** meant, and so her attitude evolved from giving what she thought was 100% to **really** giving it 100%. Some, like Alex, had raced for England and knew already the heightened behaviours and attitudes required for such a challenge.

Alex:

Working with a genuinely high-performing team in International competition was a dream. For two years my role was number one bowman and during certain manoeuvres, such as a sail change, at a particular point I would reach behind me without even looking and my number two would already have the rope I needed ready to pass to me. This was done without a word spoken. We practised and practised, understood each other's roles in depth and completely trusted each other. Because we were racing at world class level, the smallest mistakes were punished heavily; we had to perfect every manoeuvre.

One thing was very noticeable among the top teams – there was never any shouting. The further down the field teams were, the louder they got as they approached a mark. This was distracting for them and meant that people had to be told what to do, rather than proactively doing it. It also meant that they were not just focusing on their job; they were checking each other which showed a lack of trust.

If you want to win, you have to have trust.

The boat was our office every minute of the day for months. Its performance consumed us and boat speed was our single priority; so of course, we were motivated to achieve the best results we could. But we were a team comprising all types of people with different attitudes towards high performance. We had obstacles to overcome and crew to influence and inspire. Just like any workplace. One obstacle was having two very separate watches... like having two distinct departments, or teams, or shifts...

Two Watches, One Boat

Team Stelmar organised themselves into a typical two-watch system. There were (usually) 18 people on the boat. The Skipper and Navigator worked as a pair and the remaining 16 people divided into two watches of eight people: seven core crew and one legger. For a bit of fun, the watches were called 'The Grunters' and 'The Groaners' after the noises they made while grinding on the winches. Each watch had a Watch Leader and the watch system ran as follows:

06:00 – 12:00 Watch A on deck
12:00 – 18:00 Watch B
18:00 – 22:00 Watch A
22:00 – 02:00 Watch B
02:00 – 06:00 Watch A
06:00 – 12:00 Watch B, etc.

This meant that you either worked a physical 10 or 14 hour day, which rotated every 48 hours. During time off watch, you would be either eating or sleeping.

Both watches were extremely focused, efficient, effective and very, very united, but only really saw each other when one watch had just woken up and the other was keen to go off watch to eat and rest.

We thus had two distinct teams of people who had to work effectively together for the sake of the one boat. They had to behave towards each other in a 'high-performing' manner for the benefit of the whole.

However, in poorly-managed circumstances, this divide can deteriorate into teams or departments working in silos. In a worst case scenario, departments can end up doing their own thing; thinking they are superior; being protective and territorial; not communicating or supporting each other; being competitive or even hostile towards each other. This of course, is not good for the company and many organisations have to invest in a 'one team' campaign to redress the balance. Ideally, divisions or departments are prevented from falling into silo'd working in the first place.

Our two watches were different from each other. They were different in personality, culture, attitudes, ways of working, communicating, behaving. They had their own sense of humour. They talked about different things; they decided to carry out manoeuvres in slightly different ways. This was all tolerated if it was for the good of the boat. Here is how Team Stelmar kept working effectively together as one high-performing team of two watches for the sake of the one boat (one company):

a) The watches were different culturally, but respected each other.

Each watch had their own foibles and mannerisms, habits and eccentricities, especially from living together 24 hours a day. These little cultural differences could have caused problems – like living with someone and falling out over housekeeping – but we were mature enough to accept and respect the differences.

b) The watches didn't work together, but held quality handovers **every** watch change.

Although both watches only ever worked together at the very start and end of each leg, they had to work seamlessly (maintaining maximum boat speed) as they switched *five times a day*. Ten minutes before the official start of each watch, the on-coming crew would be on deck for a handover with their opposite number and to acclimatise to the conditions. This put them in the best place for continuing the good work.

c) The watches sometimes competed to 'up the ante', but never as enemies.

Once, we nearly deteriorated into becoming overly-competitive between the watches, but usually we competed with good-humoured banter which gave us an extra charge of energy and refocused us when we relaxed too much.

d) The watches had their own ways of working, but shared them just in case.

Over time, each watch evolved and developed their own systems and ways of working. In most cases, there was no right or wrong way; different methods had different merits. So each watch generally devised and tweaked their own methods but shared them with the other watch just in case.

e) The watches had an hour together every week to reunite.

We had Happy Hour every Sunday to preserve boat time as we travelled across the time zones. This was our main opportunity to share knowledge, issues, concerns and practices and generally remind ourselves that we were a team of 18, not two teams, a Skipper and a Navigator.

f) The watches held separate meetings on and off the boat, but shared top line content.

Sometimes the Skipper or Watch Leader had to have a word with just one watch or one individual (the only place to do this in private was to go to the foredeck). In port, each watch held their own debrief meetings to iron out any problems and work out how to improve. These were generally matters that pertained to each specific watch; however, the gist of the content was shared with the other watch so they had an understanding of what was going on in the wider team.

g) The watches had an overall Skipper to keep the balance.

Two watches, one boat, one team, one leader. Clive, the Skipper, was responsible for maintaining an equality between the two watches; ensuring both held the same understanding and knowledge, even though for most of the time one team was asleep and one was working. Clive was unbiased and provided the pivot between the two sides, connecting them and ensuring balance.

h) The watches were separate teams, but everything they did was 'Best for Boat'.

Despite working quite independently of each other, everything they did, every decision they made, was always best for the boat overall.

1) Best for Boat

'Best for Boat' was one of our catch phrases. We had four core axioms which were extremely clarifying and useful for maintaining high performance. They were:

1. Best for Boat
2. Eyes on the Boat
3. Keep Scratching Away
4. Control the Controllables

Best for Boat meant that everything we did, every decision we made was best for the boat. (Best for boat speed, best for boat morale, best for boat safety.) When faced with a dilemma or tough decision, we asked ourselves what was best for boat, and the answer often came clearly and quickly. It was a great decision-making tool. The alternative phrase for the workplace, would be best for company, or perhaps, best for customer.

An example of this in action is the fact that Paula was not chosen to be part of the helming team even though she enjoyed it, because she had such little experience and there were others who were better. This meant that Paula was a victim of the best for boat philosophy, but *Team Stelmar's* performance benefited as a whole.

Another example: it was 'best for boat' that we all spent our first and last week in port working on the boat rather than sight-seeing. Other holidays in the future would allow us to see the countries; this trip was about winning a round the world yacht race. Our time was best spent on the boat.

2) Eyes on the Boat

Eyes on the Boat was another great phrase that we used regularly to pull the focus inwards. This is about looking at what **you** are doing rather than what the competition are up to. Yes, it is good to be aware of the competition - or the marketplace - but not to spend too much time keeping vigil and closely observing; especially not following them or letting their tactics influence yours.

We found in the race that we often lost ground to boats that were within eyesight, behind us, especially at the start and end of each leg when the boats bunched up. This focus on what was behind was like driving using the rear view mirror. Looking behind was not as helpful as looking at what was in our immediate focus; what we were doing and where we were going. The 'rear view' was anxiety-inducing, nerve-wracking, intimidating. These emotions were not helpful to working in a motivated, confident and uncompromisingly competitive manner. Nervously watching the boats behind became almost obsessional, taking away the much needed focus and energy from driving our own boat as best as we could forwards and looking at ways of making it go faster.

Eyes on the Business would translate just as well. Be aware of competitors and market shifts, but focus closely on your own employees, production levels, goals, direction. Look inwards and forwards; don't drive the business along using the rear view mirror.

3) Control the Controllables

Possibly one of the most used phrases in sport psychology is to 'control the controllables'. Ed Moses, arguably the greatest ever 400m hurdler, went undefeated between 1977 and 1987, spanning a total of 122 finals in ten years. When asked what made him successful he simply stated:

Ain't no use worryin' 'bout things beyond your control coz if they're beyond your control there ain't no use worryin'...

Controlling the controllables is doing the absolute best you can with what you have.

In ocean yacht racing there are many uncontrollables. The weather is a big one. We could do nothing at all to affect what the weather was doing to us, or the competition, so there was no point in worrying about it, thinking about it, spending time and energy on it. We could, however, excel ourselves in getting the most out of the boat with the weather we had. What was within our control, we controlled to maximum affect. Our Navigator Nicko would look at the weather and decide which way would be best to go, we then had to make the boat go that way as quickly as possible.

We could not control the weather, the prescribed route and waypoints, the competition or the sea state. So we didn't try. We could control our actions, the way we worked, the way we sailed our boat. So we did all we could to control these to the best of our abilities. In business, you cannot control the environment, government policies, EU regulations, competitors, society trends, shopping habits, market forces; so don't waste time trying. You **can** control quality, motivation, customer and employee satisfaction, innovation, culture, etc.

Similar to eyes on the boat, control the controllables is about expending energy on the right things; achieving high performance through concentrating on our own decision making and actions.

4) Keep Scratching Away

Our Skipper introduced us to 'keep scratching away'. The theory is that a race is won inch by inch and if you keep scratching away at the lead you will slowly gain on them. In *Every Given Sunday*, Al Pacino's 'inch by inch' pep talk revitalises the spirits of a losing American Football team at half time:

> *You find out that life is just a game of inches.*
> *So is football.*
> *Because in either game*
> *life or football*
> *the margin for error is so small.*
> *I mean*
> *one half step too late or too early*
> *you don't quite make it.*
> *One half second too slow or too fast*
> *and you don't quite catch it.*
> *The inches we need are everywhere around us.*
> *They are in every break of the game*
> *every minute, every second.*
> *On this team, we fight for that inch*
> *On this team, we tear ourselves, and everyone around*
> *us to pieces for that inch.*
> *We CLAW with our fingernails for that inch.*
> *'Cause we know*
> *when we add up all those inches*
> *that's going to make the f****** difference*
> *between WINNING and LOSING*
> *between LIVING and DYING.*

Powerful stuff. This speech is iconic and has positively inspired many sports and business people. It is used frequently in sports psychology and high-performance training. 'Inch by inch' is motivational but also practical in that rather than focusing on winning the whole round-the-world, 35,000-mile, ten-month long yacht race (which is strategically motivational in the long term), it is about fighting for every inch, racing mile-by-mile, focusing step-by-step, scratching away at the mammoth, seemingly insurmountable task ahead.

More than twice we scratched away and made significant, noticeable progress[11]. For the rest of the time, we scratched away and made small, but critical, headway. Some legs were won by seconds in time - boat lengths in distance - even after six weeks and 1000s of miles of sailing. Some competitions are won by split seconds (Formula One) or millimetres (target shooting). Every inch counts. Every ocean mile. Every action.

Businesses need their long-term goals and far-seeing visions for motivation and direction, but operationally have to work inch-by-inch, day-by-day. Teams need to keep scratching away at their goals. Individuals need to keep scratching away at their performance targets. Leaders need to keep scratching away at their strategies. Businesses need to keep scratching away at their customers and competitors, pricing structures, products, and portfolios. Fighting for all those inches makes the difference between winning and losing, living and not-living.

VMG – Velocity Made Good (Right Speed, Right Direction)

VMG is a yacht racing expression used to describe the optimum speed achievable towards a goal, 'mark' or buoy, taking into account wind angle and wind speed. Velocity Made Good is the most efficient use of effort towards a goal; the opposite being wasted effort and time spent going the wrong way.

When sailing, if the wind is coming directly towards the bow, then the boat cannot sail towards the wind or at an angle either side of the wind direction by about 40 degrees (depending on the individual boat). Crews in this situation have to 'tack' the boat; zigzagging towards their goal. Each boat varies (according to length, weight, build, etc.) as to its optimum speed in any given wind-speed/wind-direction combination, therefore many boats have VMG 'Polar' charts

---

[11] Once, after getting stuck in a wind hole in the Canary Islands on the first leg, and once after dropping Karen off at Puerto Williams and regaining eight places in a week.

which graphically depict the optimum boat speed to wind angle for maximising performance towards the goal. The expression 'sailing too close to the wind' comes from this physical circumstance. Too close to the wind, and although heading towards the goal, progress is slow. Equally, sailing too far from the wind will mean ending up in totally the wrong direction and not making progress towards the target. There is an optimum trade off between boat speed and distance sailed, and that optimum is VMG.

If business success was compared to a yacht race, there would be a finish line to reach ahead of the competition and buoys (targets) to go round en route. Sometimes fleet progress would be fast as the boats sail away from the wind, being pushed along with their great spinnaker sails up, and sometimes progress would be frustratingly slow, as each boat tacks against the wind. The wind is the force, whether good or bad. Leveraging the wind's force to the best of your ability is what yacht racing is all about.

The analogy then is that businesses need to 'sail' at their optimum angle according to the 'climate' at the time. If businesses sail too close to the wind they will lose speed. If they get distracted and sail off the wrong way, although appearing very busy, they will make less progress towards their goals. A little deviation from heading directly forwards **may** be beneficial such as: innovating; new product development; reviewing ways of working; possibly being a little bit creative. But heading off-course, losing focus of the finish line or marks, will slow a business down and deviate it from its core purpose.

Ideally, organisations have their own version of a 'Polar Chart'. This would depict the guidelines within which they operate; the no-go zones which deaden progress and their framework (ultimate angle to the wind) for achieving maximum speed with the most efficient use of energy and time.

Push v Preservation

Similar to sailing close to the wind, there is a fine line between taking calculated risks and carefully protecting people, boat and equipment. To win a race (or succeed in business, or feel alive) sometimes risks have to be taken. Conservative sailing in a yacht race - or in business - will rarely win trophies, respect or admiration. But risks have to be taken, balanced with the possibility of damaging people or equipment.

Adventures, challenges and white-knuckle experiences are undertaken with calculated risk; individual adventurers usually sign a disclaimer 'signing their life away'. They know that by participating in risky activities they have a greater chance of injury, but living on the edge is what makes them feel alive. There is a window in a Queenstown adventure agency claiming that 'if you are not living on the edge you are taking up too much room', and Helen Keller[12] famously said: 'Life is either a daring adventure or nothing at all'. Do we dare to try or try to dare?

Boats (their equipment and crews) have to be pushed to achieve maximum boat speed. The 70' boats in the Volvo Ocean Race sometimes hit 40 knots; they are on the edge of their manufactured capabilities, reaching **perhaps** maximum potential for that design of yacht. Much faster, and the control is gone; crew and boats could get seriously hurt. Too cautious though and the competition will overtake. It is a question of knowing when to push and when to preserve, at the right time, and for the right length of time.

Team Stelmar were a little too conservative early on in the 2004/5 Global Challenge. The more we pushed, the more we realised we could push. You don't really know what you (or the business) are capable of until you push, so it is a matter of pushing just to the limit and then knowing where the line is. Or pushing just once past the limit and then knowing to

---

[12] Helen Keller, 1880 – 1968, was an American author, activist and lecturer. She was the first deaf-blind person to graduate from college.

back off a little. Daring to try. But at what cost? If we irreparably damaged a sail on the yacht race we were deducted points. If we damaged equipment then it was likely we would have to do without for the rest of that leg. If we damaged a person, then the risk wasn't worth taking. We learned where our boundaries were and tried to push to the edge of them without going over. Certainly, the more you know your people and environment, the more calculated your risks can be and the less likely you are to push too far. But if you don't push, you don't get anywhere worthwhile.

Getting the Basics Right, then Getting the Basics Better

The phrase 'back to basics' is used by many companies to refocus on getting the fundamentals right again, when perhaps they have begun to lose concentration (and therefore quality) on their core purpose. Take the Post Office for instance; they are essentially about getting postal services and deliveries right; the most basic, fundamental services that the Post Office was set up to do – **not** travel insurance, or foreign currency, or banking. A supermarket is about selling everyday items off the shelf, not mobile phones, or financial services, or even home delivery. A brewery is about brewing good, drinkable beer not sponsoring public events.

As a strategy, 'getting the basics right' certainly focuses the workforce on getting right what they fundamentally exist to do. Produce widgets. Serve customers. Fight fires. In the Global Challenge it was all about sailing: changing sails, trimming the sails and helming. They were our three fundamentals. We had to get those basics right to be worthy of just being in the race. However, once those basics were right – which was achieved during the training sails – then the focus was on getting the basics **better**. If those three things – changing sails, trimming the sails and helming – were our bread and butter jobs for winning the race and for preventing costly mistakes, then we had to get them dead right. Every time. Time and time again. We had to concentrate on changing the sails, trimming the sails and helming as best as we could. Controlling the controllables.

This continuous improvement [13] was achieved through discipline, fanatical attention to detail and analysing every move.

Throughout the race, we made almost 1000 sail changes. We looked to trim the sails every ten minutes and we helmed continuously; there was plenty of opportunity for analysing and reviewing our three basics! So we did. We went about it with discipline and fanatical attention to detail. We briefed and debriefed every major manoeuvre. We reviewed every action and we learned all the time. Despite reviewing, analysing and debriefing to a 'ridiculous' extent, we continued to acquire fresh knowledge.

All businesses have their own 'basics'. If organisations boiled everything they did down to the core rudiments of what they do, then they may be left with one, two or three things to concentrate on getting right, and then work on getting better. These basics should then be measured, reviewed, analysed, pulled apart and rebuilt again and again and again, so that they are as perfect as they can be. And then they should be reviewed again some time later, with fresh eyes and fresh thinking. Hardly anything man-made is perfect. There is always scope for improvement.

Getting the Edge

*What is it **exactly** that gives an individual or a team or a business the edge over the competition?*

All professional athletes and sports teams like to have the edge on the competition. Businesses too. The 'edge' may be anything from a unique selling point (Volvo's sturdiness), to

---

[13] See also: 'Kaizen' (Japanese expression for continuous improvement), TQM (Total Quality Management), Six Sigma and CIP (Continuous Improvement Process) for examples of working in this way; though be aware that continuous improvement can counteract 'radical innovation' – great leaps of innovation.

having a head start as the original product (Post-it, Viagra, Sellotape), to longer stride length (Usain Bolt[14]), psychological superiority (boxing) or holding the 'upper hand' (poker).

In companies, the phrase 'unique selling point' is used to define the *difference* between a company's product (or proposition) and a rival product. This difference is not necessarily better, it is just a difference. It is why one customer will buy Dyson instead of Hoover. A unique selling point gives one company the edge over another, but there are plenty of other ways for businesses to gain an edge.

Red Bull have the edge by being the original (re)creator of an energy drink and then maintaining the lead by sponsoring events (Formula 1, Red Bull Air Race and free surfing to name three). Google hold their edge by allowing employees to spend 30% of their time on innovation. Apple has an edge because of their exquisite designs. When the first banks opened to the public on Saturdays they had the edge... for a while. When Tesco started home delivery, they had the edge, until the other supermarkets followed.

Unfortunately 'edges' can be copied and will only remain a leading strategy while they are unique.

On *Team Stelmar* our edge was 'fanatical attention to detail through measurement, review and improvement'. As mentioned in the previous section we concentrated on getting our three basics better – changing sails, trimming the sails and helming – by continuous improvement.

As an example, Nicko wrote a computer program which measured the accuracy of the helming every second. A traffic light system showed whether the helm was on course (green), slightly deviating now and again (orange) or deviating more dramatically (red). Too many reds and oranges after ten minutes and we would change the helm. (Sometimes helms had bad days.) Another example: despite collecting data continuously via our computers, we still had a laminated

---

[14] Broke 400m record in 2008 Beijing Olympics.

template on deck that we filled in every ten minutes with data such as wind speed, wind angle, boat speed, heading, sail plan, etc. This gave us a psychological edge by reminding us on deck every ten minutes how we were performing. Another example: we briefed and debriefed every major manoeuvre (such as changing a sail) even on the 500th sail change, even on the 167th day at sea. Regular discipline. Constant feedback and new knowledge. This gave us our edge over the competition.

Lessons on High Performance from the Boat to the Boardroom

Two Watches, One Boat

Your company may well consist of different teams, departments, locations, countries, shifts. Prevent them from turning into silos. Work on connecting them, gluing them together into 'one team/one boat'. See 'Two Watches' Chapter for a list of tips.

Best for Boat

Is everything you do, every decision you make, 'best for boat'? Use this as your judging criterion until it becomes habitual.

Eyes on the Boat

Have some axioms that will help clarify, simplify and compel high-performing behaviours. 'Eyes on the Boat' helps to pull focus inwards - making teams concentrate on what **they** are doing and where **they** are going, rather than worrying too much about what's in the past or what the competition are up to. Don't drive using the rear view mirror.

Control the Controllables

The weather was outside of our control. We worked on getting the best performance whatever the weather was doing. Only spend time and energy working on what is within your control. Reduce time and energy worrying about everything else.

Keep Scratching Away

Every inch counts. Reduce mammoth tasks to do-able steps. Fight inch by inch. Play the Al Pacino excerpt to your team. Find other inspirational music or film clips to stimulate your teams into running at altitude.

VMG

Sail at the optimum angle for achieving the best results. Do not stray too far from your core purpose but allow for some experimentation. Know the no-go zones which kill progress.

Get the Basics Better

What are your business's basics? Work out the fundamental one, two or three things that are your basics. Work on getting them right, but then keep working on getting them better through 'ridiculous fanatical' attention to detail. Debrief them, analyse them, pull them apart and rebuild them time and time again.

Get the Edge on the Competition

What is your edge? The thing you do to give you the advantage? Keep looking for more edges.

High Performance Exercises

1. Think about what your business equivalent is to putting in a 3rd reef:

- In this Chapter there was a description of a high performance scenario where Team Stelmar had to put a 3rd reef into the mainsail – basically one of the hardest and most loathed manoeuvres on the boat. What is your business equivalent of putting a third reef in? One of the hardest and least liked jobs?

- Talk it through with your colleagues.

- Do you complete this task in a performing or high-performing manner?

- Can you improve your approach, your attitude, your actions, your communications in this business scenario?

2. Think about what your edge is on the competition:

On *Team Stelmar* we were fanatical about data logging. We devised a computer software program that logged boat data every ten seconds. We collated as much data as we could before we set sail. We data-logged every ten minutes onto a laminated sheet on deck. The latter operation was more about gaining a psychological edge on the competition.

Steve Smith, a British Olympic medal winning high jumper, used to get up at 05:00 to give him the edge on the competition. By getting up at 05:00 Steve ensured that he could focus on his differentiator, which was getting the right nutrition into his body three hours before his first session at 09:00. Ultimately none of his competitors were going to this length psychologically and physically. This gave Steve the edge and filled him with confidence.

- What's your edge on the competition? Can it be better?

- If you don't have one, can you get one?

3. Doing the Basics Better

- There is getting the basics right, which is standard performance.

- Then there is getting the basics better, which is high performance.

- What basic things does your business do every day, so much so, that they get overlooked and neglected?

- Pick a basic and pull it into tiny pieces.

- Review it and analyse it to the finest minutia.

- Bit by bit, what can be improved?

- On the boat, for us, it was packing the spinnaker sail.

- We reviewed this and slightly changed the way we did it, many, many times.

- This continuous evaluation and improvement reduced the possibility of it not unfurling correctly each time we put it up

4. Control the Controllables

- In a team meeting, take a large piece of paper and draw a boat on the sea, or a business in its environment

- With the team, review what is within the realms of the business's control and what is outside the controllable area

- Write these on the inside or outside of the drawing as appropriate

- Then review the non-controllables

- Does anyone spend too much time reviewing, watching or thinking about these factors?

- If so, can they work smarter by diverting their efforts towards internal controllables?

5. Best for Boat

- Introduce the concept of *Best for Boat* to your team or colleagues

- Strength test your decision making against it for the first month until it becomes habitual

Chapter 3. Strategy and Tactics

Definition

THE WORD 'STRATEGY' COMES FROM the ancient Greek word: *stratēgos*, which in itself derives from *stratos* (army) and *ago* (leading). 'Tactic', comes from the Greek word: taktikē, which is the art of *organising* an army, in other words the *method* by which the battle is fought. A strategy is generally a long-term, proactive, analytical plan devised to beat the enemy; tactics are the various actions undertaken to achieve the strategy. Sticking to the military analogy, an example strategy to beat the enemy could be by attrition during a long, harsh winter (Stalingrad) and some tactics to achieve this are in the positioning of the troops, the management of the troops (e.g. shooting deserters), the clever deployment of the Panzer tank divisions, etc.

Both terms originate in the military and Sun Tzu's *Art of War* is one of the most famous strategic references[15]. Back in the 6th century BC, strategy was defined by Sun Tzu as follows:

A style of thinking; a conscious and deliberate process; an intensive implementation system; the art of ensuring future success.

---

[15] Sun Tzu – see translation by Lionel Giles. The *Art of War* is one of the oldest books on military strategy. It is the first and one of the most successful works on strategy and has had a huge influence on Eastern and Western military thinking, business tactics, and beyond. He taught that strategy was not planning in the sense of working through a to-do list, but rather that it requires quick and appropriate responses to changing conditions. Planning works in a controlled environment, but in a competitive environment, competing plans collide, creating unexpected situations. (Wiki reference)

'The _art_ of _ensuring_ _future success_'. Strategy is an art, not a science; the art of being several moves ahead of the enemy. Strategies are designed to ensure future success; to achieve victory; to place the army, boat or company in the best possible position to win. Sun Tzu recognised the importance of positioning in strategy and the fact that position is affected by both the objective conditions of the physical environment and the subjective psychology of the players on both sides. Armies, boats or companies essentially have to work out: (1) what position they are in in the first place and (2) how to advance that position. The proposal for getting from one to the other is the strategic plan. The method and actions to get there, are the tactics. This is why a SWOT-type analysis is used by companies to work out their (physical and psychological) Strengths, Weaknesses, Opportunities and Threats to best understand their current position. This is then evaluated against their vision or goal, which is where they want to be. Strategy planning is the route from one to the other and tactics are the means of getting there.

The _quality_ and _inventiveness_ of the strategy, the 'art of ensuring future success', are the determining factors; tipping the balance between winning and losing.

All men can see these tactics whereby I conquer, but what none can see is the strategy out of which victory is evolved. (Sun Tzu)

Strategy and Tactics in the Global Challenge

In the Global Challenge there was no 'war' as such, but there were certainly battles, skirmishes, strategies and tactics, whereby each boat fought to conquer and achieve victory over the others, leg by leg, in the long campaign. Skippers had overall race strategies, plans to win the Global Challenge, but inevitably these differed in _quality_ and _inventiveness_. Generals in battle (and skippers in the Global Challenge) achieve different rates of advancement because of their skills at strategising and their ability to lead the tactical execution.

They are human beings with differing expertise and experience, with varying strengths and fallibilities, different principles and beliefs, responding to a moving situation. Perhaps if the skippers had read the *Art of War* before they left, their strategic planning would have been more robust and they would have stood a better chance. Who knows. It would be interesting to stage a race with two fleets of boats, a control fleet and a Sun Tzu fleet. As it was, the skippers planned their strategies as best they could to place their boat in what they believed was the optimum position to win.

The winning Skipper's strategy was to sail his own race, and not be influenced by the other boats. (see p.148) This obviously worked for Andy Forbes of *BG*, but it was a risky strategy; an all or nothing approach. We assumed he knew the risk and calculated it accordingly. It was certainly brave and inventive (and probably more interesting on board), and it did achieve success. This is why strategising is an art. Should leaders have daring plans, risking complete failure but potentially gaining great advancement, or should they play the conservative game, fighting the battle carefully and cautiously, inch by inch? History has proven that both strategies work.

In addition to having a sound strategy, the Global Challenge competitors also needed a competent Skipper and crew. All the boats were exactly the same, with the same rules, equipment and weather information, so the only difference between coming first and 12th was either in the strategy, or the people. The crew had to be consistently competent and confident to be in with a chance of winning such a series of races, leg by leg. Assuming the crews were more or less equally competent and confident by the end of the race, the difference that remained between the boats was strategy and tactics.

Strategy and Tactics from Boat to Boardroom

We have briefly used the analogy of war in describing strategy and tactics, because the terminology – and much learning - originates from the military. However, this is a book about round the world yacht racing, not war, and there are more relevant parallels to be drawn between competing in the Global Challenge and competing in business. Both have strategies and tactics, winners and losers, and a lot more in common besides. To clarify the correlation, here are some metaphors:

The Boat	=	The Business
Skipper	=	Leader
Watch Leaders	=	Middle Management
Watch Teams	=	Divisions/departments/ work teams
Core Crew	=	Permanent Full-time Employees
Leggers	=	Temporary Full-time Employees
Watch System	=	Shifts
RORC	=	Business regulators
The Ocean	=	Marketplace
Weather	=	Business Climate
Competitors	=	Competitors
Waypoints	=	Goals or deadlines
Velocity Made Good	=	Most efficient progress in the right direction
Best for Boat	=	Making the right decisions for the sake of the business
Man Overboard	=	Crisis
Southern Ocean	=	Tough times, etc.

We had, as in business, a vision, a mission, values and goals, strategies and tactics, crises and competitors. Our Mission was to race around the world. Our Vision was to finish in the Top Three and our Goals: to finish in a high-ranking position in each leg. Our Values were Safe, Happy, Fast.

Our strategies and tactics were complex and specific to yacht racing, and there is no reason to go into the details of them here, but when a boat (business) is competitively racing 24 hours a day, seven days a week, whilst responding to sea state (marketplace), weather (business climate) and crises, lessons arise which are applicable and relevant to the business world. Here are some generic points then, rather than specific strategic and tactical plans.

Stick to your Strategy... but Respond to Change

As previously mentioned, strategy is an art. One way or another, leaders have to know when to stick to their strategy and when to flex. Strategies are generally proactive and premeditated. Strategic plans are devised in controlled conditions, with level-headed decision making based on the current known facts and circumstances. However, we live in a changing world, and in business things are changing so quickly that the current catchphrase is 'the only constant is change'. So leaders and businesses have to keep up with change as a minimum, and stay ahead of change if they are to be competitive. Sun Tzu knew that preplanned strategies require quick and appropriate responses to changing conditions in the field. Planning works in a controlled environment, but in a competitive environment, unexpected situations arise - even from clashing strategies. So it is important to have a plan and stick to it, but also to know when to adapt it in response to a situational change - and not just because it looks easier or more convenient to do so.

On leg six, we had a strategy and we stuck to it. We knew initially we would be disadvantaged as we headed further north, but then we began to overhaul the entire fleet and led the race right to the finish line.

On leg one, we had a plan to sail well to the west of the Canary Islands, but when we got there, temptation was great and we actually decided to sail between the islands; it was shorter and **appeared** quicker. However, we got stuck in a wind shadow – as our pre-race advisors had predicted – and we lost many places, finally finishing the leg in 8th place.

On leg four, from Sydney to Cape Town we had a plan but halfway through the leg we changed it. Initially we were sailing the shortest route to the finish, but were losing out to the other boats; we had to review our options. We had a good, compelling reason to change the tactics backed up with hard evidence. We finished in 3rd place.

Strategy **is** a fine art. It is hard to know when to stick and when to change. In the main, strategies should be adhered to; they were devised for a reason, generally after much thought, consultancy and with a clear head. Certainly if the vision, mission (core purpose), goals and values support the strategy, then all the more reason to *hold the course*. However, there will be times – as Sun Tzu predicted – when quick and appropriate responses are necessary in reaction to changing circumstances and shifts of power; in crises such as the 2008 credit crunch for instance. Then holding the course (dogmatically) has to give way to changing course (flexibly).

The other occasion to maybe change strategy or tactics would be to seize an opportunity. In war: the arrival of more troops; the invention of a long-range weapon; an unexpected strategic alliance. In yacht racing: a change in the weather; a mistake by a competitor; a wind shift; damaged or broken equipment. In business: a hole in the marketplace; an innovation; sudden access to a new customer segment. Short notice opportunities require nimble footwork. The previously much-heralded strategic plan may have to be reviewed or completely rewritten, on condition that a company sticks to its mission, vision and values, for these are the guiding principles throughout. These provide the backbone to allow for flexibility.

Keep Eye on Big Picture

Winning the Global Challenge is about winning a 35,000 mile round the world yacht race. That's the big picture. The key strategic focus is on a ten-month long global competition where, overall, the crews have to consistently sustain extraordinary performance.

Forget about specific factors for a moment, such as medical evacuations, competitor performances, tactical errors, sails deteriorating; these are distractions. A good Skipper, a good boat, will keep an eye on the predominant goal; the big picture. This long-term helicopter view, and the attitude and decision making that comes with it, sorts the 'men from the boys' in such a high-quality field of determined, expert competitors. Only a few sailors are able to free themselves sufficiently from preoccupation with the tactical situations and boat speed to concentrate on the long-term goal.

In typical yacht racing, such as local 'round the cans' races, crews can become so preoccupied with the immediate that they neglect the future. Their focus may shift from one concern to another: is the mainsail set right? Will the spinnaker go up cleanly? Will we get across the start line in clean air? Being so busy, they miss the things that **really** matter and so hardly notice losing ground until it is too late. In contrast, there is the single-minded determination of the round the world race winner, constantly checking in with the big picture. These 'professionals' are not bogged down in doubt, indecision, and distraction. Their thinking is coherent; their priorities clear. Their attention is on the things that really matter in the long run.

With confidence gained from experience, or just plain audacity, the minute-by-minute management of the yacht can be ignored and attention focused upon the determinants of victory. With this approach, the overriding factor in each leg is known; the most likely major error is understood. The probability of success is greatly increased and the risk of disaster is greatly reduced. Keeping an eye on the big picture brings clarity, removes distractions and aids prioritisation. A leader will not lead their company to greatness all the time they are concentrating on the ground-level detail.

Chunk by Chunk

As well as focusing on the 'big picture', each boat's overarching strategy was 'chunked down' into more manageable bites. Vision and long-term goals are useful for clarity and motivation, but for employees or crew to then comprehend and execute the master plan, smaller time periods and goals have to be agreed, planned and tactically implemented. Team Stelmar, for instance, had an overall race strategy, but then also devised strategies for each leg, waypoint and weather system in order to provide focus and tactics in the more immediate term.

The most obvious way of breaking down the huge task of winning a round the world race was initially by focusing on each leg. The legs were very different from one another, some lasted for over a month, and one lasted just four days.

Some were in the Southern Ocean, skirting icebergs and Cape Horn, and some were in the tropics, crossing the equator and the doldrums. Each required very different strategies and tactics.

The next 'level' of planning was by waypoint within each leg. A waypoint is essentially a place, determined by latitude and longitude in the case of the Global Challenge race, by which boats must pass. They are like milestones en route to the finish line and, in some cases, serve to steer the boats away from known iceberg territory by directing boats north or south of a waypoint. From one waypoint to another, there may be three weeks of sailing.

There are then weather systems which affect the boat's performance for a number of days. Strategies are definitely needed to respond to weather systems, as the weather is the most influential external factor to making a boat go faster. Planning strategies by weather system involved poring over the charts and forecasts and analysing them for best possible outcome.

Within weather systems, the boat generally operated by 24-hour days. This was the natural cycle of the boat, though did not particularly affect the planning and tactics. Next were watches and six-hourly schedule updates. At watch changeover, after every four or six hours, there would perhaps be a slight change in watch tactics and ways of working, but again, there was no significant strategic difference. There was also the danger that when the six-hourly race updates came in, there would be a reactive effect upon decision making and preplanned tactics. On *Team Stelmar* we tried not to let the 'skeds' we received four times a day affect our plans by making 'knee jerk' decisions. Finally, time was broken down into reviewing boat performance every hour by completion of the log, and then also every quarter hour as the laminated performance template was filled-in on deck.

The main chunks requiring specific strategies were: each leg; each waypoint; and each weather system. Within these, were tactical manoeuvres. And within each 24-hour day, watch, hour and 15-minutes, were tactical actions.

The dichotomy of thinking on the Global Challenge, from the long-term helicopter view, to the short-term, detailed execution of tactics, was where success lay. We tried to keep an eye on the big picture without getting distracted, but also planned in detail for every 15 minutes.

Consistency

Success in round the world yacht racing depends on consistent success in the individual legs of the race. The basic requirements for success are: a competent Skipper and crew; boat speed equivalent to that of the upper 20% of the fleet; and a clear understanding of the overriding strategic and tactical principles. Racing against crews with strong abilities, all capable of winning individual legs, means success depends on consistency, avoiding mistakes and recovering swiftly from errors of judgment.

Confidence provides the determination to prepare properly, to sail effectively, to avoid major errors and to finish high on the results tables repeatedly. Confidence coupled with mental toughness prevents distraction from immediate tactical problems and allows for concentration upon the outcome of the whole race. But victory at this level requires more than adapting to different conditions, more than boat speed in light and heavy air, more than windward and reaching ability, more than a combination of tactical and strategic skills, because such skills, both individually and in combination, are possessed by most of the competitors. The regular application of these things, consistently, leg after leg, is possible for only a few. Andy Forbes, the Skipper of *BG*, for instance, won five podiums in seven legs.

At the start of the race, there was a larger disparity between the teams. They had prepared differently, with different skippers, and there were different levels of ability among the mixed crews. New leggers were almost as able as the core crew. However, as the race wore on, the skippers and crews grew in competence and confidence; clever strategising and lack of mistakes became the determining factor between winning and losing. It was then down to the consistency of finishing highly in all the legs that determined who won the overall Global Challenge. Even boats that had good results such as ours, with a first and third place, also had bad results which in our case evened out to 6th place. Boats which performed consistently averagely or badly finished below 6th place.

This realisation dawned on us when the race settled into its rhythm, about halfway around the world, after two legs. One error could cost a boat the whole leg, because the standard of racing had increased to such a high level of competency. Very few mistakes were made, and when they were, they were costly (as it was for *BP* on the last leg). The pressure was then on, for all crews to perform to very high standards, for every minute and every manoeuvre. There was no margin for error.

Plan – Implement – Review

There was a productive rhythm to the race because in between each intense racing leg was time on shore for reflection and recuperation. We stopped in some of the most magnificent places in the world – Buenos Aires, Wellington, Sydney, Cape Town, Boston and La Rochelle.

These were really inspirational settings full of history, culture and physical beauty; perfect for rebuilding the team and boat.

For many of our stopovers we had about three weeks time 'off', however two of these were spent working on the boat. In the first week we did all the primary jobs: checking and repairing the sails (five people full-time); carrying out an inventory and ordering new equipment; dismantling the bunks and sending them to an industrial launderette for cleaning; checking and fixing the rigging; thoroughly cleaning the whole boat inside out, top and bottom; attending functions, protest hearings and visiting schools. The next few days were usually spent doing personal admin and housekeeping, followed by about three to five days of sightseeing. Then we would be back at the boat for a week doing the pre-race preparation jobs such as: reattaching the bunks and sails; loading about 2000 meals; restocking the boat; taking VIPs out sailing; practising the race start; attending functions, ceremonies, press conferences and award dinners; and other admin and general preparation.

In addition to this workload the Watch Leaders and Skippers held one-to-one and whole-watch debriefs to iron out any issues and gain further understanding of their crew. Plus there were two new 'leggers' to welcome, train and talk with so that they were fully functioning team members as quickly as possible. We also always held a full crew debrief to discuss the leg and decide on changes and improvements for the next leg. These would often take half a day and sometimes be quite heated, but always very productive. This was a chance for everyone to have their say, clear the air, put forward ideas and agree a way forward. Where possible, the two new leggers would be part of this process too so they understood our reasoning behind the way we ran the next leg.

This cycle of sail – debrief – sail – debrief, was a useful process. It enabled us to practise, then reflect, then improve, throughout the race, in addition to mini debriefs held during the leg itself. In planning, there is a cycle with these stages: plan, implement, review, plan, implement, review, and so on. The stopovers allowed us to process our thinking and lift our heads up out of the day-to-day racing. Any strategies or tactics we had tried on the leg were reviewed and we learned from them, adapting where necessary. The next leg's strategy and tactics were then discussed and agreed.

In business, there are sometimes cycles of activity that occur naturally. If not, then it could be productive to build in some 'firebreaks' from the daily routine of activity; time out for breathing space and review of the strategy and tactics, adapting and improving before moving on.

Lessons on Strategy and Tactics from the Boat to the Boardroom

Go to War

If you need focus, and determination, and robustness, plan your business strategy as if you are going to war. Plan how to beat your enemy. Take a hard line. Take it seriously. Think about: your deployment and management of troops; what is in your arsenal and how you can add to it; what advantages can be gained from the terrain; what the enemy are likely to do; what attack and defence moves your business is capable of executing. Read a translation of Sun Tzu's *Art of War*.

Plan to Win

Strategy is the 'art of ensuring future success'. The point of having a strategy is to be best placed to win. Plan to win, don't plan for planning's sake, or because you have to.

Stick to your Strategy – but Respond to Change

Stick to your strategy – most of the time. If the strategy was thoughtfully preplanned with well-conceived ideas, if it supports your mission, vision, values and goals and if there is no compelling reason to change it, then hold your course. However, if there is a fundamental change in circumstances then be agile with quick and appropriate responses and communicate them to everyone.

Keep an Eye on the Big Picture

If you are a leader, don't be preoccupied with the operational detail. Rise above, look ahead and have the confidence to ignore all else but the determinants of victory.

Chunk by Chunk

Break down giant ambitions into bite-size chunks. Then plan and execute to those chunks, delegating if possible, but only to people who understand the bigger picture.

Consistency and No Mistakes

To win a long race, or a series of manoeuvres, you have to be consistently successful. Reliable, unfailing, unswerving, constant. This requires a certain mindset where error is not an option.

Plan, Implement, Review

Plan your strategy. Implement it (or part of it). Review it. Adapt if necessary. Create time out from the routine to refresh and review.

Strategy and Tactics Exercises

1. Work out your position now and the position you want to be in

1. Do a detailed and honest SWOT analysis[16] (Strengths, Weaknesses, Opportunities, Threats)

2. Also do an external situational analysis covering:

   − Markets

   − Customers

   − Competition

   − Technology

   − Supplier markets

   − Labour markets

   − The economy

   − The regulatory environment

   − Long-term trends

3. Work out where you want to be. Either…

   − Refer to your vision or long-term (3–5 years) stretchy goals if you have them

   − Generate them if you don't

2. Devise a Strategic Plan

1. Work out your best strategy/strategies for getting to where you want to be which is of high quality but also inventive

2. Draw up a strategic plan/route-map. Three useful questions are:

   − What do we do?

---

[16] There is also PEST analysis (Political, Economic, Social and Technological) or STEER analysis (Socio-cultural, Technological, Economic, Ecological and Regulatory) if more appropriate.

- For whom do we do it?
- How do we beat the competition?

3. Have working groups discuss and produce the tactics for each chunk of the strategic plan

4. Get buy-in from the whole company by sharing it in an engaging, graphic and memorable way

3. Review your Consistency

- Does your company or team experience peaks and troughs of quality?
- Can you work out why?
- What can you do about it?

4. Review your Mistakes

- Specifically, and with examples, what mistakes are being made by your company or team?
- Can you work out why? (See Six Sigma for a range of quality management tools and methodologies)
- What can you do to reduce or stop them?

5. When to Stick to the Strategy and when to Flex?

- Draw up judging criteria to help decision making with the above. For example: Is there a real and considerable threat to our business?
- Place this on a one-page decision-making aid with the company's: Vision, Mission, Priority Goals and Values
- Add a thought bubble: Is there a **compelling** reason to change your strategy?
- Do a situational SWOT analysis if you think it will help, reviewing both internal and external conditions at that time
- Use all of this as a reference tool for when you are deciding whether to stick to your strategy or adapt it

Chapter 4. Crisis Prevention and Management

Definition

CRISES CAN HAPPEN ANYTIME and anywhere; in business, in families, in societies, in localities – and most definitely on boats, giving rise to the phrase: 'worse things happen at sea'. Most definitions ascribe three common characteristics to crises, stating that they all contain: a threat, an element of surprise and short decision times.

In general, a crisis can be described as a situation in which things are very uncertain, difficult, or painful; especially a time when action must be taken to avoid disaster or breakdown; and/or a critical moment when something very important for the future happens or is decided.

In business a crisis is defined as: 'a major, unpredictable event that threatens to harm an organisation and its stakeholders'. The United Kingdom's Department for Business, Enterprise and Regulatory Reform (2008), describes a crisis as:

...an abnormal situation, or even perception, which is beyond the scope of everyday business and which threatens the operation, safety and reputation of an organisation.

The concept of unpredictability is common in most definitions; however, although crises can be unpredictable, they should not be unexpected. Crises can be prevented, planned for and managed. Gonzalez-Herrero and Pratt[17] describe a four-phase crisis management model that includes: issues management, planning-prevention, the crisis, and post-crisis. This Chapter is not just about crisis management, but also crisis prevention and post-crisis reconciliation.

The UK's Department for Business, Enterprise and Regulatory Reform goes on to say:

The department advocates that businesses treat crisis management planning with the same attention as other business plans.

...The crisis should be dealt with as an operational management issue that is simply being undertaken in extreme circumstances. The crisis management framework for response is normally based on existing management structures and responsibilities. It must also reflect (or improve upon) existing lines of communication, both within the company, and with other organisations which may be affected. This approach, when developed in conjunction with the operational managers, will confirm ownership of plans and prepare the proposed framework for practical implementation. (United Kingdom, 2007)

This advice advocates that companies predict and plan for crisis; making crisis management planning as important as other business planning; enhancing operations, structures, responsibilities and communications in order to manage and control the outcomes; but how many companies actually do this and prepare for their own 'man overboard' scenario?

Crisis Prevention and Management in the Global Challenge

Of all the crisis preparations the Global Challenge teams undertook, the 'Man Overboard' drill was the most prolific and exacting. First, the likelihood of a man (or woman) overboard was fairly high, but secondly, in practising the drill

---

[17] Gonzalez-Herrero, A., & Pratt, C. B. (1995) 'How to manage a crisis before or whenever - it hits'.

again and again, it achieved a (crisis-oriented) discipline within the teams, thus preparing them for behaving in an orderly and practised manner in other crises. The beauty of the drill, in preparing for one specific situation, was the wide-ranging application the knowledge had on the different crises actually experienced. The crews were thus (more-or-less) programmed to behave in a certain way when crises happened on board. The *basic* principles were essentially the same:

1. Let the whole boat know as quickly as possible there was a crisis, what it was and where

2. Assess the whole situation

3. Make the boat as safe as possible

4. Deal with the particular incident in a safe, proficient manner

5. Diffuse the crisis

6. Generate a continuity plan

7. Deal with the post-crisis fallout

8. Communicate clearly throughout – with the crew and with the outside world

9. Learn from it

There were certainly plenty of crises on our race, and in the race prior to ours. In the 2000/1 Global Challenge *Quadstone* heavily collided with *Save the Children* in Wellington, NZ and *Quadstone* had to retire from the leg. Skipper Alex Philips later resigned. Both boats had to be extensively repaired in New Zealand. There was also a major incident on board *Veritas*. The boat was hit by a freak wave in the Bass Strait and a few of their crew were injured; one losing the top of his finger, and one fracturing his left femur, right ankle and left elbow having been pushed through the steering wheel by the water, resulting in immediate medical evacuation, plastic surgery for Robert Brooke and many operations for Charlie Smith.

During our race, there were more than a few crises, some of them involving serious medical evacuations. Our boat suffered twice; *Unisys* evacuated John Masters by helicopter near New Zealand and *Save the Children* had to stop racing at one point to evacuate a crew member with a broken hip. We also had crew with broken bones, fractured ribs, concussion, severe rope burns, torn muscles, broken contact lenses, squashed fingers, seasickness, and our Navigator had to have an operation on his leg to remove a haematoma whilst we were racing. We also ripped most of our sails, snapped one of our spinnaker poles, broke or bent many of our stanchions, suffered a knock-down in the tropics and dealt with waterspouts. There were plenty of crises which we 'managed' but also potentially quite a few which, through prior planning and training, we 'prevented'.

The Global Challenge pre-race training provided some crisis simulations which had to be worked through by the crews, providing them with tough learning environments. There were also the Man Overboard and other drills as part of each boat's training regime and teams conducted their own training and crisis prevention planning. On *Team Stelmar* we recreated medical situations and took part in the 'Sinking Ship scenario' (see pp 19-20). The Global Challenge Business and the officiators, the Royal Ocean Racing Club, had a degree of responsibility for supporting the boats from the outside world. There were systems and structures in place should a crisis occur, and training and discussions to avert disaster too. This was the fourth Global Challenge Race and many lessons were learnt from the earlier races, as well as other round the world yacht races such as the Volvo Ocean Race and the Vendée Globe. As an example, the route for the race in 2004/5 Global Challenge was different to the previous race. The first leg, instead of going to Boston, went to Buenos Aires. This was to avoid the hurricanes off the east coast of America at that time of year.

'Worse things happen at sea' is a phrase that has arisen because the sea is a relentlessly dangerous place, and any boat or crew sailing the world's oceans will face harsh environments and powerful forces. Gale force winds and 40' waves. Tornados and electrical storms. Freak waves and icebergs. Crises are almost inevitable and certainly expected at sea, the question is – how to either prevent or properly manage the crises when they do occur?

Crisis Prevention and Management from Boat to Boardroom

According to research in 2006[18], in the five years to 2011, 83% of companies will face a crisis that will negatively impact their share price by 20 to 30 percent. Some crises may be immediate and unexpected, some may burn slowly over time, some may be obscure one-offs and some just perceived, but crises can *'threaten the operation, safety and reputation of an organisation'* as well as be detrimental to profit margins, and therefore threaten companies' actual existence. In 2008-9 the credit crunch hit and most companies suffered financially, to the point of closure in many cases. This is an example of a severe (thankfully rare) global financial crisis. Other crises may be more specific, such as the one experienced by Exxon in their 1989 oil tanker spillage.

Company crises vary greatly and may be of little or great significance. Other crises outside of the corporate environment will also vary widely from case to case, but there are similarities in each. First, the three common characteristics: a threat, an element of surprise and short decision times. Second, the typical planning and prevention required: communication planning, responsibility planning, health and safety checks, crisis scenario planning, issues management, training, etc. And third, the typical responses during crisis management as mentioned previously:

---

[18] Oxford-Metrica for Aon.

1) Let the relevant people know as quickly as possible there is a crisis and what it is

2) Assess the whole situation

3) Make the overall 'environment' as safe as possible

4) Deal with the particular incident in a safe, proficient manner

5) Diffuse the crisis

6) Have a continuity plan

7) Deal with the post-crisis fallout

8) Communicate clearly throughout – internally and externally

9) Learn from it

What did the Global Challenge crews do and discover, that businesses can learn from?

The Calm before the Storm

PREVENTION = Preparation. Practice. Planning.

'Practice makes perfect'. 'Practise, practise, practise'. 'Perfect planning prevents poor performance'. 'Be prepared'. These phrases are common to the ear, but perhaps less common in practice. Practising crisis scenarios, rehearsing 'what ifs', drilling emergency procedures, preparing for disaster recovery, planning for business continuity... is about being prepared. Being prepared for potentially the worst disaster the organisation will ever experience, possibly one that threatens its very existence. This is the time when great leadership and teamwork under pressure are vital to avoid disaster and breakdown. When businesses plan for success, forecasting profits and generating long-term goals, they should also plan and prepare for the downside: crises which will negatively affect their operations, profit, reputation and safety.

Not only should crisis scenario planning be part of general business planning, but also there are benefits to be gained from doing it. Irrespective of the size of the crisis or organisation involved, these benefits include:

1) Chance to assess the organisation's strengths, weaknesses, opportunities and threats (SWOT) from inside and outside the organisation, in an objective, measured manner

2) Review and improvement of structures, chains of command, communications, operations, safety procedures, etc.

3) Faster and more effective action and decision making during crises

4) Generation of techniques, actions and decisions for damage limitation

5) Continuity business planning to reduce disruption and minimise impact

6) Generation of new ideas which may improve operations in non-crisis times

7) Better institutional resilience

8) Compliance with regulatory and ethical requirements, e.g. corporate social responsibility

9) Better management of incidents or injury

10) Ability to prioritise e.g. using a 'triage' system

11) Improved staff awareness of roles and expectations

12) Improved staff knowledge

13) Increased ability, confidence and morale

14) Advanced risk identification, and so mitigation

15) Enhanced reputation as a reduced-risk organisation in the eyes of public, press and shareholders

16) Appreciation of post-crisis fallout and solutions to it

Scenario planning is essentially rehearsing for the real thing so that if a crisis should occur, the organisation and the people – especially the leaders - are ready for it. Crises are unpredictable but should be expected and therefore planned for.

In the Global Challenge we **knew** we would experience crises, so we verbally discussed and physically rehearsed several different scenarios, until we were programmed to behave in a certain way, no matter what befell us. One of the biggest learnings to come out of these pre-race preparations was around chain of command including clarity of roles and trust...

Leadership and Chain of Command

As mentioned in the Leadership Chapter, different styles of leadership suit some situations more than others. Often these preferences are inexact as there are pros and cons to the different styles, but during a crisis, strong, visible, decisive, up-front leadership is much favoured. Almost a militaristic style is required to bring about discipline and control in an otherwise potentially chaotic situation. The first hours after a crisis breaks are the most crucial, so working with speed and efficiency is important, and a decisive, directive leader promotes that way of working. In crisis there is often noise, confusion, uncertainty and a lack of confidence. Strong leadership helps alleviate these barriers to resolution and a commanding no-nonsense style of communication – with no hesitation, no questioning, no answering back – is appropriate in the early stages. Practising for this is about *mastering* crises; priming for efficiency and effectiveness in the toughest of times.

The chain of command is also important. One leader can cover and command only so much in a short time. In Team Stelmar's pre-race practices and dry runs, the chain of command became clearer and clearer the more we carried out drills and crisis scenarios. If initially the chain of command is not quite clear, practise, practise, practise and it soon becomes evident who should do what; what the team's strengths are, what the networks and links need to be, what the roles are and who exactly should be in (and out of) the chain of command (and therefore the primary communication lines). Drilling enforces discipline. Discipline produces clarity and efficiency.

Once the chain of command is determined, there has to be trust up and down the line. Again, practice will help. During practice the team can see who is best placed in what role – no matter what their day jobs are, so the leader's crisis planning should include drawing on people's strengths and skills. Trust comes next. If the right people are allocated to the right jobs, then those people should be trusted to fulfil their roles, and with trust comes more speed and efficiency. There is no time for double-checking or closely managing in the heat of a crisis. It's about delegating and moving on.

Communication is of course vital during and after the crisis, both internally and with the outside world, and the communication must be clear and concise. (See below)

Finally, leaders need to make plans for getting out of the crisis. Business continuity, damage limitation, crisis diffusion and resolution, and post-crisis clean up. At this juncture, the decisive, commanding leader can afford to change to a more consultative style and encourage two-way communication once again, taking on board advice and information; planning reconciliation strategies with their advisors and allowing their team to regain control, and so, their confidence.

For Team Stelmar, in practice and actuality, the early stages of a crisis were alleviated with strong leadership, a clear chain of command and trust.

Communication

Shortly after each of Team Stelmar's medical emergencies, the boat was placed under a communications embargo by the Global Challenge office – with no satellite communication allowed in or out (phone calls and emails) until the Challenge Business could verify and control the flow of information to avoid unnecessary worry and panic back home. **All** of our close contacts were called, as well as our sponsors, and each situation was explained in clear, matter-of-fact terms with no spin. Information was released to the press and a factual explanation was posted on the race website. The other 11 boats were also informed. Only then were communications re-opened between the boat and the outside world. This was a little tough on those on board, but the crew knew it was for the best. It meant that everyone closely and emotionally concerned heard the story first from a factual, objective source before rumours, exaggerations, emotions or gossip started to spread.

In business, the first communications internally and externally are critical to set the right tone, before the wrong messages spread, potentially causing more damage to reputation and sales. Many companies haven fallen foul of this advice and suffered considerably as a result. The companies that got it right however, no matter how grievous the disaster, bounced back, sometimes with a better reputation than before, winning round public and press opinion with their honest and speedy reactions. Sometimes it is not the crisis itself that causes damage; it is the way it is dealt with.

Take two giant companies Exxon and Dell. Back in 1989 Exxon had a huge oil spillage causing great damage to the local environment and inducing a media outcry. Exxon were slow to react to the public and the media; they did not have a crisis communication plan or team in place and the CEO himself did not actively help with PR and thus was perceived not to care. Exxon suffer even now from a negative reputation from this incident. More recently Dell's laptops got a reputation for 'exploding'. In this case, the people took it upon themselves to spread the word electronically, blogging about 'my Dell hell' and quickly informing others on the net about the issues. Now, with the world wide web and email, the spread of news is dynamically fast and companies have to get in immediately with their reconstructive messages before the public do so with their deconstructive (but often honest) ones.

A positive example of great communication was with the American company Odwalla, who back in 1986 were at the centre of an E Coli poisoning scare with an apple juice product:

Within 24 hours, Odwalla conferred with the FDA and Washington state health officials; established a schedule of daily press briefings; sent out press releases which announced the recall; expressed remorse, concern and apology, and took responsibility for anyone harmed by their products; detailed symptoms of E. coli poisoning; and explained what consumers should do with any affected products. Odwalla then developed - through the help of consultants - effective thermal processes that would not harm the products' flavors when production resumed. All of these steps were communicated through close relations with the media and through full-page newspaper ads (Dwyer, 1998).

That's more like it.

Crisis management planning needs to cater for urgent, genuine and appropriate communications as early as possible within the crisis, to both internal and external stakeholders. Failing this, the void of silence will be filled by uninformed, potentially damaging, opinions. Communication has to be clear, factual and as informative as possible under the circumstances with frequent updates. There should be no spin. There should be transparency. If a company communicates falsely in these times, and is later found out, greater and long-lasting damage to their reputation can result.

After experiencing their own 'Dell hell', Dell concluded in 1987:

- Customers are in control. Work with them and learn from them

- Real conversations are two-way

- Think before you talk — but always be yourself

- Address any form of dissatisfaction head on

- Be aware that any conversation can become global at any time

- Size doesn't matter - relevance does. Just as one journalist can trigger a news cycle, one blogger can do the same

- Don't be afraid to apologize

- Develop direct links to customer community (IdeaStorm for Dell), listen for how we can improve

- One customer is part of many communities

- Teamwork, transparency and frequent consistent communication are key in this new world

- No shortcuts are possible. Implementing business change requires much effort across departments[19]

Communication planning also needs to take into account functional communication to allow for the flow of information to pass in and out of the 'command centre', enabling the right decisions to be made. Methods for damage reporting and systems checking, networks with communication links inside and out, and ways to

---

[19] Mar. 11, 2008 article on CustomerThink.com: 'You Can Learn From "Dell Hell." Dell Did', by Mei Lin Fung, Institute of Service Organization Excellence, Inc.

communicate clearly, without misinterpretation, across geographies and cultures should also be organised.

In the Global Challenge, there were global considerations and time zones to take into account. The website was a great portal for everyone back at home – a constant source of information and updates 24 hours a day, meticulously maintained by the Race Office. Communication between the fleet was also excellent. Radio communications, emails and satellite phones were all used to enable boats to support each other and come to each other's aid; we were our own safety net. For example, in 2004/5 both *Samsung* and *Save the Children* went to the help of *Unisys* to give them further medical supplies. Unfortunately, in *Team Stelmar's* case, there was no additional physical help the other boats could provide, but their messages of support and encouragement were extremely welcome even so.

Weathering the Storm

Crisis Management

It is not always the crisis that has the most capacity to destruct; it is how it is dealt with.

Crises **will** happen – especially at sea – they are an inevitable part of life. They can often be prevented. They can be prepared for, planned for, drilled and rehearsed, but one day, the real thing will occur – often with no notice - requiring the best possible management. Strong leadership. Effective teamwork. Great systems. Fantastic communications. The best of every operational aspect of a racing yacht or a company has to come into play. There is no wimping out with a crisis. There is no softly-softly management. There is no more time for coaching or training or hesitating. Crises are brutal and unforgiving. The management of them needs to be of an equal and better strength.

On *Team Stelmar* we had a genuine call of 'Man Overboard' within ten hours of the race starting, in the middle of the night. Both watches were still finding their feet so early in the race, and team development was still embryonic. If it hadn't been for all the MOB drills in the lead-up to the race, it probably would have been quite a shambles above and below decks at that point. Half the crew were battling a force ten gale on deck, already stretching their strengths and skills, and the other half were strapped in their bunks below in fitful sleep. The Skipper was a good leader, but young and only on day one of the race. None of us expected to be hit so soon. But we were a practised, drilled team. We went to our jobs and did what we had to do almost without thinking. We were disciplined to do so. We had structure, roles, a chain of command, a certainty in **everyone's** head as to what needed to be done. We functioned well. The first thing in crisis management then, as already covered above, is to be prepared.

Part of the preparation is risk evaluation and instilling safety procedures. Our values were 'Safe, Happy, Fast' and our life-jacket rules were to wear them at least when the winds exceeded 20 knots, when the spinnaker sail was up and between sundown and sunrise. Our 'man overboard' on that first night was OK because of our boat rules. He was still attached to the boat by his life-line. In a less fortunate incident, Dutchman Hans Horrevoets, 32, fell from *ABN Amro Two* in the 2006 Volvo Ocean Race and failed to regain consciousness after being lifted back on the boat. *ABN Amro Two* was sailing in five-metre seas and 30 knot winds.

So our MOB drilling (preparation and practice) and safety rules (planning), supported by our team values (safe, happy, fast), collectively put us in a good place for that first-night trauma. We:

1. Let the whole boat know as quickly as possible there was a crisis, what it was and where

2. (Shouts of 'man overboard!' to the whole crew is standard practice)

3. Assessed the whole situation

4. (Difficult at night and with only seconds of time)

5. Made the boat as safe as possible

6. (If we had time we would have fully hove to and stopped the boat)

7. Dealt with the particular incident in a safe, proficient manner

8. (Pulled the man overboard in whilst clipped on and supported by crew)

9. Diffused the crisis

10. (Got medical attendance, assessment and care. Debriefed and calmed the on watch. Supported the on-deck crew with the off watch)

11. Communicated clearly throughout – with the crew and with the outside world

12. (Shouted clearly over the noise and pressed the MOB emergency button, which sends out an automatic MOB signal including our latitude and longitude. Informed the Race Office shortly afterwards that the MOB was recovered and OK)

There were mop-up activities, but within minutes we had the situation back under control, albeit with the crew rather shaken and feeling more vulnerable than they had when they set off just hours before.

Choose your Attitude

As mentioned in the personal development Chapter, we can choose how we react to the cards life deals us. Sometimes there is good news, sometimes bad, and we can choose to respond to both with a positive attitude and constructive actions. On *Team Stelmar* we were extremely unlucky to have two separate medical evacuations within the space of one week. We had not expected such a double blow when we were doing so well. We could have lamented this and navel-gazed at our lack of luck, perhaps even blaming people's actions and decisions. We could have panicked and chased our tails during the critical early moments of each disaster. But there was no blame and no panic. Even at this early stage in the race, 70 days in, the team were so well-trained, developed and united, that they instinctively knew how to deal with each catastrophe, as a group and as individuals with a positive attitude and constructive solutions.

In crisis situations, role models that exude control, calm and objectivity are effective in preventing the spread of panic or blame. Instead they can infect others with a sense of maturity and decorum in response to dangerous, uncertain or painful situations. The natural 'mob' reaction may be to give way to fear and lack of resolve; but it takes courage and a cool head to stand ground in a crisis. Scaremongers need to be managed, and role models used and praised.

Leaders also need to be aware of the shadows they cast during a crisis. Lamenting the situation verbally and physically will not produce courage or confidence in their teams, without which everything can fall apart like a stack of cards. One strong leader can pull together a shambolic, despairing group of individuals - think of Maximum in *Gladiator*, pulling together the combatants in the Arena and winning against the odds.

In the 'Turn and Turn Again' article that was in the *Daily Telegraph* on December 21st, Team Stelmar were upheld as a resilient team, inspiring others in the fleet and in the wider world. It was around this point that the sponsor company Stelmar were in fact undergoing a takeover by OSG – Overseas Shipholding Group – and they also took heart from our response to the second crisis:

BATTLING BRITS TURN AND TURN AGAIN

by Brendan Gallagher

Trouble on the high seas leaves Stelmar Playing Catch-up in the Global Challenge.

In the best tradition of Brits fighting the elements in remote parts of the world at Christmas, Team Stelmar were heading back out into the treacherous Southern Ocean for the third time in two weeks yesterday after a second medical emergency threatened to end their participation in the Global Challenge, the round the world yacht race for amateur crews.

The crew... confounded yachting experts by opting to continue the second, and hardest, leg of the race from Buenos Aires to Wellington.

They now face a daunting 5,000 mile race against time to arrive in Wellington before Jan 23, the organisers' cut-off date if they wish to continue the race on Feb 6...

"There is almost no room for error and they are now three crew members light, but don't write them off yet. They have already shown themselves to be an incredibly durable and close crew. To turn around yet again and retrace all those hard-earned miles takes some doing."

After the Storm

The article (above) describes Team Stelmar as being an 'incredibly durable and close crew'. The crew certainly suffered more than their fair share of crises, but they remained tight as a team, and kept their issues within. Our main sponsor contact, David Chapman, now Chartering Manager for OSG (previously Stelmar) states:

One of my major 'takeaways' from watching you as a team was how 'together' you were, how 'what happened on the boat stayed on the boat'. Other teams commented on it with grudging respect.

Team Stelmar were an incredibly tight team. Thanks in the first part to a good mix of personalities, but secondly, it was down to the positive attitude they collectively developed from the start, and the Skipper's leadership.

In the fallout after a crisis - once the storm has passed – there is still work to be done. The more palpable trouble may have been dealt with, but there is still potentially 'below the surface' damage to structures and people. In the extreme, 'post traumatic stress disorder' is now known as a condition brought on by emotional, physical and/or psychological trauma. Once the energy and focus fade away after a crisis, people can then suffer from shock, stress or demotivation. This calm after the storm needs to be just as carefully managed as the crisis in the eye of the storm. People can be RE-motivated with a crisis, but DE-motivated after one. (see Motivation Chapter p.302). Teams need to check and support each other (including the leaders) through the fallout. Leaders ideally also create a new focus and fresh energy, perhaps by reinventing team goals.

After *Team Stelmar* dropped off Flash after his accident, the crew had to get back to where the incident had happened; a place they dubbed 'Waypoint Flash'. This took five days and refocused them on getting to that point. After that though, they had to decide whether to retire or continue racing. They were encouraged to retire, as this was the most logical and apparently safer option. What they actually decided to do though was to continue racing which boosted the morale of the team and many people watching. Finally, they had to 'just' get to Wellington within their given deadline, as safely as possible - but it was going to be tight. Three crew members down by now, and thousands of miles behind their competitors, the team knew that their chances of winning the Global Challenge were now in tatters. Their goal of winning the leg to Wellington was impossible. Even their aim of having a decent finish was not achievable. So they reviewed their situation and adjusted their goals. From that point on they had a renewed sense of purpose.

Team Stelmar changed their immediate goal. Their new objective was to get to Wellington, safely and by sail power, before the deadline. This was going to be tough in itself. They also changed their **race** goal to winning legs instead of the whole race; to finish in the top three in each leg, rather than in the final results. Finally they also had to adjust their personal ambitions towards achieving their lifelong dream; they learned the hard way.

In crisis there is opportunity. Opportunity to grow, learn and innovate.

Team Stelmar learned a lot of lessons that December and January. They learned the hard way about life, luck, stamina, friendship and themselves. They learned more about getting the most out of the boat during the slow, lonely haul to New Zealand as they took the opportunity to experiment, practising different ways of working. More importantly, they grew. They grew as a team, and they grew as individuals.

Post-race, three years on, the crew know they experienced their fair share of crises, but they don't regret it. In fact their lives are enriched by the more extreme experiences they had compared to the other teams. The crew are still close, and the individuals are more confident, capable and fulfilled. In crisis, there **is** opportunity.

Lessons on Crisis Prevention and Management from the Boat to the Boardroom

PREVENTION = Preparation, Practice, Planning

Crises are not predictable but they should be expected and therefore planned for. Make crisis management planning part of your business planning. Have a crisis focus group working out the enhanced disciplines required in emergencies. Rehearse scenarios with various teams using different crises. Be prepared. Don't forget there are major benefits to doing this. (See p.228)

It's Not the Crisis, it's the Response to it that Matters

The crisis itself may be inevitable and unstoppable, but the impact needn't be. Are you going to be a company that dies by the public and press opinion, or one that actually becomes stronger? Have a clear communications plan. Be genuine and transparent. Don't be afraid to apologise. Remember the web.

Don't Panic!

Discipline replaces panic.

No Blame

Choose your attitude. You can be constructive and positive and remotivated by a crisis, or negative, despondent and finger-pointing. One makes the company pick up and you feel better, one doesn't. One has energy for moving on, one doesn't. No blame. Debrief, learn and move on. A mistake is only a mistake if no-one learns from it.

In Every Crisis there is Opportunity

See the opportunities that crises can create and make the most of them. Opportunities to grow, to learn, to innovate. Crises can be good. They can help people sharpen their swords, help companies sharpen their operations, add adrenaline and stimulus, dispel 'fat' and complacency, generate new ideas, provide lessons for growth and produce short cuts.

Triage

Work out your priorities in a crisis. Plan and act accordingly.

Have a Continuity Plan

In your scenario rehearsals and planning, plan for business continuity – what if systems fail? What if communications break down? What if a product line has to be recalled? How is your business going to continue when the crisis hits?

Mop-Up after the Storm

Damage may still spread after a crisis, it is just more insidious. Once the noise and drama of a crisis is over, sometimes a deeper harm grows as people suffer from post-crisis stress, depression or demotivation. Have a plan ready for post-crisis management. Have some tools in the toolbox for re-energising and refocusing the troops.

Crisis Prevention and Management Exercises

Crisis Prevention Scenario 1: Pre-Race

You are the Skipper/management team of *Team Stelmar*.

- What do you need to think about pre-race regarding crisis prevention and management?
- What resources can you use to help?
- What actions do you need to take?
- How much of the crisis planning is down to the Skipper versus the team?
- How can the team get involved too?
- How can you engage the team in understanding the plans?
- How often do you review the plans?

What from the above can you apply to your workplace?

Crisis *Prevention* Scenario 2: Man Overboard!

The Man Overboard (MOB) drill is well rehearsed in the boating world.

- What is your equivalent at work? (A likely crisis that requires swift response and a collective effort to resolve)
- What is your drill if this happens?
- How would you engage your team in the drill?

Crisis Leadership

In a crisis think about:

- What needs immediate response?
- What needs medium-term control?
- What needs clearing up afterwards?

These may require different styles of leadership.

<u>Immediate response</u> generally suits leading from the front.

- Decisive, visible, delegative, commanding, directive
- Ahead of everyone else, telling people what needs to be done or ensuring that the right things are happening

<u>Medium-Term Control</u> generally suits leading alongside.

- Consultative, collaborative, teamwork
- Now that there is breathing space, what to do to get the situation under more control

<u>Clear Up</u> generally suits leading from behind.

- Supportive, empowering, coaching
- Allowing others to regain their power and confidence and save face
- Asking the right questions for people to find and explore options themselves
- Thanks and recognition, debriefs and learnings
- All three styles are equally strong
- Most situations suit one style more often over another
- All three styles can be used several times in one day
- Use them in the scenarios below

Crisis Management Scenario 1: Flash!

- Leg 2: Buenos Aires, Argentina to Wellington, New Zealand

- Toughest leg, Southern Ocean and Cape Horn, estimated 38 days at sea

- Already during the first medical evacuation the week before, *Team Stelmar* lost 19 hours of racing time, dropping from 3rd to last place, miles behind the rest of the fleet

- Rounded Cape Horn, in one week, impressively caught up and overtook seven boats to 5th place, crew in good spirits

- 13th December – 16 days into leg two

- 56°19'.14 S/97°32'.97 W

- 4000 miles east of Wellington, 1033 miles west of Cape Horn, 1000 miles north of Antarctica, 2000 south of Easter Islands

- Southern Ocean, storm and hail, beating against 38 knot winds and huge waves

- Boat doing 8 knots, 3 reefs in mainsail and smallest storm sails up

- 07:12 Groaners on watch since 06:00, Grunters preparing to go to bed

- 'Man Overboard!' shout

- Flash had been on the foredeck tightening the leech line of a foresail

- A huge wave threw him against the rigging, smashing his arm and sending him over the side

- He was clipped on and wearing a lifejacket

Exercise:

1. *What are your immediate priorities as Leader (Skipper)?*

2. *What are the medium-term tasks?*

3. *What are your 'clean up' jobs when the crisis is under control? (You will need to make assumptions about the actual events)*

4. *What can you apply from this to your workplace?*

Crisis Management Scenario 2: Knockdown

- In the tropics, nearing the equator, off the west coast of Africa, heading south

- The weather is typically hot and oppressive for long periods, then sudden squalls appear with little warning

- The squalls bring with them a shift in wind direction, a dramatic increase in wind speed and then rain

- The team are hoisting a spinnaker

- The squall hits the boat, the sail is caught in the wind halfway up the mast, overpowering the boat and pulling it over onto its side (a knockdown)

Exercise:

1. *What are your immediate priorities as Leader (Skipper)?*

2. *What are the medium-term tasks?*

3. *What are your 'clean up' jobs when the crisis is under control?*

4. *What can you apply from this to your workplace?*

Actual Events

Here is what Team Stelmar actually did in the scenarios – not necessarily the right course of action, just the action we took in the circumstances.

'Flash' Scenario

<u>Immediate Priorities</u>

- MOB procedure

- Off watch woken and dressed

- Medic prepared

- Stabilised boat – turned to running downwind to stop the boat slamming against the waves

- Pulled Flash on board

- Lowered him down foredeck hatch

- Immediate First Aid in the sail locker and quick assessment of damage

- Carried him aft and held him on the saloon table

- Cut off his drysuit, mid-layer and thermals

- Further assessment by Ruth (Medic), helped by Kate (Physio)

- Informed Global Challenge, suspended racing at recorded latitude and longitude

- Phoned for advice from Derriford hospital who specialise in first aid at sea – lots of satellite phone calls

- Checked charts for navigating new route options

- Allocated three people to stay on deck and kept them informed

- Determined injuries, applied dressings, gave painkillers and medication

Medium-Term Tasks

- Rebuilt a bunk for him and dismantled the one above to help with access (3 hours later)

- Strapped and cushioned him in

- Altered course to nearest land at 10:57 local time (4 hours later)

- Rotated people on deck

- Hot teas all round

- Continued to inform Global Challenge

- Held team talks – motivation, revised strategy, consequences

- Communications embargo between the boat and the outside world for 24 hours

- Sailed 1000 miles back to Cape Horn

- Kept up Flash's spirits with jokes, Top Trumps and a pulley system for chocolates!

- Maintained medical observations and medication

- Continued to inform: Global Challenge, Skipper's wife who was flying out to meet us, Flash's family, our friends and family, *Daily Telegraph*, Sponsors, Chilean and Argentinean authorities, rest of fleet

- Supported each other

- Planned arrival jobs

- Checked if others required medical attention whilst on dry land (Paul needed cortisone injection and went with Flash to the local hospital)

- Got official RORC approval for 'outside assistance' to take on board more gas, food and diesel

- Evacuated and said goodbye to Flash

- All crew had hot shower and meal at a local hotel

- All crew then helped to restock the boat, shop for more food, liaise with local authorities, etc.

Clean Up Jobs

- Returned to Waypoint Flash, up the Beagle Canal and out into the Southern Ocean once more

- More team talks – motivation, revised strategy, consequences

- Team meetings to discuss options and implications of whether to continue racing or retire from the leg

- Researched options and reviewed opinions sent to us via email from professional and unprofessional sources

- Took the decision to continue racing with the proviso we immediately headed further north nearer to the safety of shipping lanes and further away from icebergs and storms

- Produced electronic and hand-drawn charts to plot progress

- Revised our goals for the leg and for the race

- Devised ways to maintain discipline and focus and therefore motivation

- Determined to experiment with operations and sail combinations whilst we had the chance

- Rejigged the watches, so that they were as balanced as possible

- Decided to give everyone a 'night off' by allowing one person at a time to sleep through the middle night watch from 02:00–06:00

- Celebrated Christmas and New Year

- Kept in touch with Flash and his family

- Continued frequent communications with all outside contacts

- Responded to requests for interviews and quotes for the website and for Press

- Kept an eye on individual motivation and stress

- Supported one crew member who became clinically depressed

- Kept cheerful with some silly games such as 'Hazelnut Bowls' on the side deck

- Maintained radio contact where possible with the rest of the fleet, though signal strength was poor

- Maintained the discipline of the daily log, pumping the bilges, etc.

- Held fitness sessions, such as sit ups, the 'plank' exercise across the cockpit and weight training with sail bags

- *N.B. Global Challenge MOB drill is as follows:*

- Whoever spots the MOB, shouts 'Man Overboard!' and points to where the person is. They do this until the person is recovered, never breaking eye contact with the casualty

- A flotation device and marker (Dan buoy) is thrown to them

- The helm heaves to, to reduce the power in the sails and stop the boat

- Jobs are then carried out by whoever is the nearest/most appropriate:

- Depress the GPS MOB button, start boat engine, inform the helm the engine is on

- Boat hook, lifting strop, tribuckle and scramble net collected from below decks and got ready on deck (all equipment to help get the casualty back onboard)

- Headsails dropped and mainsail held on the centreline of the boat

- Helm turns the boat into the wind and steers towards the MOB under engine power

- Medic prepares

- A swimmer gets ready just in case

- A bunk is prepared

- Someone at the bow calls back to the helm with distance and direction

- Helm pulls up to the windward side of the MOB

- The MOB is recovered safely

Chapter 5. Teamwork – The Basics

Definition

HOW DO EIGHTEEN PEOPLE, AGED 18 to 60, from all walks of life, who have never met before, sail competitively and successfully 35,000 miles around the world? Teamwork.

Sailing encompasses all the key ingredients of good teamwork: vision; values; planning; opportunity; challenge; shared goals; support; duty; responsibility; recognition; motivation; delegation; leadership and communication. If there was a visual image summarising teamwork, it could easily be an overhead shot of a racing yacht with a busy crew all doing their bit towards the team goal. A team is not just a collection of individuals and teamwork is not just a group of people all working towards one aim. Real teams have members with complementary skills and generate synergy through a co-ordinated effort which allows each person to maximise their strengths. Real teamwork is working in a way that aligns individuals in a co-operative and usually selfless manner, towards a specific purpose. It is about collaboration, co-operation and communication. If our boat hadn't had these things, we wouldn't have left the Marina!

We have split the subject of teamwork into two Chapters – *'Teamwork: The Basics'* and *'Teamwork: Moving On'* because teamwork is such a huge subject and there was so much of it in the Global Challenge. The Challenge was full of classic teamwork practices and tips (the basics), but as the race wore on, the crews experienced more and more dramatic disasters and extreme situations, and as their teamwork got subtly honed, more advanced teamwork practices began to emerge (moving on). Here are 'the basics' to start with.

Basic Teamwork in the Global Challenge

It is odd that such a team-based global challenge was spawned out of a **solo** round the world record. Sir Chay Blyth became the first person to sail single-handedly non-stop around the world the 'wrong way' (westwards) in 1970. His 59' ketch was called British Steel – after his sponsor. Nineteen years later, Sir Chay had the vision to launch the British Steel Challenge, 'The World's Toughest Yacht Race', comprising a fleet of unique, one-design yachts, 67' long with space for a crew of 14 people. A team of 14 people. Over 2000 people applied for the 110 places available back in 1989 at a time when pay-for adventures was a fairly original idea. Following the success of this first race, 5000 applied for the next one. It was a popular concept conceived to make yacht racing accessible to anyone – especially amateurs – moulding a ragtag bunch of non-sailors into a racing team. The challenge worked on many levels and it did really turning an ordinary amateur non-sailor into a critical crew member of an extremely proficient racing team.

So, in January 2004, how did this mixed group of 200 housewives, accountants, doctors and truck drivers get sorted, trained and lined up into twelve yacht racing crews by October 3rd?

Five years before the 2004/5 Global Challenge race, people applied for places and after a successful interview, started training. The Challenge Business then observed and kept notes on all the individuals and created case files on each. After three years of this, just before the teams were announced at the London Boat Show in January 2004, the managers of Challenge Business reviewed all the case notes and distributed the participants 'evenly' across the twelve boats, allocating one Skipper, and one medic to each and then distributing by experience, age and gender as evenly as possible. Thus there was typically a range of age and experience on each boat, with a ratio of about one woman to every five men. There was also one more factor taken into account.

In the interview everyone was asked where they sat on a scale of attitude; how much they were 'doing the race to win' versus 'doing the challenge for the experience of a lifetime'. The answers were very revealing about the frame of mind of each applicant. Individual drive and ambition was perhaps all-consuming on a competitive level or gently burning away as a personal endeavour. The crew on a racing – yet experiential - challenge would be made up of both extremes of people and everything in between, and the race results then were affected by these mindsets. *(Paula notes: Interestingly I went from 100% 'doing it for the experience' to 100% 'doing it to win' as the race progressed and the constant competitiveness gripped me.)*

So at the start, when the teams were announced in January at Excel, each consisted of a professional paid Skipper and fifteen core crew with a huge range of experience and attitude and background. Team Stelmar had Nicko, our Navigator from Australia, who had a lot of Antipodean sailing miles under his belt and Alex, a professional sailor who had previously represented England. Both of these men had a great deal of experience and determination to win. We also had Sue, a secretary and ballet dancer who had wanted to sail around the world since she was a child but who actually didn't mind too much whether we came first or last, and Paula who had never sailed before, and who had her place confirmed just two months before the race started. Paula was more intent on learning and doing the right thing initially, the concept of winning was something which would develop much later.

By July 2005, at the end of the race, Team Stelmar was an efficient, excellent, super-performing race team. What happened in between? The race itself was obviously a massive opportunity to develop and bond, but there were other factors that played a part as well as proactive management and training. Here are some of the fundamental workings of the team.

Vision, Values, Goal, Brand – and all that

Team Stelmar met as often as they could in the extremely busy run-up to the race, despite holding down full-time jobs for as long as possible (everyone needed the money). On several occasions they met at Hayling Island Sailing Club to discuss strategy and team build, and it was crucial that in these early days the team got an identity, agreed their vision and values and determined their goal.

There was no history for the team to build upon; they were starting from scratch with a blank sheet of paper. They had no sponsor as yet, and so no identity. They didn't know each other and the Skipper didn't know his team. They were mixed in their backgrounds and attitudes. So on Hayling Island, through open discussions, facilitation and lots of flipchart paper, they gradually generated lists of what they wanted to achieve, how they felt, what success would look like, what their beliefs were, how they liked to work, what their rules should be, and so on. As discussions wore on, priorities were agreed and long lists of assorted thoughts were reduced to nuggets of collective thinking. Finally, the team agreed that their goal would be to finish in the Top Three, and their values would be Safe, Happy, Fast. They decided their temporary brand would be 'Team 7' as they were the seventh team to be announced at the Boat Show and it was considered to be a lucky number. A logo was designed and colours were chosen, T-shirts and caps were printed and the boat's hull and sails were temporarily branded. Under this early organisation, the team started to shape up.

The goal (to come in the top three) was slightly controversial as some team members felt quite strongly - especially in the world of competitive sports - that the goal should aim for the highest achievement; the gold medal, the number one, the finish in first place. However, with fifteen very disparate fee-paying people it was difficult to reach an agreement; some maintained that 'Top Three' was still inspirational but also more realistic and achievable. So Top Three it was, with some of the more competitive team members hanging on to 'First Place' as their personal goal. (*Team Stelmar* in fact finished 6th in the end, due to some bad luck in the Southern Ocean. They did win a leg and came third in another, and certainly had the potential to be in the top three, setting speed/distance records on four out of seven legs.)

The values: Safe, Happy, Fast, worked beautifully. They were simple and strong and there were only three to remember! Many companies come up with long wordy visions, too many goals and too many nondescript values, but 'to come in the top three' and to be 'Safe, Happy and Fast' kept us focused and clear on what we were about. We also measured ourselves against the values at least twice a week and took action if we were down on one or two. Companies should also be regularly checking and measuring against their goals, vision and values otherwise the words just become 'corporate wallpaper'. Ours were central to the way we worked and informed our decision making.

Supporters and sponsors also found it easy to hook onto our values and quote them in emails, or make banners and T-shirts out of them, or reiterate them back to us in times of trouble. The three words covered all they needed to cover. Safety was paramount and always came first. Happy and fast were almost interdependent. If we were fast we were happy, and if we were happy we tended to sail faster. Being happy meant taking pride and satisfaction in the way we were working, but also meant having lots of fun and laughter. Whether someone was competitive or in it just for the adventure, this value worked both ways. Being fast captured the performance ethos. Being fast meant remaining competitive every minute of the 24-hour days, staying focused, professional, efficient, effective and so on. This required in turn, great communication, thorough handovers between watches, trusting relationships, delegation, and all those elements of teamwork mentioned at the start of the Chapter.

So when new teams start from scratch, generating and agreeing a set of foundation blocks **together**, such as vision, values, goals and brand, it enables them to progress through the 'forming' stage and accelerate development towards high performance. Even in business, with established teams, or mixed teams of new and 'old' members, it is worth spending time reviewing and if necessary, tuning the existing foundations of the team to engender buy-in, understanding and commitment on a shared ownership basis.

Team Structure, Roles and Role Delineation

The other major piece of work we did before we left the UK was about who would take each role. There were numerous responsibilities both on deck and below deck that were necessary for the smooth running of the boat. These all had to be allocated to appropriate people, playing to their strengths. Roles on *Team Stelmar* included:

- Skipper (allocated by the Challenge Business)
- Navigator/1st Mate (second in charge)
- 2 x Watch Leaders (in charge of 'on watch' x 8 people)
- 2 x No.1 Bow (in charge of foredeck, liaising with snake-pit, calling sail trim)
- 2 x No. 2 Bow (second in charge foredeck)
- 2 x No. 3 Bow (manual labour)
- 2 x No. 4 Bow (manual labour, tying sheets)

- 2 x Snake-pit (23 ropes, 3 winches, liaising between helm/Watch Leader/foredeck)

- 2 x Cockpit (mainsheet, trimming foresails)

- Helm (three people) per watch

- Mother Duty (one duty per week)

- Communications

- Rules (interpretation, implementation)

- Engineer (engines, systems, water-maker, generator)

- Sail maintenance and repair

- Rigger (mast, standing & running rigging)

- Medic

- Media (daily logs, website, photography, video)

- Administration (passports, paperwork, log books, customs, etc.)

- Equipment, stores, acquisitions

- Food and nutrition

- New legger liaison

- Sponsor liaison

With at least 48 roles to be covered by a core crew of sixteen, most people had three or four responsibilities which kept them busy during the longer legs and in port. Alex for instance, was a Watch Leader, primary helm (especially on start lines) and the rigger. Paula's key job was in the snake-pit, and she was also responsible for communications, mother duty (one day a week) and new legger liaison.

Once each role had been determined by the Skipper, in close collaboration with his crew, it was then vital to maintain clear role delineation. For instance, with four people on the foredeck, everyone knew exactly what their part was in each manoeuvre – such as a sail change - and they did not help the person next to them unless they were explicitly asked to do so. So, if the Number Three bowman had finished his job and saw the Number Four struggling, he remained uninvolved unless asked to help. This left the Number Three free to concentrate on his own responsibilities, the Number Four to finish his job without interruption, and meant that everyone was personally accountable for their own area of expertise, though knowing when to ask for help. Kate or Paula in the snake-pit, with three winches and 23 ropes, would have a tried and tested sequence of procedures and knew their job inside out. They were thrown if another pair of hands came in to help every now and again. With the best of intentions in trying to help, 'naïve' team members were actually slowing down the work by 'meddling' in someone else's job. This was disciplined teamwork – clear roles in the first place, sticking to the delineation between roles and knowing when to ask for help.

Covering Mother Duty and Sickies

Inevitably, despite the best of team plans, there are always weaknesses and curve balls. In business, key members of staff have maternity leave, leaders are headhunted to rival organisations, people go off sick at a vital moment in a project. On *Team Stelmar*, as with the other boats, we rotated the role of 'Mother', which meant that one person from each watch would be cooking and cleaning below deck every 24 hours. This really upset the system. With a key team member in each position we had to reshuffle the crew every day and have a secondary (and therefore less able) person in one of the roles. We would also occasionally have crew off sick, often from broken or bruised ribs, banged heads and other physical injuries. (At sea, it is difficult to catch a contagious illness.) 'Off sick' included in our case, two separate medical evacuations on the Buenos Aires - Wellington leg (see pp 56-88) on which one crew member had already jumped ship, meaning we were three crew members down. We did the best we could in these circumstances.

Firstly, with injured crew, safety was our number one priority and so naturally they had time 'off' to recuperate. This often meant they would take on mother duties until they were better, which kept them below deck. It also meant that everyone on deck was fully fighting fit, so if there was a crisis, everyone was able to pull their weight without holding back because of a cracked rib or bad back. In our two medical evacuations, again safety came first so the decisions were 'no-brainers'. We got the crew member off as quickly as we could.

With the mother duty system we trained up a 'number two' for each and every job on deck. They worked closely with the primary job-holder, and shared knowledge and best practices all the time. During particularly crucial times, such as gybing the spinnaker sail, we learnt to get the 'mother' up on deck during the manoeuvre, even if that meant waking the off-watch mother to cover for a while. This gave us the 'A' team at critical times and was 'best for boat' despite not being best for the two mothers!

Finally, our hardest time was covering all the roles while three crew members down on the Southern Ocean leg. The first obvious move was to get the Navigator and Skipper more involved in the day-to-day deck jobs. We also redistributed the crews so that the two watches were more even and got the mother up on deck more often. Importantly, we also kept a close eye on the health, safety and happiness of the remaining crew as they had to work harder in extremely demanding and demotivating conditions. Motivation and rest became priorities.

So to summarise in covering for absence:

1. Health, safety and recuperation came first

2. 'Number twos' were trained up to cover every role

3. Primary and Secondary role-holders worked closely together and shared **all** knowledge

4. People were pulled out of 'routine' jobs (cooking/cleaning) temporarily to help in critical times

5. The 'leaders' became crew when numbers were down

6. Close attention was paid to general wellbeing and motivation during the toughest times

All these boat solutions are applicable to business situations, yet often only the first point is adhered to. Points four and five are ways of working 'out of the box', using an innovative approach to cover for absence or crises. Not only do these two points solve the situation, they also stir up a tired and complacent workforce by demonstrating adaptability and the fact that leaders can work the 'shop floor'.

New People (Leggers)

The standard Global Challenge practice was to have a core crew of 16 including the Skipper, and two new 'leggers' on each leg. These leggers often came from the sponsor companies and gave BP, Sony, Samsung, etc. a chance to get involved by having their employees win places on the race. It was easy to train and adopt the leggers for the early legs, but as the teams got more practised, the difference between a new legger and an old crew member became greater – in skill, but actually, more importantly, in attitude. On *Team Stelmar*, we started off with two leggers, but after Mike quit the boat in Buenos Aires, and our two medical evacuations on leg two, we then had to have four. This was quite a disadvantage for us as we had to prepare double the amount of new people – two on each watch – and get them fully racing fit as quickly as possible. A quarter of our team was new on each leg. We were very lucky to have such lovely and willing people as our leggers, but nonetheless, they were a big disruption, seven times, to the proficient working of the team.

There were stories about leggers who were not made to feel welcome on their boats, which must have made it very difficult for them. But we had decided to welcome and ease them in as much as possible – after all, the more confident they were in our company, the better they would perform. By the end of leg two, our boat was quite notorious, and thanks to the media coverage of our amazing recovery following our two medical evacuations, the new leggers were slightly in awe of joining Team Stelmar, about whom they had been reading in the *Daily Telegraph* over their breakfasts at home. One legger described it as walking onto a film set when he finally joined our boat, he had been reading about us so much and keenly following our progress on the website. So our leggers were understandably nervous about joining the team and worried about letting us down. We had to counteract those feelings as soon as possible.

Leggers would often arrive in Port about one to two weeks before the start of their leg. From Wellington to Sydney we had: Rona, Adrian, Karen and Nigel. From Sydney to Cape Town we had: Sarah, Ben, James and Rob. After Cape Town 'Flash' (one of our medical evacuees) rejoined us and so we had three leggers for the rest of the race. Our induction started by giving them a welcome committee right from the airport if we could. We would go there and hold up a big Team Stelmar banner. This made them feel immediately appreciated and part of the team. (Like sending a bouquet of flowers to the home of a new employee.) We would then socialise with them to break down any barriers and get to know them personally before the sailing training had to take precedence. We also ensured that: the Watch Leader and Skipper held one-to-one conversations with them; they were included in all the in-port meetings, socials and work parties; we trained them and went out sailing with them; we listened to their ideas and treated them with respect, as equals.

By the time the leg started, ideally our leggers were as primed and confident as possible. No-one felt the 'gap' between 'them and us' and we were back to being a very efficient team. In reality of course, the leggers did feel nervous and often sick at the start of each leg, and their training would continue during the race, but we did everything we could to fully integrate them as soon as possible without patronising them or being elitist.

Trust, Respect and Understanding

Paula:

When I joined Team Stelmar in July 2004 the rest of the crew had been training for four years and had worked and sailed together for seven months. I had only been on two short 'legger' training sails – on a different style of boat (the old 67' Challenge boats which had a different layout). On the 23rd July I met my team for the first time – and they met me. I wondered what they thought about getting someone like me at such short notice. I had no sailing experience. It must have been a blow for them to lose someone clued up so late[20] and then get a replacement who knew next to nothing.

On 23rd July I was due to go 'Race Training Sailing' with my team for five days on the 72' boat. I was very nervous and seasick and extremely conscious of my lack of experience. I felt like a bumbling idiot. I didn't know what things were called and even how to move effectively around the boat. It was like being new girl at school but in a racing environment with no skills. I hoped that I would not let them down. I hoped I wouldn't make a fool of myself. I hoped I wouldn't damage the boat or hurt anyone accidentally.

These were Paula's thoughts as she joined *Team Stelmar* for the first time, just two months before the start of the ten-month race. Her crew may have been discouraged to have such a late replacement; her crew were probably disappointed to get someone so inexperienced; but did they show it? Did they make her feel ill at ease and like an

---

[20] Sarah Lamb, pulled out of the team mid-July, 2½ months before race start. Paula was her replacement after a phone call confirming her place on the 19th July. Paula had 75 days to prepare, learn to sail, find £35,000, get fit, etc.

outsider? No. Did they welcome her profusely, look after her and teach her with patience and understanding? Yes. Paula knew this was a good team to join.

Paula:

*I remember the first day on **my** boat with **my** team. I was told that my job would probably be in the snake-pit for the race. This was worrying as it looked very confusing. Twenty-three ropes all with different names and different functions. Then an amazing thing happened which took me by surprise and boosted me no end. Phil, the Number One Bowman on my watch, asked me to winch him up the 95' mast. I replied that I couldn't because I didn't know what I was doing and said I would get someone else. He said, no, he wanted me to do it. If we were to work together for the rest of the race we needed to trust and rely on each other. He trusted me to do it. He trusted me with his life. He knew what teamwork was all about.*

Phil was an exceptional crew member on our boat. He was tough and uncompromising but deep down a real star player. By allowing Paula to winch him up the mast on her first day, he gave her confidence and respect and started a deep trust between them that was absolutely necessary for their future working relationship. During any sail manoeuvre on the race, it was Phil and Paula on their watch who co-ordinated the actions, and when things went wrong, that strength of relationship was even more important. Phil and Paula knew exactly what they were doing, what impact their actions had on the others and usually what to do when things went wrong. They understood each other very well, could read each other like a book, predict each other's actions and often communicated without words. Thanks to that first action of Phil's, they completely trusted, respected and understood each other which made for extremely high quality teamwork.

Lessons on Basic Teamwork from the Boat to the Boardroom

Team Vision

Have a positive team vision. Communicate it. Get the team's involvement to make it their vision, not just the leader's. Get everyone to 'see' it and 'feel' it and contribute to it. Think about having a team vision as well as the company one – to keep it pertinent and local, even if it is about visualisation more than creating a vision statement.

Team Goal – To be in the Top Three

Have clear, precise goals – but not too many. Make them stretchy, yet attainable, and SMART. Link them to the company vision and strategy.

Simple, Sticky Team Values – Safe, Happy, Fast

Live by the values, make decisions by the values, measure the team against the values. Don't have too many. Make sure they are genuine and part of the real life at work, not vague and not superficial hogwash. Back them up with measurements, behaviours, awards and actions. Reward and recognise role models.

Trust, Respect and Understanding

Find ways to stimulate trust, respect and understanding straight away. This should be one of the first team tasks. Team building is perfect for this.

Early Identity

Get the team in synch early through a unifying identity – be it clothing or a brand or a name. Early identity gets individuals feeling part of one team quickly; a mindset which then has a chance to become ingrained and habitual for when it really matters. Early identity also helps outsiders looking in see a unified team.

Clear Role Delineation

Have a clean team structure with specific roles. Ensure there is clear understanding about both of these before defining exact areas of responsibility and disciplined role delineation.

Proactive Cover

Proactively arrange cover for potential gaps in the team. Share knowledge, have people shadow each other, buddy-up experts with 'disciples'. In times of heavy workload, think about using people in 'routine jobs' or the leaders to bolster the team.

Quick Inclusion of 'Leggers' (new people)

Make it easy for new people to fit in. Welcome them genuinely and totally, without patronising or prejudice. Think about how you can get them confidently performing and effectively contributing as soon as possible. Be aware of cliques and internal jargon. Think about how culturally exclusive the team is – what is the perception from outside of the team?

Basic Teamwork Exercises

Basic Teamwork Scenario 1: A New Team

- Your Global Challenge team has been announced at the London Boat Show
- 15 core crew and a Skipper who don't know each other.
- It is ten months before race start.
- The race itself is ten months long.
- It is January 2004; the race starts on the 3rd October from Portsmouth.
- The crew live all over the UK, with one living on the boat in Southampton, and one in Holland.
- Most of the crew work full-time.
- The Skipper works for the Global Challenge Business.

1. What would you do to effectively build and develop a high performance team *pre-race*?
2. What would you do to effectively develop the team further *during the race*?
3. Would you do anything post-race?
4. What factors would you have to take into account?
5. List all the actions and considerations for a 20+ month campaign.
6. What can you apply from this to your workplace?

Basic Teamwork Scenario 2: Tornado!

- Quite near the Bermuda Triangle.
- It is 'Happy Hour'; both watches are on deck for one hour, Sunday, 1800 hours Local Time
- Fancy Dress: 'Vicars and Tarts'!
- Close racing with other boats nearby

- Dutchman Rob is doing a talk on the Bermuda Triangle, talking about Flight 19 and USS Cyclops[21]

- The talk gets to the point where Rob surmises that so many craft have disappeared in the area because of freaky weather conditions/disturbances in the sea bed

- As he is explaining this theory we are pointing behind him at a waterspout (tornado at sea) that has just appeared on the horizon

- Fascinated we watch...

- It is five miles away to port

- Ten minutes later, Alex is staring at an area of unsettled water 200 metres away. He exclaims: "Look there's fish feeding!"

- Sharon says: "No, look up", and there is a dark, spiralling funnel of cloud coming down from the sky, and a twisting funnel of water going up to meet it – another waterspout to starboard, just 200 metres away

1. What factors do you need to take into account in the next 24 hours?

2. What actions do you take as a team in the next 24 hours?

3. In what order do you take them? What are your priorities?

4. What can you apply from this to your workplace?

Basic Teamwork Scenario 3: New Leggers on Board

- The Global Challenge standard is two new leggers per leg per boat

[21] Five aircraft and fourteen airmen went missing on Flight 19. USS Cyclops vanished in March 1918 with 309 men on board.

- Due to our two medical evacuations and someone quitting, we had four new leggers join us for two of the legs

- The new leggers had a varied amount of sailing experience and had been on one or two 'legger training sails' with the Challenge Business on the old 67' boats

- They were nervous about joining the team – a team that was notorious back home for surviving their two medical evacuations in the Southern Ocean

- New leggers often arrived about one week to ten days before the start of the leg

1. What considerations do you have with new leggers joining?

2. What actions do you take as a team to integrate them?

3. What can you apply from this to your workplace?

Basic Teamwork Scenario 4: St Kats

- The first public appearance for the whole fleet was in London on 1st May 2004

- The boats had to sail up from Plymouth, along the South Coast and up the River Thames into St Katherine's Dock

- They were scheduled to arrive at Tower Bridge at 1100, then 'pose' alongside *HMS Belfast* for photos, before docking in St Katherine's in the heart of London

- St Katherine's Dock is entered through a narrow lock which could hold four Challenge boats at a time

- Once in St Katherine's, the boats and crew stayed for three 'open days' including a Bank Holiday Monday

- The journey up the coast to the Thames was rough and difficult; many crew were sick and there were some small accidents

- As the boats came towards Tower Bridge it was quite foggy

- This excursion was designed as a PR and Press opportunity, and to include London in the build-up to the race

- It also allowed the public, sponsors, family and friends to come and visit the boats and the teams, chat to the crew and take a tour above and below decks

1. How would you prepare for this trip?

2. What can you apply from this to your workplace?

Actual events

Here is what Team Stelmar actually did in the scenarios – not necessarily the right course of action, just the action we took in the circumstances.

Basic Teamwork Scenario 1: A new team

PRE-RACE

- Given white CREW T-shirts to put on straight away, identifying and branding us as one team and creating a standout against the other teams
- Went straight out for a team meal to get to know each other
- Began basic logistical organisation
- Sharing contact details, locations and work information
- Sharing skill and experience information
- Rough pre-race job allocation
- Held team meetings
- Got to know each other a lot more
- Had fitness sessions including early morning runs and touch rugby
- Worked out team identity/brand
- Worked out team goal, values and boat rules
- Allocated more specific areas of responsibility
- Worked out boat strategy
- Shared knowledge and agreed tactics
- Went sailing:
- Practised, practised, practised
- Debriefed and adapted
- Experimented with sail plans in different conditions

- Practised the start line

- Tried people out for different jobs

- Designed a team website

- Produced branded team T-shirts, caps and mugs for fundraising

- Got the boat rebranded

- Started to fundraise individually and as a team

- Clive – the Skipper. Co-ordinated the team, liaised with Global Challenge Business, potential sponsors, other stakeholders and the media. Went on leadership training

- Kate – took on 'team kit', researched technical clothing, personal sailing equipment and tried to get as much free, sponsored kit as possible. Also team Physio

- Ruth – the medic. Reviewed everyone's personal medical questionnaires and had 1-2-1 conversations with us all. Went on first-aid-at-sea training. Got familiar with the comprehensive boat medical kits. Also responsible for food – researched and tried out various expedition foods, ordered all food, wrote recipe book

- Alex – the rigger. Went to Plymouth where the boats were being refitted to fit all the lines and running rigging

- Nicko – the Navigator. Consulted experts on routes, strategies, weather systems, tides, currents, etc. Began to develop boat-specific software to inform decision making. Ran the team website and team emails

- Phil – the engineer. Was sent on various courses with the engine and generator manufacturers. Learnt about the onboard systems from Challenge Business

- Vale – the Skipper's wife. Co-ordinated the support team, analysed everyone's personal fitness and designed a training regime

- Richard – produced a team newsletter once a month and contributed heavily to the team website, keeping supporters up to date

- Sue – co-ordinated the VIP sailing (we were all obliged to take part in six each, either before, after or during the race)

- All – went to team meetings, took part in team conference calls every Monday, participated in team builds, training sails and sea survival courses

- Personally everyone got as fit as they could – especially upper body strength; sailed as much as they could and learned as much as they could

- Everyone also had personal admin: saving money; paying for the race (£30k); sorting passports and visas; renting or selling houses; arranging communications with family and friends; writing wills; arranging insurance; having medical and fitness examinations; filling out forms; sorting out bill payments and bank account access; contributing to the team website and newsletters; labelling all personal kit; etc.

- Everyone chose a 'buddy' they knew they could go to for personal support

- July – Skipper announced everyone's roles

- August – food weighed, sorted and vacuum-packed over 10,000 meals

- Early September - sponsor announced just one month before the race:

- Rebranded everything, including the boat hull and sails

- Held an official boat-naming ceremony

- Met the sponsors and got to understand each other
- Took the sponsors sailing
- Researched the sponsors' company
- Late September, one week before race start:
- Everyone left home to live and work on the boat full-time
- Various parties, meetings and briefings
- Final check on all equipment, clothing, rigging, sails, engine, etc.
- Loading and careful packing of all kit, food, sails, books and charts
- Shopping for last items (chinagraph pencils, insulation tape, etc.)
- Final training and practice sails
- Safety checks and RORC[22] inspections
- Tactical consultancy on first leg
- Cleaned and polished whole boat inside and out
- Everyone signed-on and tested the satellite email system
- Downloaded charts, weather forecasts and computer programs
- Welcome and integration of first two leggers
- Everyone signed the logbook as an official document
- Everyone signed a document, telling Challenge Business whether they wanted to hear about family emergencies while at sea

---

[22] Royal Ocean Racing Club

DURING RACE

- Briefed and debriefed all the time – aiming for continuous improvement
- Measured ourselves constantly against goal, strategy, route and values
- Continued training
- In port
- Held team meetings for a long debrief, reviewing actions and deciding on improvements
- Held further team builds and fitness sessions
- Thanked departing leggers, and welcomed and trained new ones
- 1-2-1s held between Watch Leader and their watch, and the Skipper with everyone
- Unloaded and cleaned whole boat and all clothes
- Checked and repaired all equipment, sails and rigging
- VIP sailing trips
- School visits
- Various meetings, briefings, etc.
- Time off
- Admin and paperwork, etc.
- Physio, massages, fitness, nutrition, doctor and dentist appointments
- Newsletters, emails and website updates for supporter and fan base
- Reviewed charts, route, weather, leg strategy
- Agreed and communicated tactics
- Attended any race protest hearings
- Celebrated! Parties and Award Ceremonies

POST-RACE

- Stayed in touch
- Reunion once a year

Basic Teamwork Scenario 2: Tornado!

- Kept one person on vigil
- Brought down the sails and tied the mainsail to the boom
- Removed all loose objects to below decks
- Got everyone possible below deck
- Skipper, helm and person on 'Tornado Watch' only left on deck. All clipped on
- (One person popped up to video for a bit – had to be done for post-race glory!)
- Radioed the other boats nearby to warn them
- Luckily we were not hit directly, but over the next 24 hours we kept a vigil with binoculars as more than one tornado/waterspout usually appears
- We saw five waterspouts
- **Basic Teamwork Scenario 3: New Leggers on Board**
- Genuine welcome and full integration with the established team
- Welcome committee at airport
- Socials to get to know them as people and break down barriers
- 1-2-1 with Watch Leader and Skipper to understand their motivations, feelings and past experience and explain where we were at as a team
- Decision on the role they would have

- Shadowing who they would be working most closely with/someone from the other watch who was doing the same job

- Training

- Sailing

- Including them in meetings, parties, talks, visits, etc.

- Buddying them with someone of their choice

- Onboard support, help and further training

- Thanks and decent goodbye

- Continued to stay in touch through rest of race

- Invited to reunions as part of the team

Basic Teamwork Scenario 4: St Kats

- Whole team available to take part

- Checked boat ready as first trip to sea since refit

- Made sure all kit was on board

- Checked charts and route

- Weather planning

- (Stopover in Ramsgate to pick up another crew member and sort out a minor medical emergency - a broken contact lens in Newton's eye)

- Co-ordinated with the other yachts for the arrival in London

- Got changed into branded shore kit for the arrival

- Cleaned and tidied boat before arrival

- While waiting in the lock at St Katherine's Marina London, the Skipper announced each team member as they came up on deck

- The crew wore full team uniform for all three days

- Welcomed as many people as possible on board for tours
- Sold branded mugs and shirts to raise crew funds

Chapter 6. Advanced Teamwork

Definition

IN THE PREVIOUS CHAPTER WE covered the fundamentals of teamwork. This Chapter looks at the further development of teams as they moved into 'high performance'. One theory regarding the evolutionary cycle of teams, suggests that teams evolve from forming to storming to norming to performing; in our point of view from the race, we then moved on to *high-performing*. High-performing teams are not just functioning; they are functioning consistently successfully, efficiently, effectively and elegantly. They are top of their game - like the gold-medal-winning Jamaican men's relay team in the 2008 Beijing Olympics rather than both the baton dropping US relay teams. Like the Team GB cycling, sailing or rowing teams who between them won 14 golds; 26 Olympic medals in total.

In high-performing teams there is deepening synergy, spontaneous interactions and a surpassing of expectations and results. Great teams transcend the need to have everything spelled out in detail. They master processes. They are open to continuous improvement. They embrace challenges, opportunities and constructive criticism. They achieve goals but then can change goals. Hands-on leadership becomes redundant. Talents mesh, individuals collaborate unselfishly and amazing results are achieved. There is a deep sense of trust and loyalty, confidence and belief.

These summarise the behaviours and attitudes of Team Stelmar by the end of the race.

Advanced Teamwork Development in the Global Challenge

All 12 teams in the 2004/5 yacht race started on a level playing field. The crew members were distributed as evenly as possible across the 12 boats, none of the skippers had led a crew in a round the world yacht race before, and all the boats were exactly the same – down to the laser-cut steel hulls and central supply of equipment, rigging and sails. The main differences between the teams were the people. The difference between coming first or last was in their teamwork. Some teams gelled more quickly than others, some teams disintegrated a little mid-race and most teams went from strength to strength, learning and developing as the race progressed. Eighteen diverse people started the race on each boat; 12 cohesive teams finished ten months later. Team Stelmar in particular went from strength to strength, evolving from a good team to a great team.

On leg two of the race, Team Stelmar suffered from two separate medical evacuations in the Southern Ocean, (see pp 56-88) ending up four crew down, two weeks and 2,000 miles behind the other boats and battling for 52 days in the hostile, freezing 'furious fifties'[23]. Not only did the team have to suspend racing and supervise both medical evacuations, but they then had to muster the determination, courage and motivation to sail off again twice and continue with fighting spirit when the rest of the fleet had left them far behind and the sensible option was to retire. The other boats sailed into Wellington weeks before *Team Stelmar* and the crews were sightseeing around New Zealand when the *Team Stelmar* crew arrived, at two o'clock in the morning of the 21st January, battle weary but triumphant after 52 days at sea.

Team Stelmar were already a good crew, functioning reasonably well, before this disastrous leg of the race. The quality of their teamwork was evolving around the same pace

---

[23] The 'roaring forties', 'furious fifties' and 'screaming sixties' reference the 40–60 degree latitudes in the Southern Ocean, but also the wind strength in knots and the typical height of the waves in feet.

as the other eleven crews. On leg one they were learning more about each other, debriefing and reviewing their systems, improving processes and communications. However, what they went through on leg two accelerated their development and drove the quality of their interactions beyond the other teams. They had 'been there, seen it, done it and literally got the T-shirt' and now they were well set to rise higher. In actuality, *Team Stelmar* accumulated the most points – bar the winning boat *BG* - out of all the fleet for the rest of the race.

The fact is, teams who successfully handle serious adversity and come out the other side wiser and brighter, are catapulted forward in their development. They have learned so much more about themselves and the environment in which they work; they have pushed boundaries and questioned credos; gained great confidence in themselves and their peers and experienced such tough extremes that challenges afterwards seem within their capabilities. After **three** extra weeks in the Southern Ocean, having completed two medical evacuations – one against the armed authorities of Chile – going back into the Southern Ocean on leg four, from Sydney to Cape Town, was less foreboding for them. While the other teams were apprehensive about re-entering the Southern Ocean, Team Stelmar were looking forward to it – their attitude was: 'bring it on!'

By leg seven - the last leg from La Rochelle to Portsmouth - Team Stelmar's teamwork was almost perfect (there is always room for improvement). The systems were running smoothly; communication was effective; actions intuitive; teamwork instinctive; meetings and leadership superfluous. They had been through 'hell and high water' together and, as a result, were an extremely high- performing team at the end of the race. The other crews were no doubt also significantly practised after completing the Global Challenge, but there was nothing like the extreme highs and lows that Team Stelmar experienced to push them into excellence.

Advanced Teamwork from Boat to Boardroom

Admittedly, it is a rare workplace that provides such taxing circumstances as the Global Challenge in which teams can be pushed to develop. There are certainly thousands of organisational teams who have to work through very tough situations (9/11 fire-fighters, police and paramedics) or work extremely effectively under pressure (e.g. in operating theatres). There are also the millions of teams in workplaces everywhere who face day-to-day challenges and have to use advanced disciplines in order to work efficiently together. The sooner these teams can evolve through the early stages of orientation and develop into high-performing teams the better. The company benefits from effective teamwork, of course, but the teams and individuals also benefit from a sense of pride and job satisfaction that goes beyond financial remuneration.

The Global Challenge teams inevitably developed quickly. They were presented with training scenarios and had numerous real situations to work through right from the start; so learning and development were swift. In the typical workplace however, team development is often much slower, to the detriment of company progress and employee motivation. Team development in itself can often be neglected yet there are many productive techniques and actions that can be taken to accelerate team 'building'. There are also plentiful lessons that can be learned from other worlds where teamwork is of the highest standard, such as in sport, the armed forces or extreme challenges. 'Experiential learning' is one way that a team can develop quickly in pressure cooker situations that intensify and speed up the learning and lots of companies provide these nowadays - from fire-fighting to igloo-building. There are many less extreme ways of developing teams too, such as getting everyone naked – well, metaphorically anyway.

Nakedness!

On the Global Challenge race many people were seasick. Some of the world's best sailors are seasick (Peter Blake[24], for example). Being sick is unpleasant and embarrassing but a very human, natural thing to do.

Sailing is a great leveller; it breaks down hierarchies, removes labels and barriers and equalises people.

On our boat we had a 59-year-old Director of Scottish Widows with a cut-glass accent, but when he was on the winch in his yellow drysuit, he looked and behaved like everyone else.

We also had an awesome guy called Phil who worked the foredeck. He had extremely high standards and expected the same of everyone else. He was inspiring but also quite intimidating. When he was on mother duty, he used to put on some yellow marigolds. Those washing-up gloves turned Phil into an equal.

Ruth, our esteemed medic, won admiration for the way she handled our various medical ailments. But when she was ill and we had to look after her, she somehow became less super-human.

One of our sponsors was called Adrian and he was the owner-director of a very successful company. We could have treated him like royalty; after all, he was paying in part for our trip. Instead he had to muck in with the rest of us – including cooking and serving up our meals.

---

[24] Sir Peter James Blake, KBE (October 1, 1948–December 6, 2001) was a New Zealand yachtsman who led his country to two successive *America's Cup* victories. He previously won the Whitbread Round the World Race in 1989, and the Jules Verne Trophy in 1994 by setting the fastest time around the world of 74 days 22 hours 17 minutes 22 seconds on catamaran *Enza*. He was sick at the start of every leg. two successive *America*'s *Cup* victories. He previously won the Whitbread Round the World Race in 1989, and the Jules Verne Trophy in 1994 by setting the fastest time around the world of 74 days 22 hours 17 minutes 22 seconds on catamaran *Enza*. He was sick at the start of every leg.

Back to being sick. Forget the clothes, the labels, the public schooling, the job title, when someone is being sick you cannot help but feel for them and treat them as fellow human beings. Sickness strips people down to their vulnerable, 'naked', true selves. It's not nice, but it is human. Quite often, when we are booked for a corporate sailing event we get asked about seasickness. While we can sympathise that it is a horrible thought to be sick in front of colleagues, there is nothing better for breaking down barriers or hierarchies and bonding the team! Seasickness is not life-threatening; it is uncomfortable and perhaps slightly embarrassing. It is a natural, understandable reaction in the circumstances with which we can sympathise, comfort and sometimes (depending on the team) actually laugh about.

During a physical challenge, participants often bare their souls and reveal their true feelings - pain, fear, anger, tiredness. This is when individuals within teams really stick together and bond for life. We empathise, support and look after each other. The physical comfort alone breaks down barriers. It is very difficult to go back to aloof attitudes and superficial hierarchies after such experiences. So get your employees and leaders naked somehow! Take them to the edge of their comfort zone, do physical challenges with them, get them to talk about their fears and hopes...

Individual 'I' versus Team 'We'

The team is more important than the individual in high-performing teams.

Towards the end of the race Stelmar team members knew they made a valid contribution to the team – they understood they were cogs in a fabulous machine, but they also knew they were personally appreciated and independently responsible for their part of the whole. The team *was* more important than the individual and the individuals selflessly accepted that, knowing that they were still significant players.

At a talk given by David Whitaker OBE[25], he described the difference between a new and an established team as follows:

If you tell someone in a new team that the team is more important than the individual, then the individual will not be happy and think "what about me?"

If you tell someone in an established team that the team is more important than the individual, then the individual will think, "well, yes of course", because they know they can be an individual within that team. Mavericks, for example, can be carried within good teams.

Great teams work so well that the individual team members do not feel swallowed up, insignificant or invisible but very much important players, with their own unique personalities, skills and expertise which are appreciated and valuable to the team's success.

Paula:

Believing I was an exclusive individual when I joined Team Stelmar, I hated all the conformity - the marching to the beat of the drum wearing team uniforms for team photos. The 'me' in me rebelled. I resented the 'teaminess' of the team. However, by the end of the race, I was proud to be part of my team. I was part of the great Team Stelmar.

Psychometric tests often evaluate people in terms of their team player personalities – how they fit into the whole team make-up. People can be classified as plants, shapers or ENTPs for example[26]. This analysis enables the team to understand the people types within the team and how natural preferences and styles can work best together. An individual's attributes ideally complement those of the rest of the team and add to the strength of the unit. The whole becomes greater than the sum of the parts. The team 'we' is

---

[25] Coach to Team GB hockey team when they won gold medal at the Seoul Olympics 1988
[26] See Belbin and Myers Briggs. ENTP = Extrovert Intuition Think Perceive

greater than all of the individual 'me's; though unlike the over-used saying, there **is** an 'I' in team. It's about achieving synergy.

Synergy is the highest activity of life; it creates new untapped alternatives; it values and exploits the mental, emotional and psychological differences between people.[27]

Working to People's Strengths

In personality profiling, there is no such thing as a weak or useless personality type. All types are equally valuable because they are complementary; working in unison with all the other personality types to create a balanced, fully-resourced team. Once a team is complete, the key is then to put the right type into the right role. There is no point in putting a 'completer-finisher' in an entrepreneurial role, or a 'plant' (creative) in to finish off a project, this would cause frustration and malfunction within the team.

On *Team Stelmar* there were the fundamental roles to fill - such as Navigator and Medic - but also less obvious ones such as: communications, media, motivation, quality control, etc. Filling the functional jobs required care, thought and attention to people's skills and experiences, but personalities were also taken into account. Some roles for instance were extremely physically demanding, requiring great physical and mental tenacity and courage. Another role – in the snake-pit – required good communication skills (it was in the middle of the boat liaising with the foredeck and cockpit) and multi-tasking dexterity. So the actual job expertise was important, but the more subtle personal skills were equally essential – if not more so; *expertise can be taught, attitude cannot. Over* the course of a competitive, ten-month long yacht race, the right personalities (and attitudes) had to be in the right jobs.

In the workplace people are often recruited or promoted because of their expertise and knowledge but not necessarily

---

[27] Stephen Covey: 7 Habits

because of their attitude or *potential*. On *Team Stelmar* one of the Watch Leaders – Mike - was appointed because he had a maturity of years and a reasonable amount of sailing experience. However, Mike, with a fair amount of technical knowledge, was not such a good people manager. On only the first leg, his watch deteriorated under his management and, disappointed with his performance, Mike walked off the team at the first stopover. Alex on the other hand, who was a less 'obvious' candidate to Clive for Watch Leader, definitely had the qualities required to take over the dysfunctional team. He was easygoing, supportive and fun but also had huge technical expertise to make the right decisions on deck. The watch blossomed again under his appropriate leadership.

Placing the right people in the right roles and working to people's strengths (actual and emotional) is an ideal scenario. Employees should be selected on a 'skill + personality' basis and careful attention should be made to their *potential* once trained, rather than to their immediate task-based expertise. Often in the right conditions and with the right coaching, strengths can be nurtured to fill the gap between current and future capabilities. Coaching treats people like acorns; with encouragement the 'oaktreeness' within can grow.

On *Team Stelmar*, Alex effortlessly assumed the mantle of Watch Leader, Paula grew into the communications guru and Phil rose to the challenge of quality control. The potential was within them and there was no glass ceiling to prevent their growth. People were encouraged to work to their strengths. Sue, a ballet dancer, had excellent balance and was never sick; she became the team lynchpin in rough weather. Julian was a project manager with an eye for detail; he was in charge of passports and customs entry administration. Sarah, one of our leggers, was a slip of a girl with huge determination and a wiry strength; she ended up putting the boys to shame on the foredeck.

The strengths of the wider, non-sailing team were harnessed too. The Skipper's wife, Valeria, was a personal fitness trainer so she designed our physical training regime. Wives Peggy and Ciara came to every port and their practical skills were a huge benefit in the food packing. Everyone had their part to play, and that part played to their strengths.

Individual Responsibility

In dysfunctional teams, with poor accountability and vague role delineation, team members can duck down and become invisible in the crowd, getting away with minimum effort and minimum responsibility. There are poor employers who cannot keep track of, let alone motivate and coach, their employees. There are companies who don't even know how many people work for them at any given time. There are employees who care nothing about their jobs so long as they take home some wages at the end of the week. These people are costly passengers (see next section).

In the Global Challenge we were all **paying** passengers who had made great sacrifices to get on the race, which included paying £26,750 for each place, plus insurance and living costs etc. It was in our vested interest to participate wholeheartedly and to the best of our abilities. We were not disengaged employees. However, we were *slightly* disengaged at first. Many of us were used to being part of a hierarchical organisation prior to the race, answerable to line managers and corporate demands. We were generally 'trained' to respond - respond effectively - but respond nonetheless. We lacked the belief and power to personally take on the corporation that was the Challenge Business, the race committee, the Skipper and the sponsor. We felt dependent on the 'mother ship' for our actions and decision making, lacking complete personal responsibility.

However, as the race progressed and the team developed, our individual sense of ownership, accountability and responsibility grew. Take, for example, personal health and hygiene. As team members we felt rather institutionalised initially. We neglected to look after ourselves and allowed ourselves to dehydrate, get ill, lose sleep or become undernourished. We assumed the team, or the medic, or the management would take responsibility and look after us. But this was naïve. We realised that advanced teamwork required a mature attitude and the only person responsible was ourselves. If we failed to drink enough water one day or stayed up too long reading and neglected vital sleep, we not only had ourselves to blame but were letting down the team and that was not acceptable.

How many employees genuinely feel accountable and act 100% responsibly? Ten percent, if that? What can be done to encourage greater self-responsibility?

Trust. Genuine delegation. Coaching.

No Passengers

There is a management analogy about *having the right people on the bus* (or the boat!*)*. Assuming that the bus represents the team or the company, then everyone has to justify their seat on the bus and there should be no passengers. If there are passengers (or joyriders) then it is the responsibility of the management to 'manage them up or manage them out'; in other words, do something about it. In *Good to Great*, Jim Collins describes the bus analogy as follows:

[Executives say]...., in essence, "Look, I don't really know where we should take this bus. But I know this much: If we get the right people on the bus, the right people in the right seats, and the wrong people off the bus, then we'll figure out how to take it someplace great.

On a boat, thousands of miles away from land, it is very difficult to manage people off! As much as we wanted to occasionally, we could not force crew members to walk the plank! It was also almost impossible to lose ineffective crew in port – they were, after all, fee-paying 'customers' of the Global Challenge. On board, it was hard to manage people *up*, because in such close confines, any management had to be delicate for fear of escalating the issue. If taken badly, there was nowhere for an angry or upset person to go. But we did not want to tolerate passengers on our boat. They not only fail to perform their role and let the side down, but they also send the wrong message to the rest of the team – that inappropriate behaviour is tolerated and the leadership is ineffective at performance management.

We did have a passenger or two on our boat and they were tricky to handle for the reasons previously mentioned. We really had to do the best we could to manage the *whole* situation, not just the person involved. Any clumsy management of just the individual and the fuse could have been lit, which is not great on a 72' boat at sea for five weeks. So the Skipper and Watch Leaders had their work cut out in delicate negotiations with the individuals involved as well as placating the rest of the crew. Maybe walking the plank was not such a bad option!

Influence

On a boat, if you pull a rope something happens at the other end of it. In working in the cockpit or the snake-pit, crew had to be very aware of what was happening at the other end of their actions – for every action there was an equal and opposite reaction. The power in the ropes was massive in strong winds and they could potentially cause serious harm to the boat or the crew if they were not handled correctly, which included 'operator error'. For instance, in tacking the boat, two people release the two working foresail sheets (ropes) and two or four people winch them in the other side. If one sheet is released too quickly and the opposite side doesn't wind it in fast enough then there is an 18mm thick rope flailing violently around the foredeck where potentially one or two crew are working. On *Team Stelmar* we had some nasty accidents where rope severely whiplashed or constricted around people's torsos. To avoid this we had to be very vigilant and aware of the impact our actions had on the rest of the boat.

This physical impact was reflected in the emotional impact we had on others, something we also had to be aware of. In high-performing teams, team members are so close-knit that one person's attitude or emotions can easily affect the team's mood. Ideally all the team members (not just the leader) are emotionally intelligent; conscious of their own attitudes, feelings, body language and expressions at all times and the effect they have on the team. The shadows cast by leaders are very influential, but the shadows cast by high-performing team members can also have a significant influence:

You don't have to be a 'person of influence' to be influential. In fact, the most influential people in my life are probably not even aware of the things they've taught me.[28]

We knew each other so well on the boat we could read each other like a book. The feelings of one watch member could impact the rest of the watch because we lived in each other's pockets. We exerted subconscious influence upon each other.

Phil Beck was a powerful role model with his extremely high standards; serious, professional discipline; determination; strength and commitment. There is no doubt that he lifted the rest of the crew to his heights by showing the way and demonstrating that by really going for it and giving it 100% then life was better, the boat was more competitive and a sense of great satisfaction and pride was achievable. The most casual or reluctant crew members were inspired by Phil and raised their game as a result of his influence.

Similarly, in the workplace a team can be lifted by the inspiring behaviours of influential individuals – not only the

---

[28] Scott Adams is the creator of the Dilbert comic strip and the author of several business commentaries, social satires and experimental philosophy books.

leaders. Unfortunately, the opposite can also be true. One rotten apple in the barrel can cause widespread decay, having a significantly negative impact on the morale or commitment of those around. In high-performing teams therefore, it is vital that team members are emotionally intelligent and able to assess and manage their influence; turning negativity into constructive criticism; issues into problem-solving opportunities and infecting others with enthusiasm and excitement when they are on a roll. How to win friends and influence people? Be positive and genuine.

Identity/Brand

Wearing the same shirts doesn't make you a team[29]

Before Team Stelmar had a sponsor we called ourselves 'Team 7'. We were the seventh team to be announced at the London Boat Show and it was a lucky number. This early identification of the team united us under one banner, but we were a long way from being a high-performing team at this stage.

By the time we arrived in Cape Town, after five legs of the race, we had taken our identity to an extreme level. Most of us, including the Skipper, went to a hairdresser in Cape Town, had our hair bleached white with a neon-blue stripe dyed on one side to match our sponsor's colours. The visual impact was stunning. The external perception of our commitment was undeniable. The other teams, the race committee and the supporters and sponsors thought we were mad, but admired us for it all the same. This was not only an extreme example of our commitment to the team, but actually a genuine sign of our inward loyalty. We felt blue and white through and through. We were proud, loyal, committed 'Stelmarites'. We were fiercely protective of who we were and what we stood for. We became tribal. Think Braveheart.

---

[29] 'Creating the High Performance Team' *Buchholz and Roth.*

'Wearing the same shirts does not make you a team', but it does help to kick-start the feel of one team-ness. Agreeing a team identity in the early days is a good start. Exploring that deeply is the next step. Teams can analyse what they stand for – like any brand. Looking at their cultural ethos; what they believe in and aspire to be; what traits they are collectively known for; how they are perceived by external teams or customers; what their values are. If leaders can encourage teams to take on a deeper identity beyond the external symbols of uniform or hairstyles then the unifying behaviours, beliefs and attitudes become second nature. A biker in black leather sitting on a Harley isn't necessarily a Hells Angel, unless they think, feel, act, speak, behave and believe like a Hells Angel.

Lessons on Advanced Teamwork from the Boat to the Boardroom

Put the Team Through It

The more the team experiences, the swifter they develop and the more capable they will become. Push them. Stretch them. Send them on tough team builds and experiential learning challenges to accelerate their growth.

Get 'Naked'

Break down barriers and allow genuine human connections to be made, building trusting relationships and improving communication. Breaking down barriers to reveal the natural 'naked' person beneath the labels and layers can be started with safe and simple activities such as socialising, sharing past work successes or admitting mistakes.

Recruit the Right Attitudes

Skills can be learned; attitudes run deeper. 'Getting the right people on the boat and in the right positions' is critical to achieving team excellence. Recruit personalities and attitudes as well as skills and experience. Recruit potential and then...

Coach for Growth

Once you have the right people with amazing attitudes on the boat, coach the 'oaktreeness' out. Support and encourage people to grow through coaching to reach their full potential.

Personal Responsibility

In great teams, everyone is 100% responsible, there is no leaning on the management or deferring to others.

No Passengers

Passengers should not be tolerated on great teams. They should be helped to contribute fully by finding the cause of their disengagement and then collaboratively finding solutions. If this fails, then passengers should get off the bus.

Emotional Intelligence

All members in advanced teams should have emotional intelligence, not just the leaders. They should be self-aware and responsible, able to assess and manage their emotions and influence over others.

Identity Through and Through

Find the team's 'brand' – not only the physical, external identity but also the implicit, deeply-held values and ethos. Get the team to live and breathe its brand. Go tribal.

Advanced Teamwork Exercises

Advanced Teamwork Scenario 1: The Eve of Start Day

- It is the 2nd October 2004, 19:00 hours – the night before start day

- The team is staying in a hostel in Southsea

- The town is brimming with visitors, supporters, friends, family and the media

- The crew is nervous, excited and almost sick with anticipation

- Everyone knows they are about to embark on the single biggest challenge they will probably ever face in all their lives, leaving their loved ones behind to enter dangerous territory for nearly a year

- The weather forecast for start day is gale force 7–9 with winds expected up to 40 knots

- The race start is 19 hours away at 14:00 hours on the 3rd

- The actual start is critical – at the fire of the cannon by Princess Anne, all 12 heavy, powerful, steel-hulled yachts will jostle for position along the start line

- The world will be watching to see which yacht crosses the line first and takes the lead

Exercise. To achieve advanced teamwork...

1. What factors do you need to take into account in those 19 hours?

2. What actions do you take as a team in those 19 hours?

3. What can you apply from this to your workplace?

Advanced Teamwork Scenario 2: Sydney Debrief

- It is the 3rd leg of the race

- *Team Stelmar* finishes in 8th place; we arrive in Sydney seconds behind *Sark* and just minutes behind *Samsung*

- We are all disappointed, especially after the sweet taste of success when we were in first place just 24 hours earlier

- We felt that 8th place did not reflect our skills and effort

- We had been determined to do so much better after our 8th place (9th after our penalty) on the first leg and 11th place (due to two medical evacuations) on the last leg

- We held a team debrief in a local conference room

- We were all in bad moods; we didn't want to finish that low again

Exercise:

1. How should the team debrief be conducted?

2. What sorts of things should be reviewed?

3. What should be said to the next four leggers about our performance to date?

4. What can you apply from this to your workplace?

Advanced Teamwork Scenario 3: Someone not Pulling their Weight

- It is the 2nd leg of the race

- The team is in the Southern Ocean after 28 days at sea with about one month's sailing to go

- They have had two medical evacuations and are three crew members down, 2,500 miles behind the rest of the fleet

- One of the remaining crew members claims to be clinically depressed

- They take to their bunk frequently to read whilst the other five struggle on watch in freezing storms, working hard to compensate

- They walk off deck when they want to

- They are uncommunicative, difficult and moody

- The watch work very hard in dangerous and uncompromising conditions, knowing that the depressed crew member is tucked up in their bunk and reading a book, day after day...

- This is the last straw for a team who have suffered so much recently

Exercise:

1. What do you do?

2. What can you apply from this to your workplace?

Advanced Teamwork Scenario 4: Last Leg

- It is the 7th and last leg of the whole race, from La Rochelle (France) to Portsmouth

- We have been competitively racing for nearly ten months

- We have three new leggers

- The leg is only three days long

- We start at 14:00 UTC on the 13th July 2005

- On the 14th July it is Paula's birthday

- At 15:30 local time on the 15th July we see land – England for the first time

- At 14:22 GMT on Saturday 16th July we finish

Exercise:

1. What needs to be taken into account to achieve advanced teamwork on this special leg?

2. What can you apply from this to your workplace?

Actual events

Here is what Team Stelmar actually did in the scenarios – not necessarily the right course of action, just the action we took in the circumstances.

Advanced Teamwork Scenario 1: The Eve of Start Day

- We all still had a fair amount of personal administration and preparation to do
- We stayed focused and didn't go into town
- We didn't party or drink that night
- We mainly retreated into our shells and got on with what needed to be done
- We went to bed early but sleep was elusive
- We tried not to think of the encroaching weather
- We visualised success and worked on what needed to be done to have a successful start

Advanced Teamwork Scenario 2: In Sydney

- The debrief was a tough one, but sometimes things need to be said and emotions need to come out
- There were arguments and intense debates, but no blame
- There were some extreme suggestions (like just having the leggers do mother duty so the established crew could concentrate on sailing the boat) which were stimulus to some great discussions
- The Skipper participated as much as the crew
- All opinions were equal and considered with respect
- We allowed as much time as was necessary to get it all out and come to agreed solutions
- Only one person at a time was allowed to speak

- New leggers were frankly told about everything

- They committed to try as hard as us to achieve much more in the next leg (we came 3rd)

- We reviewed everything and made sensible revisions to our teamwork

- We agreed to have a solid strategy for the next leg and stick to it

Advanced Teamwork Scenario 3: Someone not Pulling their Weight

- We were obliged to treat it as genuine depression – in case it was

- Luckily one of the crew was a psychiatric nurse and he advised us on how to cope with it

- We gave them space, but made sure we kept communicating with them about what was happening on deck so they felt included

- The rest of the team had to swallow their doubts and irritation and also assume that it was a genuine case of depression

- Watch Leaders and the Skipper all helped to support the team and be positive

- The watch they were on held several team chats over mealtimes to clear the air

- They were encouraged to come on deck during calm conditions to get them 'back on the bike'

- In port, a more formal debrief was held with them to check whether it might happen again on future legs

- The whole watch discussed together how they might continue from there

- The watch and Watch Leader did the best they could to resolve any outstanding feelings and move on

Advanced Teamwork Scenario 4: Last Leg

- The leg was treated with as much importance and severity (but no more) as all the others – it carried the same amount of points and would affect the final positions

- The team kept cool and professional, despite the pressure and the emotions associated with going home

- Paula's birthday celebrations were planned – but not to detract from the racing – it was only a three-day leg and every minute counted

- The team agreed some short-leg tactics: no showers (holding fresh water made the boat heavier); minimum clothing and personal items; the **least** pivotal watch members to be on mother duty once each

- No other special, new procedures were introduced, the team was working well as it was, there was no point in changing a successful formula

Chapter 7. Motivation

Definition

WHERE DOES MOTIVATION COME FROM? And what exactly is it?

Motivation comes from a variety of internal and external influences which affect our thoughts, emotions and actions, prompting us to take action either towards good things (pleasure) or away from bad (pain). Different people are motivated in different ways.

There is debate around how much motivation comes from intrinsic versus extrinsic sources. John Adair [30] the management guru suggests it is a 50-50 split, whereas some [31] would say that there is no such thing as internal motivation – it all comes from outside influences. In work, intrinsic sources of motivation would be self-generated such as finding work interesting and challenging, feeling responsible and proud. Extrinsic sources include pay, promotion, praise and punishments. On the boat, we had similar internal motivations – pride in our performance, the desire to push the boat faster, satisfaction in completing a perfect manoeuvre, etc. External influences included the physical sight of us racing past competitor boats (you can't beat that feeling!), sailing into Sydney Harbour, and receiving trophies for various achievements at each leg's award ceremony.

Motivation is often viewed as being *needs* driven. People have a need for satisfaction, power, respect, esteem, love,

---

[30] See 'Adair on Teamwork and Motivation'.
[31] For instance Stephen Reiss, professor of psychology at Ohio State University.

affiliation and so on and they will find the drive (motivation) from somewhere to acquire these things. Maslow's [32] 'hierarchy of needs' suggests that we would find the motivation at different levels of need; from the most basic (physiological) needs of life such as finding warmth, food and shelter, to the 'higher' needs of self-esteem and self-actualisation:

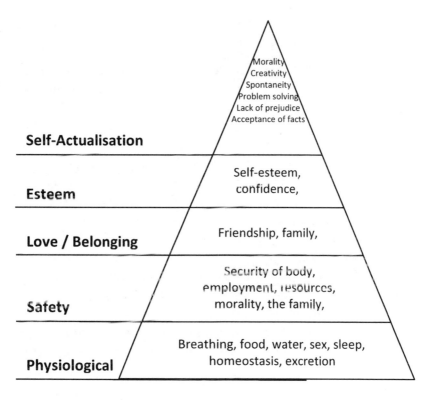

Self-Actualisation
Morality
Creativity
Spontaneity
Problem solving
Lack of prejudice
Acceptance of facts

Esteem
Self-esteem,
confidence,

Love / Belonging
Friendship, family,

Safety
Security of body,
employment, resources,
morality, the family,

Physiological
Breathing, food, water, sex, sleep,
homeostasis, excretion

Maslow's Hierarchy of Need

Certainly on the yacht race, motivation was less about the basic physiological needs for warmth and shelter (which were severely lacking) and much more about fulfilling the higher needs of confidence, achievement and self-actualisation.

Another widespread theory is that people will always seek to maximise their pleasure and minimise their pain. They will

---

[32] American psychologist

thus be motivated, for instance, to sell hard and earn more money to buy a new car or to go on holiday. Conversely, they will also be motivated to run fast to get away from potential pain. Tony Robbins[33] states that there are only two things that will **move** you – *Inspiration* or *Desperation*. This really boils down the multitude of motivational drivers to two succinct, opposing feelings which then generate thoughts, decisions and actions to either increase pleasure or reduce pain. Inspiration (such as becoming pregnant) may motivate someone to give up smoking; desperation (such as falling ill) may do the same – with the identical result.

Another way of looking at motivation is to consider the opposite - demotivation. What demotivates people? To what extent, why and how? The quantity and sources of demotivation are varied and the impact severe. It can take a lot of effort over time to build motivation, but very little to take it away. The smallest factor – possibly blown out of proportion – can easily and quickly demotivate, causing disappointment at least or depression at worst. Demotivation may result in a feeling of general malaise, a lack of energy, a loss of confidence, a lack of will and a waving of the white flag – 'I give up'. Demotivation is unsympathetic and destructive. In reading this Chapter, for every tip or point about how to motivate, read into that – how **not** to demotivate. Motivation can inspire people to achieve extra-ordinary results leaving them feeling sky-high with success. Demotivation can completely destroy the will to succeed, work or even live.

Motivation is the will, the drive, the attitude, to do something remarkably demanding like 'the world's toughest yacht race' whilst striving to win (and keep smiling)... no matter what.

---

[33] Anthony Robbins is an American self-help guru who runs motivational workshops with thousands of people in attendance, such as 'Unleash the Power Within', which includes walking on hot coals.

Motivation on the Global Challenge

The Global Challenge **is** a tough challenge. To sail all the way around the world, the 'wrong' way against the waves, in the hardest and most unforgiving environments such as the Southern Ocean; through storms, freezing sleet, snow and hail; miles from anywhere or anyone; with no such comforts as fresh food, warmth or dry socks; while being beaten and bashed physically every minute, awake or asleep, as freezing 40' waves crash over the boat taking your breath away... hardly gin and tonic sailing! It is extreme. Add to that Team Stelmar's experiences of 'high highs' and 'low lows' and you get a crew of ordinary human beings determinedly fighting against the elements **three times** around Cape Horn in pure 'survival mode'; trying to stay just warm enough, just safe enough and just content enough to get through the next ten minutes, let alone the eight weeks of the leg.

At these times, the vision of finishing in the top three takes a back seat; what does take precedence is getting through the watch (four or six hours on deck) without hurting too much physically or emotionally. Motivation switches from *inspiration* (to win) to *desperation* (to get through). It is survival time. This is a very different set of motivations, feelings and behaviours. The bigger picture of racing against 11 other boats around the world, contracts down to just the one boat in that time and place; looking after number one and keeping an eye out for team mates. This tunnel vision helped us focus on the more immediate and pressing issues, cutting out the peripheral 'nice to haves' which would have wasted precious energy at that time.

The motivational vision and long-term goals would come back when we had a chance to take a breath. The order of priorities just re-jigged, as they do in life. One day we were sailing as fast as possible for first place, three hours later we were sailing as fast as possible to save Flash's arm. (We knew we had a week to get him to hospital and with 1000 miles to cover, it would take us about that. In those conditions, sailing using wind power was actually faster than motoring with the engine.) Our motivations changed as a result of external circumstance. The inward drivers of pride, competitiveness and 'job satisfaction' were replaced by ethics, integrity and affection for Flash. We were not demotivated at this point; we were **re**motivated by a different set of drivers. We were still driven, determined and focused. We still had motivational attitudes which inspired us and kept our spirits up.

This happens in life and in business. Visions and goals are fantastic for long-term motivation, but when crises hit, short-term survival has to kick in and the drivers for motivation will change. A need for esteem and power by achieving corporate success through realising a strategic goal can quickly be replaced by a much more basic need for 'warmth and shelter' should the company flounder. Look at when the 'credit crunch' hit in late 2008. Prior to the financial meltdown, the London City boys and girls were motivated by the thought of collecting the latest Aston Martin or Ferrari off the production line; a month later they may have been out of a job and more motivated by the thought of supporting their dependants and paying their mortgage. How fast life can change.

As difficult and painful as it can be, becoming remotivated through desperation or a negative change in circumstance is not as bad as becoming demotivated. At least with inspiration- or desperation-induced motivation there is still a 'will' - an inner strength to survive. With demotivation there is a lack of will and an inner tendency to give up. This is much more damaging and difficult to remediate.

In our situation with Flash we experienced a change of motivation at the time of the crisis, but we were still motivated. This gave us the energy, determination and strength to carry on, to turn around (again) 180 degrees away from the finishing line in New Zealand and towards help in Argentina instead.

However, once the immediate crisis was over, when we had dropped Flash off at Ushuaia and turned around again to go back out into the Southern Ocean three crew members down, we were hit by a great lethargy and depression. One crew member became clinically depressed and many others went down with an amount of depression at some time or other in the weeks that followed. This demotivation was a much worse state of affairs and it was very difficult to lift everyone back up to full fighting spirit; the lack of motivation - the internal malaise - prevented some of the crew from even trying. Sailing towards Argentina we rallied together to achieve our new goal of helping Flash and our teamwork was exceptional. Sailing away from Argentina, we began to idle, bicker and fall apart because there was no inspiration or desperation any more. The effect was powerful and negative – definitely something to look out for in the future and something that businesses must try to avoid at all costs.

So, how did the individuals on *Team Stelmar* stay motivated (and **not** get demotivated) through circumstances such as:

- Seasickness and Man Overboard within ten hours of the race starting
- Coming 8th on the first leg with a goal of finishing in the Top Three
- Two separate medical evacuations around Cape Horn
- 52 days in succession in the Southern Ocean
- Thousands of miles and two weeks behind the rest of the fleet
- People quitting and wanting to quit
- Fear, danger and darkness

- Disasters, broken equipment and shredded sails
- Doldrums and 45° tropical heat
- Living in close confines with 17 strangers
- Tornados, storms, sleet, wind chill and 40' waves?

And stay extremely competitive and keep smiling? **How?** Different people are motivated in different ways, but here is a list of the positive external and internal influences on Team Stelmar:

External Factors

1. Great leadership
2. Supportive team
3. Having strong and simple vision, values, goals
4. Sticking to the rules
5. Role models
6. Large and active fan club and supporters outside the boat
7. Great communications
8. Physical, tangible, visible progress from A to B
9. Advancement shown on charts, schedules and racing past other boats
10. Winning awards and trophies, winning legs, (the dream of) winning the race
11. Self-policing culture
12. Humour/fun
13. Knowing that the outside world was watching and following our progress
14. Competition against the other 11 boats
15. Weather – either great weather for sailing or great weather for feeling good

16. Good results

17. Music[34], speeches, poems

Internal Factors:

1. Inner determination and personal drive

2. 'Racing not Cruising' competitive attitude

3. Not being in the lead and therefore not complacent

4. Courage

5. Survival instinct

6. Wanting to prove oneself

7. Pride, honour, recognition

8. High standards/personal goals

9. Faith

10. 100% commitment attitude

11. Optimism

12. Personal philosophies

13. The personal desire to role model for others/show others what 'I' am capable of

Motivation from Boat to Boardroom

Although life on board the boat was extremely tough and therefore very uncomfortable, we were at least taking part in an amazingly motivational challenge – a round the world yacht race. (More people have been into space than have

---

[34] We were not allowed to play music on deck in case it distracted the On Watch. We did play a bit when we were not fully racing, such as when we dropped Flash off. One popular track that motivated us was Baz Luhrmann's Suncreen Song: *Everybody's Free (To Wear Sunscreen)* which included the line: 'Sometimes you're ahead, sometimes you're behind, but the race is long, and in the end, it's only with yourself.' Also the poem 'Don't Quit' was spot-on for remotivating people internally. See p351

raced the wrong way around the world.) We were all 100% committed; enthusiastic volunteers because sailing, or taking part in extreme challenges, were personal ambitions. The world was watching, the media were covering our stories and we were sailing across the equator twice, into places like Sydney and Cape Town, seeing dolphins, Cape Horn and the Aurora Australis en route. This was clearly motivational stuff.

Whereas in the workplace - with a much more comfortable and forgiving environment – it can conversely be harder to motivate people. Both working and crewing can be mundane, with the same repetitive and uninteresting tasks to be done, but employees are likely to be less committed to the overall goal, less inspired by the vision, less engaged with the culture and values, less competitive and ambitious in attitude and have less stimulation overall. The workplace is typically a more mundane, safe, stable, predictable place than the dynamic environment of a racing yacht at sea.

However, other than the race itself, there were numerous ways that the *Team Stelmar* crew were motivated – 30 are already listed – and all of these can be adapted by teams and leaders at work. The external influences are more tangible and so easier to affect, but with the right recruitment, employee engagement and inspirational leadership, the internal motivators can also be cultivated and grown. Different people are motivated in different ways and the need for motivation will change (inspiration/desperation) but motivation is important for progress, and success, and personal satisfaction; demotivation is a killer of these.

Motivated crew/employees:

- look for better ways to do a job
- are more quality oriented
- are more productive
- are happier
- are more committed and loyal

Demotivated crew/employees are lethargic, disruptive, rebellious, unhappy, unproductive, even deeply depressed. Here are some lessons from the boat that can be taken into the boardroom.

Motivational Leadership

The subject of leadership already has a dedicated Chapter in this book, however *motivational* leadership warrants a specific mention here. An influential source of motivation is inspirational leadership – not just from the leader with the highest ranking job title, but all sorts of leaders including middle managers, team leaders, project leaders and even thought leaders; people with influence; people whom other people look to for reference on how to behave (think and feel) in certain situations. These leaders cast bigger shadows than other people. (see Leadership Chapter p.145) Their actions and words, facial expressions and visible emotions will have a greater effect because of their disproportionate influence (their shadow). Therefore if leaders are themselves motivated, they will send out strong positive signals and motivate others - almost through osmosis. So motivational leadership rule number one is: 'Be Motivated Yourself'.

Motivation is transmittable between people but also between the external influence and the internal feeling. Cause and effect is at work: positive cause and motivational effect. When Clive our Skipper was upbeat we were infected by his high spirits; we then 'relaxed' and had more fun; which made us act exuberantly; which then put us in a good mood and we pushed harder (like physically dancing to music will make you feel good emotionally.) But when Clive was in a bad mood, we all caught it, which lowered our spirits; made our movements heavier and communications brusque. This then negatively affected our performance. Leaders can have a strong influence, without perhaps realising it, just by being and thinking differently, small nuances in their expressions or tone will be picked up by the team. Thus they need to be emotionally intelligent and aware of the shadows (or sunshine!) they cast over others.

Leaders will have a natural influence over others because of their position and the way they behave, but there are plenty of other 'tricks' they can use proactively to generate motivation (and prevent demotivation).

Ideally, the first step is to understand what motivates each individual because different people are motivated in different ways. On our boat we had people who were doing the Global Challenge to win a major yacht race, people who just wanted adventure and people who wanted to escape from their home lives. Phil was motivated by executing a perfect sail change. Ruth was motivated by being held in high regard by her crew. Sharon was motivated by having fun. Nicko was motivated by getting the numbers right. Paula was motivated by genuine delegation. Alex was motivated by boat speed. Newton was demotivated by getting out the Genoa sail. Rich was demotivated by what was happening at home. Paul was demotivated by the continuous pain in his arm. And so on. We, like everyone else in the world, had our own switches or 'hot buttons'. Leaders need to understand these to 'play' the individuals - like a conductor with an ensemble of different instruments which require different handling in order to create a symphony.

A leader in business should find out what it was that motivated each employee to apply for work at the organisation in the first place and then what retains them. Money or location? Praise or challenges? Prospects or security? What makes them have a good day and what makes them not want to come into work? What makes them work harder; what makes them give up?

To understand people, leaders must genuinely listen to them with open ears and open minds. This alone is motivational for employees. Through honest listening and close observation leaders will then understand what makes people tick and be able to manage them – and inspire them – accordingly; giving people challenging tasks, coaching, praise, or responsibility as appropriate. Patting people on the back for a job well done, or berating them for not doing better – each will motivate depending on the individual. Some people are motivated by winning; some are motivated by losing and wanting to do better. Jose Mourinho had this down to a fine art in his individual management of the Chelsea players before he moved on. He 'played' each team member beautifully; encouraging, berating, consoling, pushing, as he saw it, because he knew his team so well.

Great communication is also vital in motivational leadership. State of the Nation speeches, conferences and Q&As are one-off devices, but regular, good communication is the lifeblood. Constructive reviews, debriefs, feedback and performance management; realistic, no-spin updates; face-to-face engagement; saying thank you; talking to employees with respect; demonstrating knowledge about the marketplace, the competitors, the customers; giving supportive comments in passing; no-nonsense updates during times of difficulty; timely communications when necessary; visionary inspiration; walking the talk; etc.

If a leader is personally motivated, understands and leads people as individuals, and is a great communicator, then they are likely to be good motivators. Here are other lessons from the boat.

Positive Role Models

As well as leaders, individual people – role models - can have a motivational effect on their peers. Many people, who are theoretically not in leadership positions, are capable of being inspirational through their words, deeds or attitudes. These characters are often strong in their beliefs, have high standards or are driven by superior guiding principles. They have a positive influence on those around them by conducting themselves in such a way as to set a good example. They do not preach or teach, they are just themselves and by watching them or being near them, others are inspired or motivated.

We had a very strong role model on Team Stelmar – Phil – who conducted himself with the utmost professionalism on the boat and had very, very high standards. He pulled us all up to his level. We saw in him that it was OK to be so driven, such a perfectionist, whilst maintaining a sense of dignity and 'cool'. Phil was funny and tough and a party animal in port, but able to carry off a puritanical attitude to detail on board which was perfectly right in such race conditions. It was almost like being at school, where the cool kid worked hard instead of mucking around as expected and the rest of the gang took note and followed his example.

Newton, our 59-year-old, was also a positive role model. He put us to shame with his perseverance and physical tenacity when times got tough. He was also pragmatic and had a cracking sense of humour – again in times of difficulty. We all stood a little straighter with Newton around and learnt to get on with it without complaining. Clive too, role modelled respecting people. He was extremely courteous and respectful of everyone equally. There was no teasing, or talking behind people's backs with him, no matter how badly people were behaving.

This role modelling on board *Team Stelmar* worked both ways. We were inspired by the behaviours and attitudes of others, but we also wanted to be the inspirer. We didn't want to let the team down (and demotivate) by being irritable or lazy or grumpy. We wanted the better qualities in us to shine out and motivate others. So we were externally motivated by others role-modelling best behaviours and internally motivated by being role models ourselves. Equally, we tried not to demotivate the team or watch by setting a bad example. At least two people in our crew were strongly demotivated by seeing a lack of will in other team members.

They gave up if they saw others give up. We fed off each other's strength.

At work it is equally true that role models will inspire or un-inspire others. Role modelling speeds up learning and compresses the time it would normally take to see, understand and change. An outstanding role model will deliver complex or subtle positive messages without spin; people will then learn from them and choose to change without coercion or duplicity. Leaders alone don't have to take the full weight of responsibility for 'walking the talk'. Role models are everywhere and can be more believable and 'followable' than leaders sometimes. They lack the political agenda.

People's lives are also a direct reflection of the expectations of their peer group: 'who you spend time with is who you become.'[35] Our team consisted of constructive, ambitious, capable people. The combined positive attitude of 18 crew members was motivating in itself. We had a can-do culture. Maximum effort went in to everything we did. We threw ourselves into each task with 100% commitment. We were self-policing. We subconsciously approved good behaviours and disapproved bad. We didn't tolerate bad moods, bad performances or bad cooking! Collectively we cultivated an invisible ethos that was a 'racing not cruising' attitude. We were motivated by our own culture, which grew out of, and was perpetuated by, our own attitudes and behaviours. If this culture can be achieved in the workplace, then it can be self-generating, without the need for enforced communications, training or other props.

This slightly touches on the 'right person, right job' point made in the *Advanced Teamwork* Chapter. If the right people are recruited with the right attitude in the first place, then the right culture will grow as a result. Positive role models will support and police each other, and negative characters will be eased out (like a disease being ejected from the

---

[35] Anthony Robbins

human body). If there are too many negative influencers however, then demotivation of the whole team or department may result. Strong, inspirational leadership or other external influences such as reward and recognition then need to kick-in to redress the balance.

Rewards, Awards and Competition

There is nothing like a good competition to get the heart pumping and people energised into trying a little bit harder than they were before. If the Global Challenge had been a sail (not a race) around the world (like the ARC 'rally' from Europe to the Caribbean every year) then probably about 50% of the effort would have gone into it. The Global Challenge yacht **race** was exciting, inspiring and motivational because it **was** a race. It ignited people's competitive spirits and made them feisty and even aggressive. It pumped the heart a bit harder and focused the mind a bit sharper. It made people go to the gym before the race six days a week instead of two. How often is someone motivated enough to do that? It got teams practising out in the Solent in the winter when they could have been at home watching TV. It had people taking just one kg of personal kit on board, leaving behind precious luxuries, and refusing to shower because of the extra water needed. It made supporters fly out to faraway ports, hire boats and shout and scream at us across the water. How motivational?

Every six hours we were given the race positions. The numbers between 1 and 12 became vital four times a day and especially at the end of each leg. Who came first? Everyone knew. Who came seventh? Who cared. We had a fresh pump of adrenaline every time the race results came in. We were flying high when we were first, second or third. We were kicking ourselves when we were losing places.

In each port there was a fantastic award ceremony complete with three course dinner, invited guests and VIPs, film montages, and the bit we all waited for – the announcement and presentation of the trophies. There were trophies for first, second and third places, trophies for 'first across the start line', the best '24-hour run' awards and others for safety, best media footage, etc. We won 14 trophies in 7 legs; more than any other team.

We also held an internal competition between the watches for one leg (Sydney to Cape Town), with mixed success. Yes, competition fires up the muscles and stimulates the brain, but it can also have a divisive effect between teams that still have to work together effectively for the sake of the bigger picture. We introduced motivation through a competition which logged the number of miles covered by each watch. Thousands of miles were raced during 100s of watches, and over time the average number of miles achieved per hour for each watch became evident. One watch did better than the other. This almost divided the whole boat into two halves, rather than motivate the teams into a positive work ethic.

In the workplace, a little competition is an invigorating method to motivate teams or individuals, but it needs to be done carefully and for the right reasons. Also at work, awards or rewards are motivational. Celebrating success, recognising effort, upholding values, rewarding sales or innovation or customer satisfaction, they all inspire good performance – though for some people more than others. We had major trophies which were coveted and without equal (for winning a leg for instance) but also more humble ones such as 'the best onboard sail repair'. They were all appreciated and gave different teams a chance to shine in different ways.

Fire people up with recognition, praise and competition. Reward people with incentives and awards and celebrations. All motivational *on balance* if an eye is kept on those who don't win or who win too often and possibly become complacent. Some people are motivated if they are in the lead. Some people are motivated if they are in last place. So is winning a motivator? Yes, to most people. Striving to win may be more motivating for others. Complacency is dangerous. Looking behind all the time is also potentially destructive. It is hard to stay at the top. Fresh motivation may need to come from somewhere else. Different people are motivated in different ways; it's important to understand this.

Tangible Progress

Competitions need a visible scoreboard, league table or progress chart such as a giant thermometer for the 'Church Roof Fund' to demonstrate achievement tangibly. Some competitions or goals are nebulous and need to be made more concrete to inspire and be kept 'front of mind'. If a Sales Team has a quarterly sales target to achieve then this could be portrayed as a giant chart or graph, with milestones or measures of progress that can be checked off over time. If a call centre aims to deal with so many customers an hour, then a board or LED display could be up on the wall for all to see. And what about the higher management - what do they get to show their progress? Often nothing, which is a pity as they too need motivating and stimulating towards achieving success.

On the boat it was easy. We were physically sailing from A to B on each leg. On the second leg for instance, we sailed out of Buenos Aires, progressed along the River Plate, then watched the coast of Tierra del Fuego pass to starboard, rounded Cape Horn and then advanced towards Wellington, physically eating up the miles, passing other boats and travelling from one country to another. It was only as we sailed into Sydney in fact, that most of us realised what we were actually achieving. We had sailed from England to the other side of the world.

We also had charts and computer graphics to show our progress. On leg two, when we had a deadline to get to Wellington and whilst there was no competition provided by the other boats which were 1000s of miles ahead of us, we redefined our goals and created new ones. We made up two new measures of progress which plotted our speed against our own target. No longer were we racing against the fleet; we were racing against the clock – to get to Wellington before the midday on the 21st January deadline. We made up a digital time-line on the computer and Ruth, our medic, created a pictorial version with pen and paper. These became our new records of progress. Mileage versus time became our new measurement. Getting to Wellington by 21st January was our new goal.

Many people respond to incentives and often their preferred method of communication is visual (as opposed to hearing or feeling), so introducing a target and plotting progress towards it graphically and tangibly, helps a lot of people understand the targets and get motivated. Just a graphic representation of the progress is enough, if a real visual is possible (such as seeing products physically leave the store or creating a wall of customer satisfaction letters) then even better.

Management are often poor at using graphics because physical images can be regarded as immature but everyone can enjoy, learn from, and easily understand pictures. Why should the fun, inspiration, simplicity and creativity leave us when we start work? Innocent Drinks have a fabulous office environment for instance with plenty of pictures, 3-D paraphernalia and a glass-walled kitchen in the middle of the main room in which people can experiment with different recipes. Their environment is stimulating and so motivational. It is tangible and visual, creative and colourful. Can you say the same about your office environment, or the way you present your management reports or financial updates?

All in the Same Boat

'All in the same boat' is one of many idioms derived from the nautical world. One definition given on-line is: 'If people are in the same boat, they are in the same predicament or trouble'. Although this is a very negative interpretation, it is often true - ocean racing is very rarely 'plain sailing'! The more balanced definition is: people who are all in the same boat must work as a team because they face the same challenges together. Yes, 'being in the same boat' encourages teamwork, but there is also something comforting about being in the same situation together. A motivational source is knowing that your close comrades are also experiencing the same highs and lows as you. You can celebrate with them when times are good and you can take comfort with them (and belly-ache with them) when times are tough. Knowing that other people are having a better time than you are can be demotivating. Picturing people partying at home on Christmas Day and eating a full Christmas lunch was very difficult when we had to be on deck for six hours in the Southern Ocean and were eating freeze-dried expedition food.

When *Team Stelmar* dropped Flash off at Ushuaia – our second about-turn in seven days - a few of the crew wanted to get off the boat, fly home for Christmas and return to Wellington for the start of the next leg. A perfectly understandable desire in the circumstances. However, there would be two problems with this. One, the person who left might regret it later for not sticking it out with the team, and two, the crew remaining on the boat would find it very hard to come to terms with the fact that their team mates deserted them when the going got tough. Would we ever have recovered from this and reverted to the high-performing, fully integrated team we were before? Would we have felt the same trust and appreciation of those who had deserted? It is doubtful.

So, although not a very dynamic or 'sexy' motivational driver, 'all being in the same boat' helps achieve a sense of unity – of camaraderie. This can mean that when colleagues at work are absent from a particularly exceptional time, e.g. extremely busy or very successful or rapidly growing, they can miss out on the 'glue' of the memory that binds the others together. Even when companies or departments go through a really difficult crisis, it can pull people together and motivate them, whilst also helping the company have a more successful future. People who miss this may be relieved, but actually miss some of the excitement and buzz of working; they should be re-engaged as soon as possible.

'All in the same boat' is figuratively speaking, everyone experiencing the same circumstance at the same time. If one team or department is experiencing huge success and get their bonuses and go to the pub early to celebrate one day a week, and another team is experiencing the opposite and having to work overtime just to survive, then this huge mismatch will cause problems. The hard-working team will be demotivated but may also hold a grudge against the other team in the future.

On *Team Stelmar* we had two distinct watches. We ensured that we looked after both equally and if one watch suffered a major crisis the other watch would get out of their bunks immediately, get dressed and go on deck to help no matter what. We were, quite literally, all in the same boat.

Challenge

When an adventurer is asked why they put their life on the line to climb a mountain or sail solo around the world or BASE jump off the Petronas Towers, their reply will often be about living life to the full. By putting themselves in danger and pushing their personal limits - and risking death - they feel more alive. In *Mountains of the Mind – A History of Fascination* by Robert Macfarlane he puts it thus:

Risk-taking brings with it its own reward: it keeps a 'continual agitation alive' in the heart. Hope, fear. Fear, hope – this is the fundamental rhythm of mountaineering. Life, it frequently seems in the mountains, is more intensely lived the closer one gets to extinction: we never feel so alive as when we have nearly died.

In doing the Global Challenge, most of the crew felt 'more alive' than they had ever before, despite – or rather, because of - risking their lives to do it.

There is a massive difference between the emotions and feelings induced from sitting at a desk five days a week for 20 years, and the emotions and feelings gleaned from racing around the world the wrong way in a 72' yacht for a year. Flash should know – he was an accountant, and then became our number one bowman on the boat, before getting medivacked out of Cape Horn!

Of course there is a difference between the two scenarios. There is so much more adrenaline generated in sailing in 40 knot winds than attending a business meeting. There is so much more excitement and energy and emotion and thrills in sailing around Cape Horn than typing an email. The Global Challenge is an extreme adventure and most workplaces don't provide extreme work challenges. So what can be done to induce a little bit of the 'live life to the full' feeling at work? Pushing people hard. Creating tough challenges. Supporting people to reach their full potential. Setting demanding but achievable goals. Having amazing visions.

Almost contradictorily, many people thrive on being pushed and challenged rather than being given work to do that is beneath their capabilities. If stretchy, yet attainable goals can be discussed and agreed with the team or individuals, then it gives them something to strive for and something to celebrate and be proud of. Likewise, if the company has a far-reaching and ambitious, almost idealistic vision, such as Disney's: 'To make people happy', or Cancer Research's: 'Together we will beat cancer', then **engaged** employees will be motivated towards achieving it.

Even in traditionally monotonous jobs there have to be ways to raise the game sometimes; to create a challenge, a competition, a stretchy goal, allowing some adrenaline to kick in; to get employee's hearts pumping, getting them more focused, driven and energetic towards their daily work. This extra pressure may be cynically perceived as a company's crafty move towards achieving better results, but the employees benefit too by lifting themselves above their usual levels of effort; motivated towards achieving greater success, making them feel proud at the end of the shift. Challenge people. Get their hearts pumping, their adrenaline flowing, and their motivation levels through the roof.

Self-Motivation and Drive

Of course, people who are self-motivated may not need external or superficially created motivational devices; they are capable of generating their own. They will set their own goals, SMART objectives and have dreams that they can motivate themselves towards realising. They are driven by an internal engine of motivation. Somewhere inside is a voice or strength which pushes these people into action, whether it is someone unemployed getting up in the morning or a mountaineer climbing Everest. Mallory was so driven then he attempted Everest three times. Each time he said 'never again', but each time he tried again, self-driven so much in the end that he died trying (though whether he reached the summit is still a subject for speculation). Famously Mallory's motivation for climbing Everest was, 'because it's there' – an almost down-to-earth motivator for such a huge, record-breaking challenge.

As previously mentioned, the crew on *Team Stelmar* had a variety of motives for doing the Global Challenge. These initially were self-motivational. As the race progressed, the range of internal and external influences maintained that motivation.

At work, people will have different reasons for applying for the job, but then there needs to be a range of internal and external sources of motivation to keep them there. Different people are motivated in different ways.

Celebrating, Humour and Fun

Finally, we come to fun!

Humour is one of the least understood and most valid tools of management and leadership. The appropriate use of humour can diffuse, amuse, motivate, challenge and completely change the atmosphere. (Sir Brian Wolfson, Chairman of Wembley)

In agreement with Sir Brian Wolfson, humour and fun are valid tools of management, leadership and teamwork, and there is probably not enough 'official' use of it in the workplace. When times are hard, there is no need for everyone – especially the leadership - to walk around grim-faced, exuding doom and gloom. Challenge and excitement can be found in hard times; some laughter and fun will inject people with the positive energy needed to cope. Equally, when times are good there is reason for some frivolity, fun and celebrations. In good, bad and mediocre times, there is always a case for having fun because it has beneficial effects – it can 'diffuse, amuse, motivate, challenge and completely change the atmosphere'. It also creates energy; putting a spring in the step on the shop floor and a smile in the voice in the call centre. It can make things seem more accessible and do-able. It provides camaraderie between colleagues and positive memories between business partners and customers. Having fun has plentiful business benefits, **and** it also creates a good feeling. Why should work lack the sense of humour that is found outside of work? Work should be rewarding and fun.

On *Team Stelmar* we worked hard, but played hard to balance that. One boat in the fleet was considered to be a very serious, 'heads down' boat, and yet another was nicknamed the 'party boat' at the other extreme. We had the right balance of maintaining a professional, high performance attitude whilst being able to have a few laughs along the way. This helped us to appreciate our leader (who had a good sense of fun), our sponsor (who wrote us extremely witty emails about what was going on in the outside world) and helped us to like each other and thus work better as a team. We had more energy and physically moved faster and more incisively when we were in good spirits. (See *The Ups* in the *Leadership* Chapter)

Humour is motivating. A lack of fun, a lack of humour and a lack of celebrating is demotivating. When we won our leg from Boston to La Rochelle we held our emotions in check until we actually crossed the finish line, then we all went completely mad and had a big impromptu bundle on the side deck. Ridiculous behaviour for fully-grown adults but the photos say it all. The madness, the tangle of bodies and the broad grins in contrast to the photo of our more formal acceptance of the 1st place trophy at the award ceremony. The spontaneity of the celebration once we had crossed the finish line in first place was much more memorable and natural than the more considered celebrations at the official ceremonies. Food for thought in the workplace perhaps.

How many companies have 'fun' as a value? Maybe it is considered too trivolous, but actually having fun whilst working enlivens the working environment and improves working relationships. Customers also like to experience good times with their suppliers; their memory of the company will be a positive one and they will come back for more. Most of all, celebrations, awards, fun and humour are a great external source of motivation. If a company scored itself everyday on the amount of fun employees were having, versus the amount of motivation people were feeling, versus the level of production, there would be a strong correlation.

How to achieve it? Leaders can set a good example – even in difficult times. High spirits between workers and teams can be encouraged. Socialising within work or outside of work will help to break down barriers. Awards, recognition, parties and ceremonies will give people a great sense of satisfaction. Celebrating birthdays in ridiculous ways is an example of injecting a more creative form of fun. (Setting up a 'tropical beach' around someone's desk for example or giving 'slave for the day' vouchers.) 'You don't have to be happy to work here, but if you are it helps'.

Lessons on Motivation from the Boat to the Boardroom

Leaders

- Be motivated yourself
- Understand exactly what motivates each individual
- Treat everyone with respect
- Coach, support and train
- Stick up for your team
- Delegate; let people do things their way
- Say thank you. Reward achievement

Challenge

Get people's 'blood up' with challenges. Set and agree with the team or individuals demanding goals which are stretchy yet attainable. Don't make them impossible, give them too many or too often.

Compete

Ignite people by introducing competition. Competing against the numbers, against time, against competitors or (carefully) against each other will focus the mind, create a sense of fun and get people trying a little bit harder than before.

Encourage Role Modelling

Role modelling speeds up learning and condenses time. Role models demonstrate complex and complete ways to behave without being political or superficial. Positive people can infect others with their enthusiasm. Negative people will drain energy.

Show Goals and Progress towards Them

Graphically represent progress so that it becomes visible, tangible and experiential. Enable employees to see advancement. Harden nebulous concepts by using charts, graphs, pictures, thermometers, etc. Don't forget the leadership need stimulus too.

Long Vision. Short Steps for Survival

Have a long-term ambitious and motivating vision. Keep the wording sexy. Aim for the heart with it. In times of trouble, reduce visions and goals to short survival steps. Allow people to tick off achievements in small chunks when they are under it and reward them accordingly.

Engaging Communication

Engage, immerse, involve employees in company life. Connect them with the vision. Help them to live and breathe the values; visualise the aims and goals; feel the successes.

Celebrate Success and have Fun

Keep a sense of humour no matter what. Be creative, original and spontaneous with fun. Ensure that role models and leaders are emanating **genuine** positivity even through difficult times. Celebrate success in many different ways. Keep it fresh.

Motivation Exercises

Motivation Scenario 1: Karen

- You have had to make the tough decision to medically evacuate a member of your crew – Karen - because she is suffering from an unknown medical condition

- You are about to go round Cape Horn and so have to divert north, up the Beagle Canal to drop her off at Puerto Williams with the Chilean Navy

- As per the racing rules, you give the race committee your latitude and longitude and suspend racing

- You leave the race in 3rd position, divert for 19 hours, leave Karen in safe hands and come back out in last place, 160 miles behind the leaders.

- You are two crew members down (one crew member didn't get on to start the leg), now in last place and about to go round Cape Horn into the most hostile ocean in the world

Exercise:

1. How demotivated are you now as a crew?
2. What can you do to remotivate yourselves?
3. Write a bullet point list of actions and considerations
4. What can you apply from this to your workplace?

Motivation Scenario 2: Four Crew Members Down

- Leg two – Buenos Aires to Wellington
- Deep in the Southern Ocean after two medical evacuations
- Three weeks behind the rest of the fleet and out of radio contact
- One month still to go to New Zealand

- Grunters Watch Leader quit the team two days before leaving Buenos Aires

- Two people lost through medical evacuations (Groaner watch)

- And now one crew member taken to their bunk with depression (Grunter watch)

- Both watches two crew members down in extremely adverse and physically exhausting conditions

- Motivation is lacking as can only get to New Zealand, can't actually overtake any boats

- All crew members are physically and emotionally drained

Exercise:

1. As a single crew member, what would you do to motivate the team in these circumstances?

2. Write a bullet point list

3. What can you apply from this to your workplace?

Motivation Scenario 3: Christmas Eve

- Leg two – Buenos Aires to Wellington

- Southern Ocean after two medical evacuations

- Three weeks behind the rest of the fleet and out of radio contact

- Still one month, 3000 miles and 135 watch changes to go before New Zealand

- Yesterday you got to 'Waypoint Flash' at 22:30 on the 23rd December, where Flash had his accident two weeks before

- It is Christmas Eve

Exercise:

1. What can remotivate the team at this point?

2. Write a bullet point list of actions and considerations

3. What can you apply from this to your workplace?

Motivation Scenario 4: In the Lead!

- 6th leg – Boston, USA to La Rochelle, France

- In a good place

- Totally planned strategy pre-departure and stuck to it

- Took early route north, lost out initially, but then others got caught in Azores High

- Got through icebergs, Labrador Current, fog and where the Titanic had sunk!

- Our tactics were sound, we gained on the rest of the fleet, gradually overtaking to first place

- There is only about half a day to the finish, we are ahead by 15 miles, fingers crossed for our first win...

- Then the wind drops

- Change to lightweight spinnaker (0.75oz per square metre)

- Very slow going

- Suddenly a boat is spotted behind us through the binoculars!

- Boats gather behind us catching up, we see it all from the top of the mast

- The wind had picked up from behind and was pushing them along towards us

- We could see they had their heavy spinnakers up (2.2oz) suggesting they had lots of wind and were sailing quickly

- It's the 3rd July, 09:00 hours, and we are only doing 5 knots with the other's catching up fast and just a few miles to go!

Exercise:

1. What would you do to keep the team motivated and focused in these circumstances?

2. Write a bullet point list of actions and considerations

3. What can you apply from this to your workplace?

Actual events

Here is what Team Stelmar actually did in the scenarios – not necessarily the right course of action, just the action we took in the circumstances.

Motivation Scenario 1: Karen

- No-brainer to drop Karen off

- Remotivated ourselves with new targets – 1) to successfully sail around Cape Horn and 2) to catch and overtake one boat

- Cape Horn was the first focus – going round it was motivating in itself

- Catching just one boat was our next goal (one small step at a time)

- We soon overtook *Pindar* (within 24 hours)

- We then reset ourselves the goal of catching the next boat

- As we began to overtake boats with amazing teamwork and tenacity we soon adopted our old goal again - to win the leg

- We also checked up on Karen's progress as best we could, but communications were difficult

- We didn't get a good idea of what had actually happened until we reached Wellington

- She was in safe hands, flew back home, found the cause of her condition and was medically fine

- She rejoined the race to complete the next leg with *Team Stelmar* from Wellington to Sydney

Motivation Scenario 2: Four Crew Members Down

This is what you could do:

- As a single crew member, don't forget you can still have a big effect on the rest of the crew – and on the leader. The leader (or Skipper in this case) doesn't have to be solely responsible for motivation. Even he/she can get down sometimes

- Check in with yourself. How are you actually feeling? Can you find a way of improving your feelings? See the bright side?

- Dig deep and pull yourself up knowing that you will have a lot to cope with in the near future. You can cope with a lot more than you initially think

- Be a role model for getting on with it, working hard, and keeping smiling

- Try to maintain an outer appearance of positivity – this positive physical energy can then improve your internal mental and emotional energy

- Read the body language of your team members – who looks like they could do with a pep talk?

- Approach individuals who may need some support. Talk to them. Give them physical contact. Try to switch their thinking to more positive things

- Try to introduce fun or humour to lighten the mood

- Pull more than your weight on and off deck to make up for the gaps and role model excellence

Motivation Scenario 3: Christmas Eve

- We phoned Flash on the satellite phone, spoke to his parents and then all individually passed the phone around to speak with him. It cost a fortune but it was worth it!

- We took a photo of us all at 'Waypoint Flash' and emailed it to him

- We celebrated Christmas as best as we could:

- Printed off carol sheets and sung them on each night watch (they got a bit wet!)

- Gave each other a 'secret Santa' present, pulled out of a stocking by the Skipper

- Shared one bottle of champagne between everyone

- Got **both** watches together as much as we could with a Happy Hour and at watch changeover

- Were perhaps a little bit more thoughtful and kind to each other

- Created the best Christmas meal we could out of tinned, dehydrated and freeze-dried food

- Got everyone off deck except the two Watch Leaders to all sit down and eat together

- Gave the two Watch Leaders as much appreciation as we could in return!

- Took turns on the satellite phone calling home

Motivation Scenario 4: In the Lead!

- This was difficult as it can be very motivational to be in the lead, but there can also be a tendency to drop concentration, relax or even get complacent. It was still anyone's race - no-one wins until they cross the finish line in first place

- We tried not to keep looking behind. We could not affect the other boat's progress. We kept our eyes on our boat and what we were doing. Controlling the controllables

- We didn't allow any talk or action that was celebratory until we crossed the line

- As a team we tried to maintain focus, if one person slipped into wishful thinking, the others pulled them back to reality

- We stayed seriously focused, holding our nerve, until the finish line

- We sailed as per usual, attempting nothing new

Chapter 8. Communication

Definition

THE SUBJECT OF COMMUNICATION covers a multitude of languages, tools, systems, types and styles. There is great communication that engages, informs and inspires and there is bad communication that can leave people confused, overwhelmed, or even angry or offended. Communication is everything from formal memos to subtle nuances of body language. It covers explicitly informing to implicitly inspiring. It is printed, electronic, verbal, viral, tonal, structured, unstructured, one-way, two-way; it is in signs, symbols, body language, facial expressions; it can be pixelated, iconic, emoticonic, entrepreneurial; simple, eloquent, passive, dynamic, informative, educational, entertaining, unifying, disruptive, disturbing, visionary. Whatever communication is, it is important. It glues the human race, communities, families, individuals, departments. It has power and impact.

In business, there is social communication and more formal external and internal communication. External may be communicating with customers, suppliers, partners or shareholders through PR, brand, press, marketing, sales. Internal communication is about informing (one-way) and engaging (two-way) employees including face-to-face meetings and conferences, intranet, internal magazines, emails, workshops, performance reviews, briefings, knowledge sharing, training, etc.

On the boat, there was a lot of social communication. Hours and hours would be spent on deck over ten months without

TV, music or computers. Talk or silence were the only options. The 'old art' of conversation was resurrected.

More functional communication had to be concise, simple and effective.

Communication on the Global Challenge

Aside from communicating pre-race, post-race and with the world outside the boat, 95% of Global Challenge communication was either on deck, below deck or between the decks of a 72' yacht among 18 people. This created a unique communication environment with its own challenges and delights.

On deck there were essentially two types of communication – concise, action-specific talk during a manoeuvre, or general chat amongst the crew in between tasks. Below deck communication tended to be social - unless the Skipper, Watch Leaders and Navigator met at the navigation table to discuss strategy. Between decks the communication was usually quite vital, informing the on-watch of squalls (spotted on the radar), a change of tactics or sail plan, or the latest race statistics.

In this Chapter we shall look at the more functional type of communication, rather than the conversations, debates and discussions that went on to kill time. But on that point, without TV or computers to distract us, conversation was an essential entertainment medium and the quality of our conversational skills increased with practice. This demonstrated to us how much the electronic media had taken over our social lives and relationships. We even introduced 'Sunday afternoon lectures' during Happy Hour to talk about relevant local subjects such as albatross or the Titanic; we devised our own fun 'Stelmar-saurus' made up of phrases or words that were boat-specific and we introduced controversial topics for debate to wile away the less active six-hour watches.

'Functional' communication was mostly verbal on a professional (yacht racing specific) basis. We did pin memos or the occasional motivational email or poem up on our pinboard but that was the only type of written internal communication we had. We had no need to email or telephone each other of course, which was very liberating and meant that most of our communication was face-to-face. This was by far the most effective and efficient method and the potential for misunderstanding, misinterpretation and political manipulation was reduced as a result.

On deck, during any manoeuvre (such as a sail change or gybe), our communication had to be clear, concise and simple. Often we had to bellow above the noise of the wind and waves from at least half way along the boat (36'); there was no time or energy to talk for long. There was also the strong possibility of getting a mouthful of salt water if facing forward. Our communication had to be functional and very effective. During the worst weather we had to resort to hand signals which we devised between us. Again, this was extremely effective. It is great how efficient shouting or hand signalling can be – though these techniques are not so appropriate for the workplace!

On the Global Challenge we also had to communicate with the outside world now and again. To do this we had different radio frequencies, satellite phone and email. We were not allowed the internet and our access to weather reports, for instance, was controlled by a set budget per leg – the same as all the other boats. We were able to communicate with friends and family using the satellite system, although we had to pay quite a lot of money for each correspondence. With emails for example, the Inmarsat C system charged us for every symbol used including commas, spaces, etc. so we had to be conservative with our words. Also, if any of our correspondents hit 'reply' on their email we would receive our original words back plus the new text and had to pay for both. Because of this, some crew arranged to have one email contact back home who co-ordinated all emails to and from the yacht.

We could also use the satellite phone which was expensive but fun. It was odd to be asleep in a bunk in the middle of an ocean and hear the Sat phone ring. One time, after a particularly uneventful and quiet few weeks, the unusual noise took us so much by surprise that nobody knew what to do until the Skipper shouted, "Well, answer it then!" Likewise when you called a friend to wish them happy birthday or happy Christmas, the last thing they expected was the call. "Where are you?" they would ask puzzled. We could only give them our latitude and longitude in answer.

Paula:

I remember calling my friend Kate on the morning of her wedding day. We had just finished off-loading Flash into an ambulance in Ushuaia. We really were 'at the end of the world'; surrounded by glaciers and just off Antarctica. Kate in the meantime was having her hair done, just hours before getting married. What a contrast in our lives right then! But the communication across all those miles really consolidated our friendship; it was such an important day, in different ways, for the both of us.

We also had several administrative communications to complete. There was a radio chat show scheduled every day between the 12 boats. The main function of this was to check that the whole fleet was incommunicado, but it also connected the community of boats in the vast, lonely expanse of oceans and provided a great opportunity for psychological warfare! We also had to file a 'daily log' on email to the Challenge Office which then got posted onto the race website for everyone at home to read, along with the race stats that were published four times a day.

Occasionally we would also get phoned or emailed for special reports. If there had been a particularly 'interesting' event the media often asked for a quote or picture from one of the boats. We took 1000s of digital photos and some video footage (Phil had a head-cam from his sky-diving hobby and took some great footage from up the 95' high mast) and the photos also got posted on the website. The video footage was handed in as we reached each port and edited into great montages played at the leg award ceremonies. Twice we won best media award.

We were legally obliged to fill in the ship's logbook. This had to be completed every hour with data such as: wind speed; wind direction; sail plan; heading; latitude; longitude; etc. This was our version of an aircraft's 'black box', complete with all the information about our journey for every hour of every leg. (In leg two, after our second medivac we ran out of pages in the logbook because we were at sea for 52 days and had to continue writing it on plain paper.) We also had to submit reports such as safety pro-formas, progress reports if we hosted the chat show and requisition forms towards the end of each leg. The medic and Skipper both had official reports to write too.

Finally there were two written communications we did on the boat in order to focus the crew. One was filling in a laminated 'data log' on deck every ten minutes to record our speed versus boat set-up. This gave us the prompt to double-check our physical set-up if the boat speed seemed to have dropped even though the wind strength hadn't. The other was writing up the schedule results on our whiteboard below deck every six hours. These two sets of data focused the mind on a very regular basis and avoided complacency.

So as well as the expected verbal communications – social and functional – there were a number of official communications on the boats too which fulfilled race obligations.

Communication from Boat to Boardroom

As previously mentioned, we had to shout and use hand signals on the boat when necessary which is probably not best practice in most organisations! However, there was a clarity and efficiency that was commensurate with having to communicate in such an environment and some effective methods were devised that could be transferable into business...

SUMOs

SUMO is a communication tool, which usually stands for 'Shut up, Move On'[36], though we preferred our version which was: '**Speak** Up, Move On'. We adapted this original version and used it several times each week, especially during periods of internal trouble when it was important that people got to talk about how they felt without fear of reproach.

The way SUMO works is that the whole team sit together, ideally facing each other around a table or in a circle. (We used to sit around our saloon table after a meal.) Everyone gets to have their say and no-one is allowed to answer back. There is no dialogue or verbal retaliation. One by one around the team, people say whatever they want to for a short time – perhaps for up to a minute. They can say something positive or negative, something constructive or critical, about them, their peers or the situation. Anything goes. Whatever that person says must be accepted without rejoinders. They then 'shut up' and move on. The next person speaks up before moving on to the next, and so on, until everyone has spoken equally, even if is just, "I'm good and happy, nothing else to say".

The point is that everyone gets off their chest what they want to say but then the team **move on**, not only physically to the next person, but emotionally too.

This can be quite hard initially, because the natural human reaction is to respond or want to defend yourself, but once a team has got into the habit of conducting SUMOs then these

---

[36] Paul McGee claims to be the 'original SUMO guy' who propounds the 'Shut Up Move On' version

emotional reactions compose into a mature acceptance that everyone has a right to think and say what they want. Very occasionally, if there is a particularly heated or emotional topic, then the people involved can talk about it privately after the SUMO and at least the subject is then out in the open rather than left to fester unhealthily.

We practised this on the boat regularly and it was a very useful tool. It cleared the air and helped everyone to understand where each other were coming from; which was important for achieving quality teamwork. When someone had behaved in a certain way and assumptions had been made, clarity often came from them speaking up in the SUMO. Occasionally there would be a physical trauma during a watch and people would get hurt and frustrated or angry. This would come out in the SUMO and then the watch would **move on**.

Paula:

*It sounds very risky to hold a SUMO. You can literally sit there and get accused of doing something wrong which had a detrimental effect on the boat or even resulted in a fellow crew member getting hurt. Immediately, you want to explain yourself, or apologise, or excuse your behaviour. But this is selfishly just to make **you** feel better and not necessarily for the good of the team. So you learn to take comments on the chin and be mature over the emotions. It works. You can still apologise afterwards of course, if you have not already done so. SUMO is not designed to take away quality communication; it is just one of the sharper tools in the toolbox, with its own purpose, just like a chisel is used for a specific job instead of a mallet.*

In talking with many companies after the Global Challenge race we have recommended SUMO again and again. Understandably teams are wary of using it at first because it seems risky and could potentially open up a can of worms. We explain that if the SUMOs are lead well for the first few times, with very clear rules that the team are facilitated to stick to, they then work on a habitual basis and contribute towards achieving more effective teamwork.

Conciseness. Clarity.

Out of necessity, communication during tasks on deck had to be clear, concise, simple. We were often trying to communicate across distance and over a lot of background noise. In stormy weather, with the boom dipping in and out of the waves, sleet driving horizontally into the eyes and a 40 knot wind whipping words away, not much can be heard. Most of the time though, verbal communication was possible if shouted, it just had to be efficient.

For a start, we only had a limited amount of time in which to communicate. We were racing and the quicker we could complete any task the more competitive we would be. If we wanted to change a foresail for instance, the time between the old sail coming down and the new sail going up meant we weren't sailing at full power and so potentially losing distance to the other boats. Therefore we had to communicate efficiently. We also often needed to shout and so saved our voices and our energy by saying only the minimum.

The positive benefit of this brevity was that unnecessary, irrelevant words were ditched in favour of words that had a point. This meant that everything that was said was important and pertinent to what we were trying to achieve. There was no excess or background noise. Every word was worth listening to and we knew we had to concentrate on hearing it all; if not, we knew to ask for it to be repeated. Miscommunication was not an option in such dangerous conditions and in the middle of tasks that involved the control of powerful forces (wind, waves, ropes, rigging). In communicating, the speaker was responsible for checking that they were heard and the listener was responsible for responding, which was often a thumbs up or OK.

This conciseness and clarity of two-way communication was effective. It cut out unnecessary waffle, it 'did what it said on the tin' and it ensured there was understanding the other end. There was no ambiguity and very little chance for misinterpretation. It would be great if this was also true in the business world. Of course, there is a place for casual conversations and less military-like efficiency in communicating, but there is also often a case for the reduction of excessive internal communications especially when times are stormy and there is a lot of excess 'noise'.

More two-way communication would be better too. When a manager briefs a team or an employee, how often do they check understanding, let alone buy-in? Employees should also be responsible to say they hadn't heard or understood. During a tack, the helm shouts out three phrases at specific times: "Ready about?", "Helms to lee", "Lee ho!" The first phrase is shouted (not softly spoken) before the helm turns the wheel. In a professional, confident team, the crew shout back: "READY!" The helm then responds: "Helms to lee" and turns the wheel towards the lee side of the boat. By shouting: "Ready", the crew are not only saying that they are ready to do their jobs, but that they are also aware that the boat is about to tack and so look out for themselves on a point of safety (especially keeping an eye on the boom swinging round). Before a business manoeuvre, it would be great if team leaders, line managers or CEOs shouted something like: "Ready about?" and waited for a response. They would then know if their staff were ready and poised for action, or whether they were unaware, not listening or not understanding.

Hand Signals

As well as being verbally clear and concise during action on deck, we sometimes had to communicate physically because there was no way of hearing each other in stormy conditions. This even meant the careful use of a torch at night (without destroying night vision) though often the ambient light at sea under the stars or moon meant that we could just about make out shapes in the dark - it was rarely totally dark even at the dead of night. Physical communication sometimes meant just grabbing hold of someone and pointing, often that person then knew what to do. However, for more 'sophisticated' communication we devised a series of hand signals. These were actually quite simple, but covered the basics, such as a clenched fist meant 'hold', stop or wait. Circling the index finger downwards meant let out the number one sail, circling the index finger upwards, meant winch in the number one sail, and so on.

Now, unless work is carried out in a noisy environment or with people hard of hearing, there is no need for a system of hand signals. However, the point is we devised a communication system that was fit for purpose. It was innovative and appropriate to the environment we were in. So rather than unthinkingly going for the same old internal and external communication tools, or using every tool in the box, communication systems should be devised that are fit for purpose. Better still, employees could get involved in the design of communications so that they are meaningful and useful to them in carrying out their work.

Jargon

One danger of having a 'native' strain of communications is that it can cut off outsiders to the 'tribe'. Technical terminology; team, project or company specific language; in-house jokes or references to the past, can be jargon to external ears. Not to mention the common use of TLAs.[37]

Sailing has its own very specific and sometimes, quite illogical, language which has developed over many years. Ropes can be called sheets or halyards and are given specific names depending on their function, like barber hauler. To gybe is to turn the boat round, a jib however is a type of foresail. To

---

[37] Three Letter Acronyms such as the NHS – National Health Service.

tack is to turn the boat the other way, but a tack is also part of a sail. Sailing is cliquey and clubby which makes it a hard sport to take up and immediately feel at ease. The language alone prevents the easy incorporation of new people. On *Team Stelmar*, working so closely together for ten months, we also developed our own terminology and cultural references which were useful and funny to us, but bewildered a new legger. We ensured we were aware of this and tried to explain what we meant if we had accidentally resorted to Stelmar-speak in front of someone new. We also explained to leggers that we were used to communicating in certain ways and to question us if we weren't making sense.

Being aware and steering clear of jargon is common sense. The bigger point is that new people need to feel at ease if they are to function as soon as possible. If they are made to feel like outsiders, or be embarrassed by their lack of knowledge or understanding, their assimilation into the working team will be slower and less rewarding. It is hard enough to learn a new job without also having to tackle the maze of poor communications and internal jargon.

Knowledge Sharing

As well as learning about technical language or company-specific terminology, new people need to take on the knowledge held by the more established team members. A lot of knowledge is implicit, inside people's heads. An 'old hand' at work, for instance, who has been in the same job for twenty years will have accumulated a fair amount of experience; useful knowledge and expertise that is hard to identify in the mass of memories and difficult to make explicit. Even within one four-hour or six-hour watch on *Team Stelmar*, a lot could happen that needed to be shared with the other watch. The joy of our system however, was that there were five set times each day in which knowledge was shared in small, easy chunks (watch changeovers). Teams that work together on projects, especially those which are geographically dispersed, may have no prompt to knowledge share with their colleagues or with the company, and that knowledge can build and build until it becomes a huge mass of big facts and small 'nice to knows'. With the watch system, we exchanged knowledge every four or six hours so we knew everything, down to the most important little detail.

At watch changeover, the on-coming watch would be woken ten to forty minutes before they were due on watch, depending on whether they were going to eat a meal before going on deck and depending on the weather. If it was hot, the crew slept in their deck clothes and even at 02:00 in the morning would just have to put shoes on and go on deck. Ten minutes. In the Southern Ocean, the crew slept in their thermals and mid-layers and would be woken at 05:20 to wake-up, eat breakfast, ablute and then struggle in extremely bouncy conditions for 15 minutes to put on drysuits, boots, gloves, hats, lifejackets and harness.

The new watch would be obliged to go up on deck ten minutes before their watch was due to start in order to wake up fully, adjust to the physical conditions and hold a handover between them and their opposite numbers on the other watch. Watch Leader would talk to Watch Leader, cockpit to cockpit, helm to helm and so on. With only four or six hours worth of knowledge to share, this really only took about five minutes, but was definitely worth it.

We would also share 'longer' knowledge during Happy Hours. We had a Happy Hour each Sunday at 18:00 during which both watches would be on deck to have quality time together. This was an ideal opportunity to hold the longer conversations necessary between watches. Clive, our Skipper, and Nicko the Navigator were also responsible for sharing knowledge between watches as their on-duty times spanned across watch changeovers to ensure consistency. So we had three opportunities to exchange knowledge and share best practices. If companies don't have systems in place for people to download their expertise and share knowledge, then the community of workers will be less information-rich, development will be hindered and the same mistakes will be made again and again. Also those 'old hands' with implicit knowledge should be helped to get the useful stuff out of their heads and onto an explicit system such as an intranet or guidance notes or training manuals.

Positive but No Spin

As we were racing in often terrible and terrifying conditions, we had to maintain a positive mental attitude and stay focussed on achieving our goals. Similar to other sportspeople, we needed to hold onto our belief of success and strive for a victorious outcome. This meant being positive rather than negative, constructive rather than destructive, problem-solving rather than issue-raising; but not in a superficial way. Our positive energy had to be real. We didn't need superficial platitudes, we saw through false hope and spin, and putting a rosy glow to our situation was not helpful.

We needed factual communication stated in a positive way.

If we were performing badly, we needed to know that we were, we needed to know why and we needed to have the situation framed in such a way that it encouraged solutions. There was no room for navel-gazing or witch-hunting or wondering about the 'might have beens'. These behaviours were hindrances to moving forward. We had to know the facts and take positive action; not just be told the positive side and so hold a false view of reality.

Clive, our Skipper, was mainly responsible for this type of communication. When he got our schedule results in four times a day, he had to interpret them in light of our overall strategy and communicate his strategic point of view to the watches. Unfortunately Clive was the type of person who wore his heart on his sleeve, so he would often show disappointment when he was not happy with the results. This would impact the mood of the whole team and damage our hardworking ethic. A few times Clive was actually racing against his brother on the boat *Pindar*. When we got a bad result – or at one time when *Pindar* overtook us – Clive's mood would change for the worse and he would try to redress the balance which often meant interfering with successful procedures. We found it hard to manage this, and although aware of the impact Clive had when he was 'in one of those moods', we didn't really have a decent solution for it, except to try hard and sail into better statistics. This demonstrates the impact a leader's mood can have on the rest of the team and their performance.

In fact the interpretation of the daily 'skeds' generally affected the mood of the boat anyway. If we had a great result then obviously everyone was happy and motivated and jumped to tasks with alacrity and energy. If the result was bad on the surface, but actually we had done well considering the weather or the calamity we had just experienced, we then had a 'fair enough' attitude. However, when the 'sked' was bad and there was no apparent reason for our poor performance the mood on the boat became dark and the energy and enthusiasm drained, which was not conducive to high performance.

It was important therefore, that communication was couched in such a way that it was truthful, but positive. This meant communication between the crew as well as between the crew and the Skipper. Negativity was catching, and if anyone talked about failure or impossibilities or giving up, then the rest of the crew would normally step in and, consciously or not, boost the morale somehow.

This was most obvious on our second leg after two medical emergencies and a 2000 mile detour. Understandably some crew wanted to get off the boat and fly home for Christmas. The rest of the crew talked them round. There was no magic solution, it **was** going to be tough to continue sailing but the team propped each other up, taking turns to be 'Mr' or 'Mrs Motivator' and eventually the whole team rallied round and came back out on top. Ruth, our medic, who was not known for her motivational abilities, was actually responsible for placing a motivational poem on our pinboard, just when we needed it. *Don't Quit*. It worked.

Don't quit when the tide is lowest,
For it's just about to turn.
Don't quit over doubts and questions,
For there's something you may learn.
Don't quit when the night is darkest,
For it's just a while 'til dawn;

Don't quit when you've run the farthest,
For the race is almost won.
Don't quit when the hill is steepest,
For your goal is almost nigh;
Don't quit, for you're not a failure,
Until you fail to try.

Likewise, in business, communication should be factual and positive but not spun. People need to know the situation as it is, in order to take the right action or make the right decisions. Leaders or managers must be careful not to talk 'down', driving employees into a downward spiral of depression or into too much negative self-analysis. If times are hard - maybe a takeover is on the horizon, or 'reduced headcount', or customer satisfaction is low - then (bar the legalities) people should be communicated with in a matter-of-fact, but positive manner. Communicators need to be self-aware and manage their body language, tone of voice and facial expressions at these times as 93% of the message is received through these non-verbal signals. Appropriate action can then be taken with a positive mind-set.

Now and again Team Stelmar also needed a pep talk or rousing speech. Clive was good at these (see 'Leadership' Chapter). Again these pep talks were positive but not inaccurate. They were inspiring when we needed inspiration. Take a part of Clive's 'Team Tenacious' speech after the second Southern Ocean medical evacuation:

Team Stelmar – Team Tenacious

On the eve of our arrival in Wellington after over 9500nm, over 50 days and all the drama of the past seven weeks it is a strong, resolute team that looks forward to the rest of the race.

After everything that has been written and said, and everything that will be, as Skipper I want to pay tribute to the people that made this happen, day in day out – the crew.

For the past weeks the 'grunters' and groaners' have worked at the task in hand, around the clock, mothering, sailing the boat in all conditions, battling on relentlessly. It was not what they had signed up for, not what they expected; no-one could have predicted the events that transpired. Despite this, unperturbed they battled on determined to see it through. Testament to the fact that their tenacity would be rewarded we sail, not to retire but now for 11th place. A two point difference that in a yacht race as close as this will be telling.

Connecting People – Pre-Race

One benefit of communication is that it connects people. People communicate to learn, entertain, socialise or feel connected. They get a sense of belonging through communicating. Prior to the race start, Team Stelmar put into place a few systems so that the team could stay connected whilst living separate lives. This also helped with team building. The most effective form of communicating was face-to-face (see Leadership Chapter), but this was difficult as the whole team had to get time off on the same days, away from their families, work or other commitments. We still managed several gatherings over the course of the ten months prior to the race. We also held conference calls every Monday evening, emailed, connected through our internet site and telephoned for catch-ups when necessary.

These various methods of communication gave everyone the chance to stay in touch, which benefited the team in two ways: team development and project management. It was also motivational to hear about progress and listen to the excitement and commitment in the voices of the rest of the team. We were reminded now and again that we were not alone in our madness of spending over £30,000 for a pretty rough, but amazing year!

Even though the team were geographically dispersed and working in different jobs, they remained informed and involved. This could equally apply to business teams or employees who work remotely. They should get to see each other now and again through face-to-face situations – emails and phone calls are a poor relation.

Connecting People – Beyond the Boat

Beyond the close-knit community on *Team Stelmar* was a wider network of people who were also important contributors to the successful completion of the challenge. This group included: the sponsor (Stelmar/OSG); media; friends and family; the Challenge Business including Sir Chay Blyth and the race committee (RORC); supporters and leggers. It was important to inform, involve and include this group too. The more in touch with us they felt, the more interest, commitment and help they gave us.

Staying in touch was mainly via the Global Challenge website throughout the race which was updated at least four times a day, showing the route of all 12 boats plus the daily logs written by each boat. The occasional in-coming email would also reconnect the crew with the outside world – especially from the sponsor, David Chapman, who was a very supportive and witty writer.

We also communicated with the other 11 boats through a daily radio chat show, the purpose of which was to ensure we checked in on each other once a day in case there were any serious issues in the fleet. This chat show not only provided a lot of fun banter, but often contained psychological warfare in the shape of outright lies about progress or lack of it! This was all done in good humour. Again the main benefit of these chat shows was motivation, nurturing a mutual respect between the teams and inducing a sense of not being alone in the dramatic and powerful expanses of ocean.

So even in the 'middle of nowhere' (in the Southern Pacific we were literally 2500 miles from civilisation) and with limited communication tools, we had ways of staying connected thanks to satellite technology. And just that feeling of connection was a relief in the occasional moments of doubt, worry or madness![38]

---

[38] For madness at sea, see: *A Voyage for Madmen*, by Peter Nichols.

Lessons on Communication from the Boat to the Boardroom

Concise. Clarity

Be concise and clear when there is a lot of 'noise', especially in difficult times when the formal and informal communication networks are working overtime.

Fit for Purpose

Have a communication system and use communication tools that are fit for purpose. Hold a review and perhaps consult with employees and customers about what they want to hear, how they want to hear it and when they want to hear it, rather than inundating them with everything.

Jargon Awareness

The familiarity with jargon and TLAs is fairly common these days. The important point here is that newcomers need to feel welcome and part of the team in order to be confident and able to carry out their jobs. Using internal language and cultural references, technical talk, jargon and TLAs is not conducive to helping new people settle.

Positively no Spin

Communication should be stated in a positive manner but not so much that it becomes spin. Individuals and teams will make the best decisions and take the best actions when they know exactly what is going on and be internally motivated by positive phraseology.

Do SUMOs

Try holding 'Speak Up, Move On' sessions. These will need an explanation up front and strong facilitation initially. After two or three sessions the team should be able to conduct SUMOs in the way they were intended – as a 'sharp' communication tool.

Quality Handovers

Handover at each 'watch change' – be it a new project team, between shifts, between departments, etc. Pass on the context, the learnings and the best practices regularly before they build up into an insurmountable quantity of subtle, intrinsic knowledge.

Face-to-Face is Best

Face-to-face communication is much more effective for achieving buy-in, commitment and understanding. Face-to-face will also help achieve the company goal if individuals or teams have to work in silos.

Communication Exercises

Here are some exercises that can be carried out to review or improve communication.

1) List the benefits in maintaining communications with the 'wider' team (sponsors, supporters, media, etc.).

What is the wider team beyond your business team?

Do you communicate effectively enough with them?

Is there anything more you can do to improve communications with this group?

2) Do an Internal Communications audit – company-wide or team-wide or even just review your own communications. What can you improve to make it 'fit for purpose'?

3) Experiment. Go email-free and mobile-free for a day.

4) Try SUMOs – properly for a month.

5) Imagine the following scenario:

- It is Christmas day
- 'Flash' has just arrived home in the UK after an operation on his arm
- Your boat is 2000 miles short of the rest of the fleet following the two medical evacuations
- You still have a month of sailing in the Southern Ocean to get to Wellington

What type of communications would you deliver on this day?

What would be the content?

What can you take from this into the business?

Chapter 9. Personal Development

Definition

IN A BOOK ABOUT TEAMWORK, leadership and tough physical challenge, it is time to look at the individual; to reflect on what happened to the 'me' within the greater context; the single inner person in a round the world yacht race crewed by 12 teams of 18 people.

How did the individual crew members mentally and emotionally deal with the challenge? What were they thinking and feeling before, during and after such a life-changing adventure? How did they cope? How did the 'me' get a chance to develop in such a strong team environment? What made them apply in the first place? What did they learn about themselves? What changed inside them between signing up and coming home? How did they personally develop and what can we learn from them?

Personal development is about developing oneself to become a greater person and to have a more fulfilling, successful and happy life.

Personal Development in the Global Challenge

The Global Challenge was an incredible, unique opportunity for people to take part in a life-changing adventure. Sir Chay Blyth set the company up so that ordinary people could do extra-ordinary things. It made the elusive and expensive world of ocean yacht racing accessible to amateurs, but it also provided the opportunity for personal transformation through external and internal challenge.

Everyone evolves as they grow older and gain experience, but the pace and intensity of change varies from person to person. Participating in something such as the Global Challenge has a deep impact on the individual and so speeds up and enhances development. The crews who left Portsmouth in October 2004 came back ten months later as 'bigger' people than when they left; they had 'grown' more than all or most of their friends, colleagues and families they left behind. They had experienced greater events in the intervening time; probably stretched themselves further than they thought possible, reached near to their full potential, experienced higher highs and lower lows than ever before in their lives, seen and done some amazing things and at times, had to dig very deep.

They also had plenty of opportunity to reflect during the quieter days and, consciously or not, process what they were going through; making the most of the chance that the race presented them with for personal growth; thus profiting from the experience by greater self-development and learning.

The crew who left Portsmouth on *Team Stelmar* probably came back even 'bigger' than the other 11 crews. Team Stelmar went through more crises and successes. They experienced tougher times than the other boats and they experienced more awards and achievements than the other boats. They had two incredibly soul-destroying medical evacuations and two fantastically thrilling podium places. Their world see-sawed between peaks and troughs more dramatically because of the traumas they went through, and so the crew on the boat also experienced more dramatically the Global Challenge race compared with other teams.

In reunions and on reflection, the individuals from Team Stelmar realise they are much richer for the experience of being on such a difficult boat. They know that they had by far the most interesting and stimulating time, and in such a challenge, ideally you either come first or have the most enriching experience. Team Stelmar came back into Portsmouth ten months later, ten years wiser. Certainly very bonded with great stories to tell, but also personally more confident, grounded and self-assured. More comfortable with who they were and what they were capable of achieving.

How great would the world be if everyone felt this good and confident about themselves? If life was depicted as a journey with a series of highs and lows, experiences are typically hills. The Global Challenge was a mountain in comparison, and once one has experienced climbing a mountain then the hills are small challenges in contrast.

This is one of the reasons why the crews came back feeling so confident. They now know that they are capable of climbing mountains; of personally working in tough conditions day in day out; of effectively dealing with potentially life-threatening situations and, in actual fact, have sailed around the world, Cape Horn and twice across the Southern Ocean...

Paula:

In Boston, one of the last stops, my parents came out to see me. One evening we went out for a meal and at the end of the night began to go our separate ways back to hotels in different parts of the city. Typically my mother asked: "Are you all right going back on your own?" to which my reply was: "Mum, I have just sailed around the world, of course I'm all right!"

I, in fact, felt indestructible right then. How could I not?

The Global Challenge crews are often asked how they have changed since the race, and one of the common answers is that they no longer 'sweat the small stuff'. This is a very liberating change and made easier by having already had to sweat the 'big stuff'.

Completing the Global Challenge – and the four years previous to that in training and fundraising – strengthened the participant, and intensified and augmented their development; much like running a marathon would give someone a richer experience than running for the bus. It feeds the soul and strengthens the spirit. It was 'character building'. The more character building experiences individuals have – good and bad – the more able they will be at climbing life's mountains, the less they will sweat the small stuff and the more capable and confident they will feel.

The further someone develops and grows, the more they will be capable of achieving and the more fulfilling their lives will be.

Personal Development from Boat to Boardroom

This Chapter is about the person rather than the business, but of course, people are a company's greatest asset, so it is important that employees are happy and motivated, and ideally feeling confident, capable, self-assured and are able to develop personally. Some companies spend money on developing their personnel and investing in their inner well-being, which is a great benefit to the staff and to the company. Some companies could do with spending more care and attention on these matters perhaps, but really it is ultimately down to the individual to invest in themselves to stretch and grow, learn and develop. A company may provide the resources, but individuals should be responsible for their own personal development. The beliefs, the changes - and even the decision to change - come from within; the stimulus, resources and motivation can come from elsewhere. Here are some external stimuli for personal development from the

Global Challenge, starting with the point on personal responsibility.

Be Self-Responsible and 'Grown Up'

We theoretically grow up at 18, but many people hold on to *inappropriate* immaturity and childlike thinking and behaviours through into adulthood, and sometimes for all their lives. This is not to say that we should not have a childlike sense of fun and wonder and enjoy spontaneous play and immature banter. These types of behaviours are healthy and very much what life should be about sometimes - there was certainly plenty of it on the boat! (see pp 162-165).

We do not stop playing because we grow old; we grow old because we stop playing.[39]

Not being self-responsible and 'grown-up' is more about the subtle, often subconscious, childlike thinking and behaving that can occur *inappropriately*; in situations – for instance in the workplace - which require adult maturity.

Initially the race was quite intimidating. We set off in a force 8 gale on a 72' racing yacht, just as we were nervous and lacking confidence anyway, and we were probably feeling like children inside – excited and scared. We were just coping, and being seasick, and deep down perhaps wanted the security of a 'parent figure' to make it all better; to provide protection and give us someone we could lean on. But we soon realised it was down to us to be self-responsible; to manage ourselves, to make decisions, to deal with the Man Overboard on our first night, to work through the seasickness, and so we just got on with it. We were responsible for our own safety, health, fitness, nutrition and rest. If we didn't look after ourselves we let the team down. If we didn't make ourselves go to sleep when we were off watch, or clip-on when it was rough, or drink the protein drink, then we could get ill or lose energy and so be less useful.

---

[39] Benjamin Franklin.

When we are of a certain age, apart from healthy childlike 'play', we should be self-responsible. We are capable human beings and don't generally need to depend or lean on others for fulfilment, training, promotion, fitness, health, happiness. If we are fit and able, we can be self-responsible and self-reliant and this gives us more options and more control which in turn is very liberating. Our life is what we make it.

We should not blame or rely on or wait for others or for circumstances to change. We should make change happen; we should 'go for it' ourselves. *À donf!*

À Donf!

Dame Ellen MacArthur's [40] catchphrase is *à donf* which essentially translates as *full on, to the limit, go for it.*

Dame Ellen is an amazing 5' 2" lady packed with huge internal resources of ambition, drive and determination. She has been 'adopted' by the French (France is very much into sailing and the French have great admiration for sailors) and she was awarded the *Légion d'honneur* in March 2008, so her catchphrase is not surprisingly in the language of her second home. Her sign-off is *à donf* because she believes in giving it 100%, all the time. The English version is 'go for it'.

In life we are faced with hundreds of decisions every day and hundreds of challenges and opportunities every year. If we duck or half-heartedly approach these decisions, challenges and opportunities we either miss out on reaping the full

---

[40] In June 2000, MacArthur sailed the monohull Kingfisher from the UK to the USA and set the current record for a single-handed east-to-west passage, plus the record for a single-handed woman in any vessel.

MacArthur's second place in the 2000-2001 Vendée Globe is the world record for a single-handed, non-stop, monohull circumnavigation by a woman.

In June 2004, MacArthur sailed her trimaran *B&Q/Castorama* to set a new world record for a transatlantic crossing by a woman.

In 2005, MacArthur beat Francis Joyon's existing world record for a single-handed non-stop circumnavigation. Her time of 71 days, 14 hours, 18 minutes beat Joyon's, but has since been re-beaten by Joyon in January 2008. He did it in 57 days, 13 hours and 34 minutes.

rewards or have a less fulfilling life. Often the most ballsy, interesting, exciting decisions are suppressed by over-analysis - exactly because they are **big** decisions - and so people don't go for it. There were plenty of strong reasons **not** to do the Global Challenge, but for those who did, they had the time of their lives. For those who decided not to go for it, and played it safe, they are the ones who have lost out. The Global Challenge is no more. The opportunity to take part was there and now it's gone. Many people say to the crew: I wish I had done that... but they didn't. They found lots of reasons (excuses) why not.

Paula:

It is effortless to say, "I'm going to do X" or "I can't do X because..." The hardest part is to take that step to do it. Before I signed up to do the Global Challenge, these were some of my "I can't because..." excuses:

- *I have a full-time job which I love and I am very lucky to have it (I left my job)*

- *I am a shareholder and I will have to sell my shares and quit the company (I sold my shares)*

- *It will damage my long-term career (It improved my career)*

- *I own a flat in London (I rented it out)*

- *I can't afford £30,000 plus lose a year's salary (I make more money now)*

- *I could do so much more with £30,000 (It was money well spent)*

- *I need to save money for my pension/mortgage/cost of living (Life's for living)*

- *I can't go away for a year! (I can)*

- *I can't sail (I can learn)*

- *I get seasick (So what?)*

- *I'm not sure I will enjoy it/it sounds pretty scary (Scary = exciting)*

- *My mum will kill me! (No she won't) etc.*

Yes, all good reasons not to do something. You only live once and then you are a long time dead.

Where there is a will, there is a way.

No regrets.

Like many people, we were interested in taking part, for all sorts of reasons, but then we actually made it happen. It was a ballsy decision, a huge challenge, a fantastic opportunity, and we went for it.

People should use their gut feel and their hearts (not always their heads) for making big personal (potentially life-changing) decisions. *À donf!*

Not only did we decide to take on the Global Challenge, but we then gave it 100%.

100% Commitment – Play to Win, not just to Play

No half-heartedness. No excuses. If you are going to do something, then do it to the best of your ability and with your whole heart, body, mind and soul. When you feel that you are giving 100%, you are probably only giving 80%. Raise your standards. Raise your game. Play to win, not just to play.

This is powerful advice, and perhaps sounds 'over the top' to people who are shy of gung-ho enthusiasm and commitment, but this is the attitude that top people have. Top athletes and sportspeople, top politicians, top performers, top leaders, top explorers, top salespeople, because to be at the top you need to give it 100%, otherwise you are unlikely to get there. The will and the drive to achieve great heights stems from the attitude. You can have skill and strength, experience and advice, but at the end of the day, it is the 100% commitment that will create the difference between a good performance and an exceptional one. The All Blacks have it. Usain Bolt has it. Chris Hoy has it. They are 100% committed in attitude; towards their training, their lifestyle, the competitions, their fitness, their nutrition, their team. This means making sacrifices: sleep, weekends, parties, holidays and relaxing, and replacing it all with working really hard towards their goals.

On the round the world yacht race, crews had already demonstrated their commitment by paying £30,000 and giving up a year of their lives to take part. Also, it is difficult to duck commitment once you are on the boat – there is literally nowhere to hide! Everyone **has** to commit two or three times a day to go on deck for a watch. Even jumping out of a dry, warm bunk at one o'clock in the morning takes commitment... but there is commitment, and then there is 100% commitment.

For example, during the race we had to wind sails up, or trim them in, using giant two-handed Harken 15"-diameter winches. The quicker the winching, the quicker the sails were in the right state for maximum boat speed. It was possible to sit at a winch and grind. Especially when the spinnaker was flying, the 'grinder' typically had a half hour stint at the winch, winding in the thick rope frequently, while the trimmer let it out again, and so sitting down was a pleasant option. However, it was much better to stand, leaning over the winch bodily and committing full power and pace to the task. In the heat of the tropics it was tiring, and during quiet days it didn't feel quite necessary, but 100% commitment meant **always** standing up, leaning over the winch in readiness, clipped on, and then giving it maximum effort each and every time the trimmer shouted 'trim' or 'grind' for up to an hour at a time.

This is a single example of a typical small task. The team has a winning attitude when **everything** is carried out with this much determination and effort.

Choose your attitude

The longer I live, the more I realize the impact of attitude on life. Attitude, to me, is more important than facts. It is more important than the past, the education, the money, than circumstances, than failure, than successes, than what other people think or say or do. It is more important than appearance, giftedness or skill. It will make or break a company... a church... a home. The remarkable thing is we have a choice everyday regarding the attitude we will embrace for that day. We cannot change our past... we cannot change the fact that people will act in a certain way. We cannot change the inevitable. The only thing we can do is play on the one string we have, and that is our attitude. I am convinced that life is 10% what happens to me and 90% of how I react to it. And so it is with you... we are in charge of our own Attitudes.[41]

You can choose the way you react and feel about a situation. You can choose to be depressed or remotivated when a curve ball is thrown your way. You can choose to be angry or forgiving when someone treats you badly. You can choose to be upset or pragmatic when an accident happens. You can **choose** your attitude.

We choose how we react to life's events. When we had to turn around for the second time in the Southern Ocean, having already suffered one medical evacuation, then caught and passed seven boats in a week, then had to turn back **again**, we could have reacted badly – as one would expect in those circumstances. We could have sulked, cried, got depressed, blamed others, thought 'why me?', given up, or generally stomped grumpily about the boat. These are natural human reactions. Were they helpful? No. Would they make Flash feel better about it? Definitely not. Would they make us feel better about the bad hand life had dealt us? No.

[41] Charles R Swindoll.

So why do we choose to behave negatively when we can choose to behave otherwise? Clive, our Skipper, wrote:

None of us deserved or expected this, no-one can explain the reason or circumstances. As ever things happen in life, I believe for a reason and it is not what happens but how we react and handle it that makes us what we are.

We can decide to feel good or bad about what life throws at us. We can choose our attitudes, so why not make them the right attitudes? Positive, constructive ones. With a bad attitude you can never have a positive day, with a positive attitude, you can never have a bad day.

Don't Limit Yourself with Labels

Everyone has an *identity* which is given to them by other people and also by themselves. These identities are often perceptions; they can be assumptions or stereotypes; they can limit, expand or generalise: "They are crazy". "He is dumb". "She is geeky".

We often give ourselves self-limiting labels which then affect what we actually think of ourselves; what we decide to do and how we behave. 'I can't cook', for instance. 'I was never any good at navigating'. 'I am useless at remembering birthdays'. 'I am rubbish at sports'. 'I don't understand Excel'. While there may be an original truth in these labels, unfortunately people then grow into justifying the label ('See, I told you so') and soon live by them. If the labels are positive, expansive ones, then great. They can be motivating and give people the vision and inspiration to fulfil the prophecy. However, more often than not, people bequeath themselves limiting labels, which result in them not even trying to cook, or use Excel, or remember to send cards on people's birthdays. If someone thinks to themselves: 'I am going to die'. Where, then, is the will to live?

The more positive labels you give yourself, the more choices and opportunities you will have. Even when there is a grain of truth in a negative label – so what? Either, the label is not true; not totally true; you can try; or you can learn.

If you give yourself labels you will live by them. If you give yourself positive ones, you can fulfil them. If you give yourself lots of positive identities, you can choose who to be, and when.

Paula:

'I am a successful business woman. I am good at my job. I am an adventurer. I am a motivational speaker. I am a great driver. I am a loving daughter...' I am.

'I can't sail.' I did. 35,000 miles. 'I can sail.'

Lessons on Personal Development from the Boat to the Boardroom

À Donf!

Ellen MacArthur's catchphrase is *à donf*. In English it translates as 'Go For It'; they mean the same. Use your gut feel and your heart for whether a personal (potentially life-changing) decision is right for you. Don't suppress ballsy decisions by over-analysis. Take risks. Live life to the full. GO FOR IT.

100% Commitment

No half-heartedness. No excuses. If you are going to do something, then do it, to the best of your ability, and with your whole heart, body, mind and soul. When you feel that you are giving 100%, you are probably only giving 80%. Raise your game.

Keep Digging!

Dig deep when you need to but know there's miles more depth within you. We are so much more capable than we think.

Pain is Temporary, Pride is Forever

Behave always in a way that will make you proud - for always. Even if you are tired, or in pain, or just lacking the energy, these things are temporary. Your memory of how you behaved will last forever.

Peak State

Get yourself into peak state to achieve success. A healthy, fit, strong body = a sharp mind.

Time to Stand and Stare

Allow for time to stand and stare whilst going about your life. Even on the highly competitive Global Challenge when we were performing to our maximum, we had music, poetry, speeches and time spent standing on the bow to stare:

What is this life if, full of care,
We have no time to stand and stare

No time to stand beneath the boughs
And stare as long as sheep or cows.

No time to see, when woods we pass,
Where squirrels hide their nuts in grass.

No time to see, in broad daylight,
Streams full of stars, like skies at night.

No time to turn at Beauty's glance,
And watch her feet, how they can dance.

No time to wait till her mouth can
Enrich that smile her eyes began.

A poor life this if, full of care,
We have no time to stand and stare.[42]

Sleep is for Wimps!

'Sleep is for wimps' quote from Newton Scott, 60-year-old core crew on *Team Stelmar*. Sleep is sacred in the Western culture – at least from midnight to 06:00, we must be asleep! Why? Get up for sunrises, stargaze at 03:00, stay up all night with your best friend...

Play to Win

How you play is how you live your life. Play to win, don't play to play.

Outstanding Role Models

Model yourself on winners. Find different people who are outstanding at doing the different things you want to do and copy them, it compresses time and speeds up learning. Outstanding people are also inspirational to be close to.

---

[42] William Henry Davies.

Don't Limit Yourself with Labels

'I can't sail'. So? Learn! 'I am not good in the mornings'. 'I am not ambitious'. 'I am not very sporty'. 'I am rubbish at cooking'. Recognise any of these? If you give yourself labels you will live by them. You need multiple, positive labels – then you can choose what to do and who to be.

Be Self-Responsible

You are a capable human being. You don't need to depend on others for your fulfilment, training, promotion, fitness, health, happiness... If you are new, or young, or 'just' a housewife then do something about it yourself, without relying on or blaming or waiting for others.

Choose your Attitude

You can choose the way you react and feel about a situation. You can choose to be depressed or remotivated when a curve ball is thrown your way. You can choose to be angry or forgiving when someone treats you badly. You can choose to be upset or pragmatic when an accident happens. Choose you attitude.

There is only one thing stopping you achieving your goals. That one thing is yourself. If you are determined enough to succeed, then you WILL.[43]

---

[43] Quote by Alex Alley.

Personal Development Exercise

Take some time out to really, properly, deeply, honestly think about the above lessons from the Global Challenge. While they have fresh impact, make some notes about how they relate to you personally; some of them will resonate with you more than others. Then score yourself out of ten for how well you think you stack up against each one.

Congratulate yourself on the ones you think you do well and make a mental note to carry on doing them and know that perhaps you can help others do the same.

Look at the ones with low scores and perhaps pick one to work on at a time – you can't change the world in a day. Choose one that you think will have the greatest positive impact and work out what you can do specifically towards it, even if it is just taking 'time to stand and stare'. Possibly turn it into a SMART objective if you are really serious about it... how can you make 'Peak State' specific, measurable, achievable, realistic and time-based?

Use positive supporters and role models to provide you with encouragement and constructive help. Get rid of or ignore the detractors and energy sappers.

Review your progress, keep up the momentum and congratulate yourself on big and small achievements.

Go for it.

Thanks to:

Our Sponsors – Stelmar and OSG for all their support

David Chapman for his support and humour during the race and for writing our Foreword

Clive Cosby our skipper and his wife Vale for looking after us and getting us fit

The crew of Team Stelmar for all the good times

Peggy and Ciara for your collaboration

Our supporters, friends and family for sticking with us through thick and thin

Sir Chay Blyth for having the vision and providing us with the opportunity

The Challenge Business staff for helping us to get round the world

Don Krafft (Me to You) for curtailing his holiday in New Zealand to help us

Brendan Gallagher for the articles in the Daily Telegraph

Wikipedia for a lot of reference material

Neil from Seddon Group who got us started writing the book in the first place

Chris Glanfield for buying the first copy

Keith and Valerie Reid for their support, feedback and proof-reading

Also: Simon Potter, Craig Williams, Frank Nightingale, Ryan Larraman, Philippa Pride, Rupert FitzMaurice, Dougal Thomson, Deanna Panzetta, Rachael Hamilton and Harry Fortune.

Alex Alley

Alex is a highly competitive individual who, after teaching himself to sail as a child, turned professional at 19 and went on to represent England in 1991. His sailing experience now amounts to over 100,000 miles. Since finishing the Global Challenge in 2005 he is still very much involved with offshore racing. He is planning a solo race across the Atlantic as well as another round the world race, only this time two-handed. Alex is a co-founder and Director of Velocity Made Good with Paula and speaks regularly at conferences about his experiences.

www.alexalley.com

Paula Reid

Paula applied to do the Global Challenge in May 2004 and got her place confirmed with Team Stelmar on 19th July 2004. She hadn't sailed before.

Paula is into adventuring and extreme sports; she paddled hundreds of miles in dug-out canoes down the Mekong River in Cambodia and the San Juan River in Nicaragua, lived with Dayaks in Borneo and took up mountaineering in 2008.

She has been training and engaging teams and leaders for 17 years. She is a speaker, trainer and facilitator and is also a Director of Velocity Made Good.

www.paulareid.com

Velocity Made Good Ltd

VMG is an experiential training solution designed to accelerate high performance in leaders, managers and teams. VMG takes people from the *boat to the boardroom* (in workshops) and from the *boardroom to the boat* (experiential learning through sailing).

www.velocitymadegood.co.uk

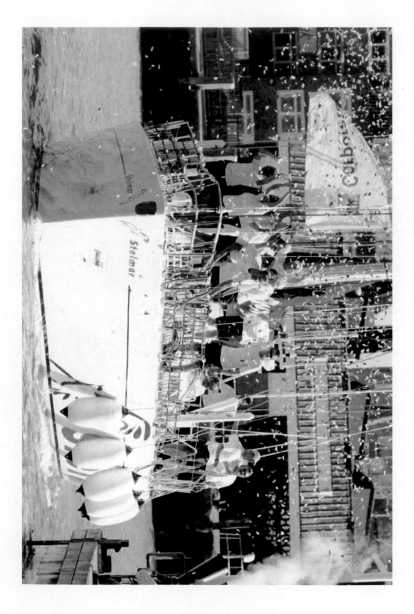